THE CHEMICAL
WEAPONS TABOO

THE
CHEMICAL
WEAPONS
TABOO

Richard M. Price

CORNELL UNIVERSITY PRESS

ITHACA AND LONDON

First published 1997 by Cornell University Press.

Printed in the United States of America

Cornell University Press strives to utilize environmentally responsible suppliers and materials to the fullest extent possible in the publishing of its books. Such materials include vegetable-based, low-VOC inks and acid-free papers that are also either recycled, totally chlorine-free, or partly composed of nonwood fibers.

Library of Congress Cataloging-in-Publication Data

Price, Richard M. (Richard MacKay), 1964–
   The chemical weapons taboo / Richard M. Price.
     p.   cm.
   Includes bibliographical references and index.
   ISBN 0-8014-3306-1 (cloth : alk. paper)
    1. Chemical weapons—History. 2. Chemical weapons—Moral and ethical aspects. I. Title.
UG447.P756   1997
327.1'745—dc21   96-24320

Cloth printing   10 9 8 7 6 5 4 3 2 1

TO THOSE WHO HAVE SUFFERED

THE VIOLENCE OF WARFARE

Contents

Preface

This book is a meditation on the relationship between morality and technology, particularly the exercise and restraint of violence in world politics. To this end it explores the development and operation of the norm in international society which proscribes the use of chemical weapons.

While I am given credit as the author, this book is the product of conversations with many minds past and present. I am grateful for the contributions of those who kindly commented on various versions of this project, including Joseph Camilleri, Sheila Jasanoff, Stephen Krasner, Jeffrey Legro, Judith Reppy, Scott Sagan, Henry Shue, Kathryn Sikkink, Takao Takahara, Nina Tannenwald, Daniel Thomas, and Mark Zacher.

I also thank in more general terms the participants in forums where versions of the project were presented: the Peace Studies Program at Cornell University 1989–1993; the 1993 annual meeting of the American Political Science Association; the spring 1994 seminar at the Center for International Security and Arms Control at Stanford University; the 1994 seminar at the Jackson School of International Relations at the University of Washington; the Social Science Research Council / MacArthur workshops on the Cultures of Security organized by Peter Katzenstein and held in Ithaca, Minneapolis, and Stanford during 1993–1994; and the International Relations Colloquium in the Department of Political Science at the University of Minnesota.

Peter Katzenstein was generous enough to supervise the growth of this project even though it was born from an intellectual tradition different from his own. In the process he challenged me to engage disparate schools of thought instead of carrying on a conversation with myself. He provided me as well with a lasting model of scholarly integrity and intellectual honesty for which I am most grateful. Christian Reus-Smit has been an invigorating intellectual companion in addition to providing penetrating comments on the project. John Ellis van Courtland Moon generously read a draft of the manuscript and provided invaluable comments; so did two anonymous reviewers. I also am indebted to those whose scholarly works provided a wealth of material, such as the authors of the Stockholm International Peace Research Institute studies on the problem of chemical and biological warfare.

I gratefully acknowledge the financial support of the Government Department, the Graduate School, and the Peace Studies Program at Cornell University; the Social Sciences and Humanities Research Council of Canada Doctoral Fellowships; and the Isaak Walton Killam Memorial Post-Doctoral Fellowship sponsored by the Institute of International Relations at the University of British Columbia.

Finally, no note of acknowledgment would be complete without thanking my family. The support of my parents allowed me to pursue my chosen profession, and my wife, Lisa, has supported the travails of this professional student with unflagging patience and love.

RICHARD M. PRICE

Minneapolis, Minnesota

THE CHEMICAL
WEAPONS TABOO

Weapons, Morality, and War

There are no moral phenomena at all, but only a moral interpretation of phenomena.
                                    —Nietzsche, *Beyond Good and Evil*

"**W**ar is hell," "All's fair in love and war"—our culture's sayings reflect the commonplace view that when nations cross the boundary separating peace from war, among the many casualties are moral and legal restraints. Humanity must, it seems, resign itself to endure the sufferings wrought by ever more powerful weapons technologies as the unavoidable burden of war twinned with the ineluctable march of technological progress. While the history of warfare offers all too many examples of this tragic wisdom, the case of chemical weapons stands out as a startling exception. Even as this century witnessed the standardization of a plethora of new techniques such as the tank, the submarine, strategic bombing, and missiles as accepted means of war, chemical weapons have thus far defied the usual pattern and instead elicit widespread disdain as a particularly contemptible and reprehensible means of conducting warfare.

Indeed, whether in press reports and scholarly discussions or at the level of public attitudes, it is generally taken as a given that there is something particularly illegitimate about chemical weapons which makes them a special problem. When the subject of chemical weapons is raised, it is routinely accompanied by adjectives such as "barbaric," "immoral," "horrible," and "inhumane," appellations that are not so indelibly attached to so many other weapons despite the suffering their use entails.

How is it that among the countless cruel technological innovations in weaponry of humankind, chemical weapons stand out as a weapon that has come to be stigmatized as morally illegitimate?[1] Why do we think differently about chemical weapons? Why have they been denied the legitimacy implied by the categorization of other means of warfare as "conventional" weapons, and, conversely, how have those latter weapons avoided the stigma of lasting moral opprobrium? What do these discrepancies mean for the practice of violence in world politics?

Throughout history, numerous weapons have provoked protest upon their introduction as novel technologies of warfare. However, as examples such as the longbow, crossbow, firearms, explosive shells, and submarines demonstrate, the dominant pattern has been for such moral qualms to disappear as the innovations became standard techniques of war. Are chemical weapons just another example of this process, and are the moral protests against this weapon doomed to fade? Or is there something unique about the proscription of chemical weapons? What are the lessons to be learned for other efforts at arms control from this apparent success?

Scholarly literature has produced a range of explanations for the varying attitudes toward the acceptability of different weapons technologies, including the hypothesis that it is easier to ban weapons on the horizon of invention rather than unforeseen technologies and the suggestion that the more closely a weapon approaches the basic effects of the fang and claw, the more readily it will be accepted.[2] Echoing this last idea, one author offers the somewhat ghoulish conjecture that "weapons seem to be accepted the closer they approximate the primitive violence of cutting, crushing, and stabbing."[3]

Although there is little in the way of systematic comparative studies of the moral and cultural attitudes that have greeted the introduction of novel weapons throughout history, one hypothesis clearly predominates: the belief that moral restraints only matter for ineffective weapons. According to this view, "the objection that a warlike device is barbarous has always been made against new weapons, which have nevertheless eventually been adopted."[4] A more explicit statement of the intricacies of this dynamic suggests the following pattern: "Technology apparently drives nations first to conceive of, then make and finally use weapons that, when first conceived, seemed too bad to be true. Once in hand, these new weapons . . . make the old ones seem less immoral than before. In the end, the further suspicion surfaces that the list of nasty weapons recognized by nations as immoral roughly corresponds to a list of nasty but relatively useless weapons."[5] Finally, the logic of the thesis further suggests that "where a rule is found prohibiting successfully some new weapon, it will usually be found that the weapon never really was of decisive military potentiality. . . . broadly, therefore, the rules that grow up are rules touching the old and more marginal weapons, not weapons which by their novelty and efficiency are more likely to be effective."[6]

If the thesis is true—that moral restraints on weapons are always destined to fade, or at least they are effective only for useless weapons—then there is good reason to believe that the norm proscribing chemical weapons is in a precarious state. The increased lethality of modern chemical agents and the greater availability of sophisticated long-range systems for their delivery have made contemporary chemical weapons an attractive military option for some nations in the international system. The use of poison gas as a terrorist weapon by a cult in Japan in 1995 indicates the attraction of chemical weapons as a potentially powerful instrument of destruction. Moreover, if it is in fact the case that normative constraints historically erode as more destructive technologies are invented, the existence of nuclear weapons should erode the novelty of the horror associated with chemical weapons.

In this book I examine what—if any—reasons we have to suspect that the norm proscribing the use of chemical weapons is any more robust than similar restraints on other weapons in the past, restraints that have eventually yielded to the ineluctable embrace of technology. To this end, I investigate the origins and development of the norm proscribing the use of chemical weapons in an effort to understand how these weapons have been constituted as a category and how they have been delegitimized. The answer is not so simple as usually supposed. Neither the view that chemical weapons are of no militarily utility nor the assumption that the taboo is simply explained by the unique physical characteristics of these weapons suffices to provide fully satisfactory accounts of the resilience of the taboo. The more nuanced investigation I undertake here improves upon existing explanations by illuminating additional dimensions of the chemical weapons prohibition—namely, the meaning of the taboo and the role it serves in the constitution of hierarchical relations in international politics—not captured by previous accounts. In the process, the book testifies to the value of constructivist approaches to the study of international relations and the relationship between technology and morality.

The Taboo and the Non-Use of Chemical Weapons

In my investigation I engage several different areas of scholarly literature, including international relations theory, especially the literature on regimes and norms and realist theories of deterrence; philosophical studies on the role of morality and ethics in international politics; the international law of war; methodological debates between rationalist and constructivist approaches in the social sciences; and works concerning the philosophy of technology and social construction of technology. In what follows, I relate my arguments here to a few selected major bodies of work concerning the norm proscribing chemical weapons.[7]

One of the pre-eminent puzzles occupying much of the chemical weapons literature is the important question of why chemical warfare (CW) was not waged by the major belligerents in the major battlefields of World War II, a conflict in which few other restraints were observed and, indeed, in which most existing prohibitions were violated.[8] A virtual consensus in this literature attributes this surprising non-use of chemical weapons to three major factors: "the two sides warned each other not to use chemical weapons at the risk of strong retaliatory action in kind; a general feeling of abhorrence on the part of governments for the use of CB weapons, reinforced by the pressure of public opinion and the constraining influence of the Geneva Protocol; and actual unpreparedness within the military forces for the use of these weapons."[9]

The argument pointing to the troika of military unpreparedness and disinterest, deterrence/fear of retaliation, and moral/legal restraints is replicated throughout the literature, with varying degrees of emphasis.[10] Although a combination of these factors explains the non-use of chemical weapons in World War II, these explanations do not offer much insight into the question of why chemical weapons—of all the destructive innovations in technology—were subject to these restraints. That is, a further puzzle remains. Even if it could be adequately demonstrated that deterrence and the fear of retaliation were decisive factors in the thinking of the decision makers of the time, there is still the question why this concern existed for chemical weapons over and above other enormously destructive and outlawed forms of warfare such as indiscriminate fire bombing with incendiary weapons or submarine attacks on civilian ships.

In hindsight it might make perfect sense to argue that enemies rationally deterred each other from using a given technology of destruction such as chemical weapons. All other things being equal, however, this mutual deterrence could presumably always or at least often be the case. Why would the belligerents of World War I not have "deterred" each other from using machine guns, since those weapons proved simply to increase the slaughter of the trenches without gaining decisive military advantage?[11] How are such deterrent thresholds defined, established, or violated?

The deterrence argument for chemical weapons restraint does not shed much light on the numerous other examples in which lethal chemicals were not used by belligerents even when their opponents possessed no chemical weapons retaliatory capability: the Spanish civil war, the Korean War, the French in Indochina and Algeria, the Vietnam War, and the Soviet intervention in Afghanistan.[12] Something else has evidently worked to restrain the use of chemical weapons.

Just as we need to explore how chemical weapons came to be understood as a deterrent weapon that might not be used, so too do we need to explain the lack of preparations to wage chemical warfare. Simply to argue that these weapons were not used because military establishments regarded themselves as inadequately prepared to wage chemical warfare leaves unanswered the question of why they were treated in this peculiar way and how such assessments could be made and become politically relevant. There are few examples in history of weapons that were not used in battle simply because an army did not have the supply they would have liked.

It is often suggested that the lack of readiness to wage CW is attributable to the lack of utility of chemical weapons. The problem with arguments that the taboo is explained by the failure of chemical weapons to be established as a decisive weaponry, however, is that the lack of decisive utility often accompanies the initial uses of new weapons. For example, the development of firearms includes a long history of sporadic use and bungled experiments. Few weapons have been decisive at their initial stages, but this lack has not prevented continued tinkering with and uses of potentially useful technologies of destruction. More damning is the fact that the empirical record renders this argument from utility untenable. As the following chapters demonstrate, the contention that the taboo has developed only because chemical weapons are not militarily useful is not sustainable, for these weapons often have been regarded by central figures as having military utility in a variety of crucial situations. To cite just one example, chemical weapons might have provided the least costly way for U.S. forces to advance against the Japanese forces that were entrenched in caves and tunnels in the Pacific islands during the latter stages of World War II. In the words of General Alden Waitt of the Chemical Warfare Service (CWS), gas was "the most promising of all weapons for overcoming cave defenses."[13]

Another argument bases the resistance to chemical weapons in the usual quaint disdain of military cultures for a novel instrument of modern science.[14] Though it illuminates several features of the World War II case, this argument does not speak to cases where chemical weapons have been employed with some gusto by armies. More important, this supposition does not provide adequate insight into the question of whether or not the prohibition against using chemical weapons is any different from the usual aversion to innovative weapons throughout history, normative restraints which eroded over time. Are there good reasons to believe that the moral prohibition against chemical weapons will not suffer a similar fate, and that it will not go the way of moral qualms against the crossbow, the firearm, and the submarine? Or is the taboo against CW only another example of the initial disdain for a novel and unfamiliar weapon that is destined inevitably to subside?

Reducing Essentialism

Authors who have approached this problem at length have sought to ascertain which qualities of chemical weapons give us good logical reasons for their proscription. Thus, it is often supposed that they arouse special dread because they cause unnecessary suffering; because they are insidious, unseen, and secretive; because they are indiscriminate; or because the effects of choking can be so vividly imagined.[15]

These explanations, however initially plausible, are ultimately incomplete, because a multitude of other weapons can always be found which offend in comparably dastardly ways. For example, one author notes that the accusation of secrecy seems odd, considering that high-speed bullets are no more visible than gas before they hit their targets.[16] And as the military historian Martin van Creveld observes, "taking an 'objective' point of view, it is not clear why the use of high explosive for tearing men apart should be regarded as more humane than burning or asphyxiating them to death."[17]

I do not argue that such qualities have nothing to do with the disdain for chemical weapons; I simply point out that given the cruelties of other weapons they do not provide by themselves a sufficient explanation of why they and not other weapons have been proscribed. How is it that we have come to regard the tearing apart of flesh by burning metal to be a "conventional" and thus uncontroversial practice of cruelty? The crucial factors lie not simply with the objective and essential characteristics of the weapons themselves but with how civilizations and societies have interpreted those characteristics and translated them into political and military practice.

Michael Mandelbaum has sought to locate the source of the chemical weapons taboo in cultural attitudes, and, like this book, his work addresses at some length the question of the legitimacy of chemical weapons in the context of attitudes toward other weapons. Despite the promise of his approach to explain the anomalous status of chemical weapons by examining deep-rooted cultural and institutional restraints, Mandelbaum finally succumbs to the temptations of essentialist reasoning: the difference between chemical and nuclear weapons is that the aversion to the former is deeply rooted in human chromosomes whereas distaste for the latter is not.[18] This genetic argument is so strained and implausible that we need to search for a more convincing account—why would we not have a "genetic aversion" to cutting steel, napalm, bullets, and shrapnel? Rational deductions for deeply rooted cultural constraints on chemical weapons are mistaken as they ignore the vagaries of history and politics. As I demonstrate here, it is political constructions in history which have shaped subsequent attitudes towards chemical weapons, contrary to rational expectations.

The shortcomings of these approaches suggest that factors other than an inherent aversion or nonaversion to the intrinsic features of chemical and nuclear armaments have played an important role in the development or absence of restraints. To be sure, chemical weapons are insidious, and they cause horrible suffering. But most if not all other weapons share similarly dubious qualities—few would argue, for example, that being torn apart by burning shrapnel is anything other than horrifying and inhumane. The difference is that most of these other weapons have not had as politically successful degrees of odium attached to them as chemical weapons—as the term "conventional weapons" implies. Indeed, the way the term "chemical weapons" has been restricted is itself by no means self-evident, for conventional explosives are, after all, "chemical," and the history of firearms is an intriguing tale of (al)chemists' recipes for gunpowder.[19] Categories such as "chemical," "conventional," and "weapons of mass destruction," in short, are not natural but are the products of politics. To fail to recognize this is to compound the way that the legitimizing appellation of "conventional" works to suspend violently cruel technologies from critical thought, insulating them by inducing a numbing acceptance by ourselves.

A Genealogical Approach to Moral Interpretations

The analysis adopted in this book to untie the conundrum of the chemical weapons taboo has as its main influence the genealogical method, one of many traditions of interpretive and constructivist social science. The genealogical method as articulated by Friedrich Nietzsche and Michel Foucault is particularly well-suited for guiding an analysis of the norm proscribing CW, for the method is specifically concerned with accounting for the origins of moral interpretations.

For Nietzsche and Foucault, the point of departure for the genealogy is the insight that institutions are contingent structures "fabricated in piecemeal fashion"[20] out of the vicissitudes of history. As a result of the marriage of chance occurrences, fortuitous connections, and reinterpretations, the purposes and forms of moral structures often change to embody values different from those that animated their origins. As Nietzsche explains:

> The cause of the origin of a thing and its eventual utility, its actual employment and place in a system of purposes, lie worlds apart; whatever exists, having somehow come into being, is again and again reinterpreted to new ends, taken over, transformed, and redirected by some power superior to it. . . . and the entire history of a "thing," an organ, a custom can in this way be a continuous sign-chain of ever new interpretations and adaptations whose causes do not even have to be related to one another but, on the contrary, in some cases succeed and alternate with one another in a purely chance fashion. The "evolution" of a thing, a custom, an organ is thus by no means its *progressus* toward a goal, even less a logical *progressus* by the shortest route and with the smallest expenditure of force—but a succession of more or less profound, more or less mutually independent processes of subduing, plus the resistances they encounter, the attempts at transformation for the purpose of defense and reaction, and the results of successful counteractions. The form is fluid, but the "meaning" is even more so.[21]

The genealogy's allowance for contingency seems intuitively appropriate for the rather jumbled history of violations and resurrections of the chemical weapons norm. Indeed, the genealogical stance accords nicely with one of the most intriguing aspects of the story—the position of the United States, which went from being the only opponent of the first chemical weapons ban (the Hague Declaration), to being the primary proponent of efforts of a ban after World War I (the Geneva Protocol), a ban that the United States sought, achieved, but then failed to ratify. This stance favorably places the genealogist "to recognize the events of history, its jolts, its surprises, its unsteady victories and unpalatable defeats"—a task especially apposite for the uneven record of the norm proscribing chemical weapons.[22]

The genealogy of the chemical weapons taboo thus seeks to remedy the deficiencies of essentialist and deductive approaches by historicizing the accepted moral interpretations of weapons technologies and the place of chemical weapons within this moral domain. This operation reflects an understanding of genealogy as an effort to find history where it is not expected to be—those moral institutions and practices that are usually thought to be exempt from the contingencies of historical tangles.[23]

Besides emphasizing the importance of historical contingency in the social construction of norms, genealogy informs the analysis of this book through the employment of two of the genealogist's analytical tools: discourses and power. Discourses, the favored analytic focus of Foucault, are theoretical statements connected to social practices. These discourses produce and legitimize certain behaviors and conditions of life as "normal" and serve to politicize some phenomena over others.

For Foucault, the production of discourses is a form of power, as it constructs categories that themselves make a cluster of practices and understandings seem illegitimate or even inconceivable.[24] This disciplinary power defines what is normal and natural and what is unthinkable and reprehensible. Prohibitive norms in this sense do not merely restrain behavior, but they are productive in that they constitute who we are: "We form our identities by conforming ourselves over time to tacitly understood norms and generally accepted practices."[25] In this way, the genealogy introduces an element of power into the study of norms, a dimension often neglected in liberal attempts to distance the normative aspects of international relations from the realpolitik focus on power.[26]

Through such discursive analysis I examine how the categorizing of weapons naturalizes or delegitimizes practices of international violence and secures identities of actors in the process. The following chapters reflect the descriptive style of genealogical analysis through the identification of contending discourses and how they change over time. More specifically, I identify features of chemical weapons that came to be regarded as essential in disputes over the definition of acceptable behavior, the naming and evaluation of the weapon, and standards of judgment to be applied in assessing their legitimacy or lack thereof.[27]

Finally, the book reflects the genealogical method by posing the interpretive questions of understanding meaning. To paraphrase Nietzsche, the purpose of such interrogations is to bring to light not so much what the taboo has done as simply what it means. Of what meanings does the chemical weapons taboo consist, and what does it reveal about the practice of violence in international politics? Such queries bring to the analysis a dimension overlooked in positivist-inspired international relations theory, which has been primarily concerned with testing causal explanations of behavior to the neglect of understanding the meaning of discursive practices.[28] And it is such questions of meaning that will inform the account of the chemical weapons taboo: what understandings have made the use of these weapons appear aberrant and avoidable whereas the employment of other weapons seems inevitable and natural? What kind of international politics are promoted by these processes of legitimation and delegitimation?

Defining Moments

The chapters that follow are organized around an investigation of important defining moments in the history of the chemical weapons norm. This book does not provide a continuous history and comprehensive analysis of all the events affecting the norm prohibiting chemical weapons. Instead, it focuses on events of particular importance which provide discursive moments characterized by bursts of rich debate and which represent discussions of the crucial dimensions of the taboo. The first such period, and the subject of the second chapter, is the era of the Hague Peace Conferences of 1899 and 1907, when the topic of modern chemical weapons was first broached in a broadly international context. Chapter 3 addresses the significance and development of the chemical weapons discourses during World War I, and Chapter 4 examines the postwar efforts to ban chemical weapons. These chapters are of obvious significance as they trace the emergence of a prohibition in international law, the first major test of the emergent norm given institutionalized expression at the Hague, and the zenith of efforts to proscribe chemical weapons through international law (at least until 1993).

Chapters 5 and 6 each counterpoise a significant case of the use of chemical weapons with a subsequent and important case of non-use. These cases illustrate how norms operate in social life. Norms may function instrumentally, such as justifying action taken for other reasons, or operating as a palpable restraint in a cost-benefit decision calculation. Norms can also have enabling effects, whereby practices are made possible that would not exist in the absence of the norms. Whether enabling or constraining, norms can sometimes being so deeply embedded that they structure action without being consciously invoked. Finally, norms can have constitutive effects through the process of securing identities. Abiding by or violating social norms is an important way by which we gauge "who we are"—to be a certain kind of people means we just do not do certain things.

Chapters 5 and 6 demonstrate how violations actually provide opportunities for us to empirically analyze the role of norms. The violation of a norm does not mean it no longer exists or that it ceases to have an impact on social behavior; what matters is how the violation is interpreted by others and what subsequent practices serve to rehabilitate or undercut the norm.[29] In Chapter 5, I examine the use of gas by the Italians against Ethiopia in 1935–1936, and the surprising non-use of chemical weapons in the European theater during World War II. In Chapter 6, I analyze the chemical weapons discourse in the Iran-Iraq conflict—where chemical weapons were used extensively—and in the Gulf War of

1991—where, despite expectations, they were not used. Chapter 6 concludes with an analysis of the implications of the Chemical Weapons Convention of 1993. These later chapters determine the effects of the creation of nuclear weapons (and other weapons innovations such as fuel-air explosives and ballistic missiles) on the taboo against chemical weapons. Has the discourse regarding chemical weapons changed since the introduction of other weapons of mass destruction, and have chemical weapons therefore become more or less legitimate?

A chief concern of this book is to place the analysis within the broader issue of the status of other weapons. The most notable comparison to another weapon of the past is poison. The genealogy of the poison taboo (Chapter 2) yields valuable insights into moral discourses on weapons technologies, their role in the structuring of international violence, and the relationship between the poison taboo and the prohibition against chemical weapons. In subsequent chapters, the comparative element of the study focuses more closely on the ways in which chemical weapons have been distinguished from their technological contemporaries such as submarines and nuclear weapons.

The sources I draw on emphasize a temporal comparison of public interpretations of chemical weapons such as appear in negotiations among or speeches by political leaders, as well as newspaper and journal articles. I have paid particular attention to the proceedings and memoranda of international forums where the question of CW has been addressed, including the proceedings of the Hague, Washington, and Geneva Conferences, and other sources such as congressional ratification debates and League of Nations and United Nations conferences.

The Argument

This genealogical study of the chemical weapons taboo remedies the errors and addresses the silences of previous approaches. The essentialist argument, which assumes that chemical weapons have been proscribed because of the intrinsically cruel characteristics of the weapon, contains a partial truth, but it cannot offer a satisfactory explanation on its own. The realist argument that "only useless weapons are banned" also fails to account for this prohibitionary norm. The inadequacies of both of these alternative explanations are engaged in the chapters that follow.

Instead, I interpret the institutional dimensions of this moral norm and how it was constructed and contested at the international level. Concerning the origins of the taboo, I argue that an appreciation of the Hague Conferences is crucial to understanding the conditions that gave rise to the chemical weapons prohibition. First, at these conferences expression was given to the emerging standards of "civilized" international society, and it is within this context of civilized international behavior that the ban on chemical weapons was implicated from the beginning. Part of what makes the taboo unique from past resistances to other weapons is that it was forged simultaneously with the notion that modern technology threatened to turn upon itself and threaten its allegedly civilized masters. Moreover, although the initial treatment of chemical weapons was embedded in a discourse of "civilization," this discourse subsequently operated as a disciplining discourse that provides the context of explanation for the violations of the taboo after World War I and arms control efforts in the 1990s.

Second, the Hague Declaration banning asphyxiating shells was unique in that it proscribed a whole category of weapons before they were even developed. As I argue in Chapters 2 and 3, this preemptive proscription altered the usual dynamics of moral protest against novel weaponry. Moreover, as I demonstrate in Chapter 4, it also provided the crucial international context for renewed efforts to ban chemical weapons after World War I. Without the Hague Declaration, these later efforts would most likely not have been concluded, and the chemical weapons taboo would have gone the usual way of moral protests against weapons innovations. This emphasis on the Hague Declaration stands in sharp contrast to its neglect in the literature, a neglect usually attributed to the supposed irrelevance of the Hague rules after the disaster of World War I.

The reincarnation of the chemical weapons ban after World War I was driven by the genuine moral rejection of CW by political leaders on the international scene. But it also owed much to a series of fortuitous events and circumstances. Although most people assume that the taboo arose naturally from distaste following the use of gas in World War I, Chapter 3 shows that what did *not* happen during World War I was more important: chemical weapons were not intentionally employed as civilian killers. The absence of a process whereby civilians grudgingly "got used to" yet another horrific means of warfare meant that the overzealous lobbying efforts of the chemical lobby after World War I worked all too well and crystallized the public's attention on chemical weapons as a special threat to civilians about which something had to be done.

The genealogical play of contingency and moral opprobrium combined over time to create an institutional legacy that legitimized a particular moral interpretation of chemical weapons. By the eve of World War II, this legacy set chemical weapons apart as a threshold weapon that it was hoped would not be used even as it was believed it inevitably would. Hope won a tenuous victory over conviction, and Chapter 5 demonstrates in various ways how the non-use of chemical weapons during World War II simply cannot be explained without an appreciation of the role of the CW prohibitionary norm.

The genealogical approach to the chemical weapons taboo offers additional purchase for understanding more recent developments in the issue of chemical weapons. Chapter 6 makes the counter-intuitive argument that the norm operated during the Iran-Iraq War—when chemical weapons were used—much as it did during World War II—when they were *not* used. Again, the disciplining discourse of "civilization" best accounts for Iraq's actions in the 1980s, as well as for various Arab nations' resistance to the Chemical Weapons Convention (CWC) of 1993. In Foucauldian fashion, some nations have inverted the disciplinary discourse that labeled chemical weapons the "poor man's bomb." Building upon the discourse of "weapons of mass destruction," these states have sought to parlay the West's disdain for CW into an extension of the discriminatory international nonproliferation regime by withholding their participation in the CWC until comparable efforts are made to proscribe other weapons of mass destruction.

In the end, the genealogical analysis of the chemical weapons discourse reveals a shift in the site at which the taboo has been contested, and I argue that this shift indicates the increasing robustness of the taboo over time. Chronicled in Chapter 3, a vociferous debate took place in the interwar period concerning the humanitarian status of chemical weapons. Some argued that these weapons were the most awful product yet of modern technology; others contended that they were the most morally desirable weapon yet devised, for they spared soldiers from the disfiguring mutilations of bombs and bullets while killing far fewer of their victims. By the era of the CWC following the Iran-Iraq and Gulf Wars, the site at which the norm is contested had shifted. No longer is it acceptable to openly question the interpretation of chemicals as abominable weapons. At issue is whether certain states should be permitted to retain weapons of mass destruction to prevent war while others are not. The resistance to the CWC by some nations is justified as an effort to extend the global proliferation regime for all weapons of mass destruction. Not only does this position assume the illegitimate humanitarian status of chemical weapons, it positively depends on them being portrayed as horrifying weapons on the order of nuclear weapons. Rather than the usual historical pattern of moral restraints eroding over time, the discursive inclusion of chemical weapons in the category of weapons of mass destruction represents an unparalleled extension of the category of proscribed weapons.

The Origins of the Chemical Weapons Taboo

Each tradition grows more venerable the farther its origin lies in the past, the more it is forgotten; the respect paid to the tradition accumulates from generation to generation; finally the origin becomes sacred and awakens awe.

—Nietzsche, *Human, All-Too-Human*

The Hague Peace Conferences of 1899 and 1907 constitute our starting point. It was at those conferences that the topic of chemical weapons was first discussed in a broadly international setting, even though such weapons had yet to be developed. Isolated precursors of chemical warfare had appeared sporadically in the history of conflict, mostly the use of choking smoke in siege warfare.[1] Such methods were so isolated, undeveloped, and generally foreign to the practice of warfare, however, that their use played for the most part a negligible role in the development of a normative discourse concerning modern chemical weapons— they simply were not significant enough to attract sustained attention.[2] A few past practices were relevant for aspects of the CW taboo; in particular, I examine the relationship between the discourses regarding poison and chemical weapons and associations with biological weapons. Before I attend to those connections, however, I focus on the story of modern chemical weapons. That story begins in earnest with the assembly of the world's major nations in the Hague at the end of the nineteenth century.

This period has been overlooked in much of the CW literature, largely because scholars assume that the widespread use of chemical weapons in World War I made the Hague Declaration (and therefore the serious study of it) largely superfluous. Thus most of the work on the chemical weapons taboo accords but a perfunctory nod to the Hague Declaration and takes as the point of departure postwar efforts to ban CW. This neglect has obscured crucial sources of the taboo that lie at the heart of the prohibition, and, if we ignore the significance of these early efforts, we risk failing to adequately understand the success of the proscription of CW.

It is usually assumed that the "age-old" ban on poison in warfare accounts for the origins of the chemical weapons taboo, an assumption that prima facie is not unreasonable. This chapter provides an in-depth analysis of the way in which chemical weapons were distinguished from other weapons of this era, and it explores the relationship of the prohibition to the ban against poison. Although the poison taboo does not entirely account for the specific ban on asphyxiating shells institutionalized at the Hague, a genealogy of the ban on poison nonetheless elucidates the operation of a moral discourse on weapons technology and its political significance in the international politics of war. Moreover, the taboo prohibiting chemical weapons has subsequently been reinforced by a belief in the more general and older ban on poison, and this process reveals the genealogical workings of a moral discourse with shifting purposes and consequences.

The Hague Conferences

On January 11, 1899, the nations of the world were invited by Russia to a proposed peace conference, one of the tasks of which was to seek "without delay means for putting a limit to the progressive increase of military and naval armaments." More specifically, the Russian circular proposed the following subjects for international discussion:

> To prohibit the use in the armies and fleets of any new kinds of firearms whatever, and of new explosives, or any powders more powerful than those now in use, either for rifles or cannon.
>
> To restrict the use in military warfare of the formidable explosives already existing, and to prohibit the throwing of projectiles or explosives of any kind from balloons or by any similar means.
>
> To prohibit the use, in naval warfare, of submarine torpedo boats or plungers, or other similar means engines of destruction; to give an undertaking not to construct, in the future, vessels with rams.[3]

Limitations for a number of weapons were discussed at the Hague Conferences of 1899 and 1907. At the conference of 1899, the delegates adopted a declaration whereby they agreed "to abstain from the use of projectiles the sole object of which is the diffusion of asphyxiating or deleterious gases."[4] At the time, these weapons had not yet actually been developed, though experimental ideas had been proposed. It is easy to conclude that the prohibition of these implements was attained at the Hague only because such weapons were of no military utility at the time, especially since the same conference refused proposals to eliminate weapons that had become militarily useful.[5] Indeed, the declaration was not seen as particularly significant by all concerned. As one observer of the conference of 1899 noted: "There was talk of including the three declarations drawn up by the first commission in a fourth convention, but it was decided not to dignify those insignificant resolutions in that way. They were to go before the conference as separate documents, hardly more important than the numerous recommendations attached to the final act."[6]

Certainly, the historical beginnings of the norm proscribing CW owe much to the fact that chemical weapons were of no military significance at the time and that the agreement to prohibit their use was thus also perceived as being of less than great importance. This is not the whole story, however. For if the delegates at the Hague Conferences did not agree to eliminate militarily significant weapons, they did agree on other kinds of limitations on weapons. We need to consider the significance and form of prohibitions on other weapons in order to determine whether there was anything unique about the initial treatment of chemical weapons in the Hague Declaration.

Proposals were considered at the Hague Conferences of 1899 and 1907 to limit powders, muskets, explosives, and field guns, but these discussions failed resoundingly to produce any agreements on weapons-specific restrictions. There were, however, agreements on limiting the use of some weapons according to the laws and customs of warfare. A Convention Relative to the Laying of Automatic Submarine Contact Mines was agreed to at the 1907 Conference. The convention prohibited "the use of anchored automatic contact mines which do not become harmless when they have broken loose from their moorings as well as the use of torpedoes which do not become harmless when they have missed their mark."[7]

The records of the conference indicate that the legitimacy accorded to mines rested in the end upon an appeal to the "imperative requirements of war," otherwise known as the doctrine of military necessity. What comes to be counted as an "imperative exigency of war" is not simply a given, however. It may seem that virtually every novel technology of warfare is eventually adopted, a phenomenon that has led some to ponder the autonomy of technology and the lack of human control over its advance. Still, the legitimation of novel weapons technologies is at least a potentially contested political construction. What needs to be understood are, first, the conditions under which the discourses arise which serve to legitimate weapons technologies as unavoidable necessities (or delegitimate them as unnecessary cruelties) and, second, the mechanisms by which these interpretations become dominant.

In the case of mines, the records of the Hague Conferences reveal a fundamental understanding: a weapon that injures the armed forces of the enemy is acceptable, whereas one that poses dangers to civilians is not. The notion of civilian discrimination, of course, has a long history in just-war doctrine, and it invites a genealogical investigation of its own.[8] I confine myself here, however, to the observation that the underlying condition that enabled this kind of distinction was the dominant interpretation of technology as a value-neutral phenomenon. According to this interpretation, technology has no moral value in and of itself; it is intrinsically neither good nor bad. Rather, the moral value of technology depends upon how it is used. The employment of mines, according to the dominant understanding at the Hague, was considered "in itself allowable"; only certain uses of certain kinds of mines were unacceptable. An absolute prohibition on all mines technologies was seen as not only impossible but undesirable as well. A fundamental distinction was therefore made between types of mines (anchored and unanchored), and the limits were designed to limit certain uses of mines.

The subject of submarine torpedoes was also discussed at the Hague in 1899, but no agreement was reached on prohibiting their use. A scholarly assessment of this issue some twenty years later nicely summarized the understanding that prevailed at the Hague and since: "The submarine is not as such an unlawful weapon at all, but the particular mode in which it is used may make it so. . . . Torpedoes at one time had their share of the execration which nearly always greets all new weapons of warfare. But long before the great war they had outlived this unpopularity, and there is now no doubt as to their legality."[9]

This treatment of mines and submarines reflects the dominant conception of weapons technologies of the contemporary era—the belief that technologies are not inherently moral or immoral. The contemporary slogan that "guns don't kill people, people do" accesses this powerful understanding of technology as value-neutral. Given this interpretation, limitations on weapons technologies almost invariably take the form of restrictions on certain uses of certain kinds of technologies. The treatment of weapons discussed at the Hague Conferences generally conformed to this understanding, whether or not actual limitations were agreed upon. For example, whereas no agreements could be reached on limiting the size or power of explosives and powders, the delegates did agree to prohibit the bombardment of undefended habitations.

The unique aspect of the prohibition against asphyxiating shells is that it did not simply ban particular uses of such shells in the usual manner (namely, against undefended populations), while legitimating their use among and against soldiers in the field. The declaration posited any use of such weapons between contracting powers as unacceptable. In the process, the ban helped to define them as a particular category of weapon and thus to politicize these weapons as a category in themselves, a phenomenon of critical importance that we need to examine in depth.[10] How was it that these weapons were not subjected to the more circumscribed prohibition applied to other weapons?

"To Disgrace Iron with Poison"

When the topic of odious methods of warfare is raised, it is not at all exceptional to hear chemical weapons and poison mentioned in the same breath; after all, the former are often referred to as "poisonous gases." It may thus come as no surprise that a very plausible explanation for the origins of the ostracism of chemical weapons is their close kinship to poison, a method of warfare thought to have been condemned throughout the ages as treacherous and cowardly. Indeed, in many scholarly treatments of CW issues, it is simply assumed that an axiomatic connection between chemical weapons and poison explains the chemical weapons taboo.

Some attempts to understand the obloquy attached to CW have taken the form of trying to explain why humans have a special psychological horror of poison. Michael Mandelbaum has taken this approach and has sought to understand the "special kind of moral opprobrium" reserved for chemical weapons by examining the deep-rooted cultural and institutional reasons for mankind's aversion to toxic substances.[11] Despite the difficulties of Mandelbaum's study, his treatment of the issue raises several important puzzles.

First, can we give a more complete political account of the origins of the poison taboo itself? If so, an interpretation of the meaning of those origins may highlight the discursive mechanisms by which this norm has become so deeply ingrained, in turn sensitizing us to discursive practices important to the norm proscribing chemical weapons. Second, how valid is the assumption that the chemical weapons taboo can be explained by the fact that chemical weapons are perceived to be a kind of poison? If the contemporary use of chemical weapons seems indelibly identified with other poisoned weapons as an utterly horrible and unacceptable practice of warfare, we can still inquire about the extent to which the identification of contemporary chemical weapons with poison lies at the origins of the moral opprobrium they have incurred. Analyzing the ahistorical identification of chemical weapons as poison leads us to examine whether the crucial condition for the origins of the chemical weapons taboo was the intrinsic quality of the first gas weapons: were gas weapons seen as little more than variations on poison and therefore subject to poison's traditional restraints?

At the Hague Conferences of 1899 and 1907, widespread international agreement was achieved on the systematic codification of the rules of warfare, a first among modern states. Three major conventions resulted from the conference of 1899, one of which—the Convention with Respect to the Laws and Customs of War on Land—contained a prohibition on the use of poison. Among the methods of warfare that were "especially prohibited" by Article 23(a) of that convention was the employment of "poison or poisoned arms." The sources of this prohibition were twofold. The first was a generally accepted notion of a customary prohibition on poison that had existed throughout the ages. In the opinion of one scholar, the prohibition on poison in Article 23(a) of the Hague was "handed down immemorially among all peoples having any degree of civilization."[12] The second source consisted of more contemporaneous attempts to explicitly codify the prohibition as a written rule of international law. By all accounts, the delegates at the Hague Conference of 1899 saw themselves as attempting to reach international agreement on rules of warfare which had been given their first systematic legal expression at the Brussels Conference of 1874. No formal agreement had been reached at Brussels, but many of the rules codified at that conference served as the basis for the agreements reached in 1899.[13]

Significantly, the ban on poison embodied in Article 13(a) of the Brussels Conference was reached without controversy. Whereas the consideration of other rules was marked by substantive debate catalogued in the conference report by Sir A. Horsford, British delegate to Brussels, discussion on the ban on poison was not so documented, for the simple reason that it did not present any points of interest.[14] Evidently, no justifications were needed to support a ban on poison. By the era of the Brussels Conference, the moral taboo on the use of poison was an uncontested norm.

An examination of the proceedings of the conference of 1899 confirms the uncontested status of the norm against poison. As at Brussels, the ban on poison was marked by little discussion; the prohibitions of Article 23, including that on poison, were adopted unanimously, and there seems to be no record of any debate on the specific prohibition on poison.[15]

If we consider the tremendous hold of this moral interpretation of poison, however, we may appreciate more acutely its meaning and significance for the practice of warfare and its relation to the taboo on CW. By the close of the nineteenth century, the prohibition on poison provoked no controversy. This development is echoed in the academic literature, where the meaning of banning poison remarkably has gone quite unexamined. As the author of one of the most probing treatments on the subject states, "consultation of standard textbooks and military manuals on the meaning of poison and poisoned weapons further confirms how little explored this field is."[16]

So absolute is the reign of this interpretation, I suggest, that in the realm of warfare the practice of treating poison as a human technology has largely gone into desuetude. Poison seems not to be conceived of as a military technology in the traditional sense, whereby its moral value would depend upon how it were used. Poison seems to constitute a different category of technology whose use is regarded as morally undesirable in and of itself: not just some uses, but *any* use in warfare—in international politics—is unacceptable.

The common associations of poison with cruelty, secrecy, or perfidy are often taken as reason enough to account for this distaste. Indeed, we can see such associations in the forerunner of the Brussels rules of warfare, the 1863 "Instructions for the Government of Armies of the United States in the Field," a manual issued to the Union Army during the American Civil War. Known as the "Lieber Code" after its author, it proscribed the use of poison by virtue of Article 16: "Military necessity does not admit of cruelty—that is, the infliction of suffering for the sake of suffering or for revenge, nor of maiming or wounding except in fight, nor of torture to extort confessions. It does not admit of the use of poison in any way, nor of the wanton destruction of a district."[17]

The association of poison with such characteristics as cruelty and unnecessary suffering undoubtedly sustains the contemporary disdain of poison as an illegitimate means of warfare, but it is problematic to assume the sufficiency of these "reasons" to account for the origins of the ban on poison. Again, how it is that we understand poison as causing "unnecessary suffering," whereas a plethora of other horrible weapons have by converse definition come to be accepted as resulting in "necessary suffering?" This question becomes acute when we recognize that in European civilization a robust consensus stigmatizing poison—such that questioning this taboo is virtually unthinkable—has obtained only in relatively recent times.

Since ancient times, references to poison as a dastardly substance have occurred in a variety of locations and cultures.[18] In Homer's *Odyssey*,

Athene explains that Ilos denied Odysseus a poison to smear on his arrows out of fear of the gods.[19] In the Hindu Laws of Manu (ca. 200 B.C.–A.D. 200) it is written that when a king "fights with his foes in battle, let him not strike with weapons concealed, nor with (such as are) barbed, poisoned, or the points of which are blazing with fire."[20] The Romans often condemned the use of poisoned weapons; the infamy of such implements is captured pointedly in the revealing remark by Silinius that poisoned spears and such are to be condemned for they "disgrace iron with poison."[21]

Encountering such evidence of ancient strictures against poison, most contemporary observers attribute a universal and age-old character to the taboo against the use of poison. But although evidence exists of a long tradition of opposition to the use of poison and poisoned weapons, it is by no means clear that this tradition reflects a robust, uncontested, and universal prohibition, a taboo uniquely and primordially rooted in human nature that has effectively curbed the use of such methods in all places since time began.

Alberico Gentili's classic seventeenth-century survey of the law on poison marshals an impressive array of opinions to support his contention that the use of poison is contrary to the law of war. It is important to note, however, that he seeks to counter a group of dissenters who do not share his opinion: Heptacometae, Getae, Parthians, Ethiopians, Africans, Caspians, Scots, Gauls, Turks, and Florentines to name a few. Despite his wish "that it were so," Gentili in 1612 was not able to treat the prohibition of poison in warfare as "a matter which is not in doubt". but was compelled to address the subject as in need of demonstration and defense.[22] Baldus, for one, argued that it was allowable to kill one's enemy with poison.[23] In fact, defenses of using poison and poisonous weapons were being made as late as the middle of the eighteenth century.[24] And indeed, even Gentili was to grant an exception to the illegitimacy of the use of poisons—namely, in wars of extermination![25]

Poisons and poisoned weapons were known and used from Europe to Asia, through Africa to the New World.[26] Gentili's numerous examples of the use of poison show that the idea of resorting to poison was not unheard of, even in Renaissance Europe. Indeed, even so exalted a personage as Leonardo da Vinci recommended to the ruler of Milan that one good way to deal with a hungry enemy was to poison the fruit trees on his line of march.[27] One commentator lamented that during the period from the eleventh to the fifteenth century a strong mark of the "defalcation of proper principles" was the "frequent use of poison."[28] Grotius's treatment of the subject in 1625 admitted that natural law allowed the use of poison, and his argument against poison suggests that the prohibition was not universally heeded: "Nevertheless from old times the law of nations—if not of all nations, certainly of those of the better sort—has been that it is not permissible to kill an enemy by poison."[29] This theme was echoed in Gentili's argument that poison was illegitimate because it was a weapon typical of barbarians and savages.

I do not argue that the use of poison was a widespread, uncontroversial, and universally embraced method of warfare—far from it. My point is that the significant formative period for the robust and taken-for-granted prohibition against poisonous weapons in Europe is more recent than is often supposed: "It is fairly clear that, until the fifteenth century, the European law of nations did not know of any rules prohibiting in warfare the use of either poison or poisoned weapons. Conversely, little doubt exists that, by the beginning of the eighteenth century, if not earlier, these rules came to form an accepted part of the laws of war as applied between civilised nations of Europe."[30] In similar spirit, Louis Lewin explains the increased protests against poisoned weapons during the sixteenth and seventeenth centuries as arising from their increasing prevalence in warfare. One result was the Strassburg agreement of 1675 between the French and Germans which prohibited the use of poisoned and otherwise unusually configured bullets.[31]

The question is, then, how to account for the relatively recent universal acceptance of poison as an absolutely unacceptable weapon of warfare. What is the meaning behind this understanding, and what are the conditions under which the rubric of "unnecessary suffering" is successfully invoked over and above the legitimizing discourse of "military necessity?"

In his analysis of the source of the poison prohibition, Schwarzenberger argues that the contemporary understanding of poison as something that causes death or injury "excludes death or injury to health by means of force, whether the cut of a sword, the thrust of a spear, the piercing of the body by an arrow or bullet, or injury inflicted by explosion or blast."[32] This definition in terms of *force* echoes the eighteenth reason (of twenty) for the poison taboo cited by Gentili: "Since war is a contest of force, it ought not to be carried on with poisons, which are distinguished from force."[33] This notion provides a crucial clue in uncovering the genesis of the ban on poison. Poison has come to be understood as not constituting a form of force as ordinarily conceived.

Why the distinction between force and weapons such as poison? Margaret Hallissy has argued that the image of poison issued from men's fear of its potential role as an equalizer by which women could upset the dominance of men. Women could use to advantage their arena of control—the household—via the food the victims ate and the medicines they took. Unlike death by the contest of physical strength, as idealized in the notion of open battle, death by poison brings no glory. As Hallissy explains:

> The idea of the deceptiveness of women is essential to understanding the image of poison. Poison can never be used as an honorable weapon in a fair duel between worthy opponents, as the sword or gun, male weapons, can. A man who uses such a secret weapon is beneath contempt. Publicly acknowledged rivalry is a kind of bonding in which each worthy opponent gives the other the opportunity to demonstrate prowess. Such heroic rivalries must be between equals, between the same kinds of creatures. . . . The dueler is open, honest, and strong; the poisoner, fraudulent, scheming, and weak. A man with a gun or a sword is a threat, but he declares himself to be so, and his intended victim can arm himself: may the best man win and have the public glory of being acknowledged the best man . . . Poison is an insidious equalizer of strength in the battle of the sexes. The poisoner uses superior secret knowledge to compensate for physical inferiority. A weak woman planning a poison is as deadly as a man with a gun, but because she plots in secret, the victim is the more disarmed.[34]

The image of poison, on this account, is that of an instrument of female power, a potential equalizer in a battle for domination which needed to be demonized as witchcraft to ensure that the physical contest of brute strength determined relations of domination. This reading would appear to be confirmed by two aspects of Gentili's treatment of the issue: not only does his case against poison include an argument condemning "incantations and magic arts, which are included under the head of poisons," but he also disavows the use of such means "because rivalry in arms is thus done away with, since there is then no trust to be put in arms; and so war is done away with, since it is rivalry in arms."[35]

Schwarzenberger has sketched other historical influences that may have served to delegitimize poison. His account ends with an astonishing argument by Grotius:

> The anti-Borgia propaganda, first used by an ultimately successful faction in the Vatican and their lay confederates and then employed for anti-Popish purposes in general could only gain in impetus by the assertion of the villainy and illegality of weapons used by this admittedly unholy family. Moreover, the mercenaries who hired out their services to the highest bidder could not but look with professional disfavour at weapons which deprived them of a sporting chance to escape death if, in battle, they were not killed outright, but merely lightly wounded. To them, the inevitable

fatality of a poisoned wound was as good a reason as any why the use of this weapon was unprofessional. Yet, theirs was not the only trade union. Princes at large considered that poison was a weapon against which, even when they were in the midst of powerful armies, they were largely helpless. In a remarkable *Cui bono* argument, Grotius explained in this way the origin of the rule on the prohibition of the use of poison.[36]

Apart from these historical practices, the very publication of Grotius's influential treatise of 1625 itself is likely to have contributed significantly to the prohibition on poison. The relevant passage reads: "Agreement upon this matter arose from a consideration of the common advantage, in order that the dangers of war, which had begun to be frequent, might not be too widely extended. And it is easy to believe that this agreement originated with kings, whose lives are better defended by arms than those of other men, but are less safe from poison, unless they are protected by some respect for law and *by fear of disgrace*."[37]

In 1758 Vattel offered a similar defense of the prohibition of poison weapons, arguing that they only made war more deadly without gaining either side an advantage.[38] A more recent study has noted that "the rule entered into international law primarily because medieval monarchs were often eliminated by their rivals via poison in food or drink. Poison was thus a very individualistic method of doing away with an enemy."[39]

Indeed, this method could have been quite debilitating for the conduct of politics in the structure of fragmented allegiances and family feuds that characterized medieval and Renaissance Europe. During the age of princes, the nature of war, weaponry, and politics tended "to exaggerate even further the importance of a very few individuals, creating what amounted to a historical star system."[40] The practices and rituals of warfare, including duels (the institution of individualized combat par excellence), "served to define the individual identities of the trans-European aristocracy."[41] Often born of personal rivalries and dynastic intrigue, wars of this period frequently also were waged in a personal manner, as rulers led campaigns on the battlefield themselves. In short, as one historian of the period has summarized, it was an era in which wars were ultimately personal matters.[42]

During this period of fluid violence, the personalized campaigns organized by military aristocracies were especially susceptible to the killing of leaders. The armies of princes were largely comprised of elite corps of knights sworn to be loyal only to their princes[43] or, later on, of mercenaries whose allegiance was a fickle thing indeed, as so memorably captured by Machiavelli.[44] Quite absent were the feelings of transcendent loyalty inspired by nationalism and patriotism.[45] In such circumstances, the use of poison to eliminate the prince was a quick method of ending a military confrontation. Recalling the deaths by poison of no less than nine of Charlemagne's successors and five popes of that era, one author has remarked that "the writings of these ages seem to show that poisoning was *à la mode* as a weapon of political murder, or vengeance."[46]

Thus emerges a political explanation for the efficacy of the prohibition on poison: poison was perceived as a threat to the practice of warfare as a circumscribed and personalized contest of force by those in control of the most powerful means of force. In other words, if the political practice of war was to remain "the sport of kings," an institution that legitimated the right of the powerful to prevail and conferred advantages and status upon those who had the most physical wealth and power (technological sophistication, economic wealth, manpower, and so on), then techniques that could undermine that practice could not be tolerated. Poison threatened this social institution because its easy accessibility and the inability to defend against it could leave princes vulnerable to assassination and perhaps disastrously disrupt the lives of taxpaying peasants.[47] Moreover, should the use of poison be tolerated, it also threatened to undermine the class structure of war, for a relative commoner could possess significant destructive capacity without the elaborate and expensive knightly accoutrements of horse, armor, and the like. To castigate the use of poison as not being "noble" or "honorable" was literally to reveal how it violated a particular cultural conception of warfare and its place in politics.

A similar sentiment lay behind the historic condemnation of the bow as a weapon, epitomized in the Second Lateran Council's ban of the crossbow in wars among Christians in 1139. Such weapons enabled a cowardly weakling to kill noble warriors from a distance without engaging in manly, hand-to-hand combat. "One reason why the bow was disliked was precisely because it was cheap, hence accessible to anyone and hardly worth bothering with as a status-symbol."[48] Relations of authority involved imputing status to means of contesting power that were exclusive to a relative few while denying status to those that were all too common. Poison could be a great equalizer and subvert the hierarchy of power: with the poisoning of water or food supplies, princes and potentially their populations could be destroyed by otherwise weak adversaries without a "war" in the sense of the "fair fight" implied by legitimated contests of strength.

The use of poison posed the kind of problem raised by nuclear weapons—the possibility of efficient killing without a technological means of defense. Poison differs, however, in that it is low cost and technologically simple, and thus widely available. Biological warfare offers similar advantages, but the spread of disease as a weapon carries the dangerous potential of turning on its own users.[49]

Rather than attempting to eradicate war as a political practice among the most powerful, the historical response to poison has been to gradually eliminate it as a legitimate option of force. In this respect, the "inevitable" if "natural" tragedy of war is revealed as a carefully preserved social institution. The consolidation of the poison taboo is related to the increasing concentration of legitimized coercive means at the hands of the centralized sovereign state and the concomitant elimination of other means of violence.[50]

In a sense, civilians have been a beneficiary of the genealogical creep of the poison taboo from its origins in political relations of domination to an unquestioned ban that applies to all people everywhere at all times.[51] Any use of poison, even against soldiers, has come to be understood as an unacceptable practice of warfare. The use of poison has come to be stigmatized as immoral in and of itself. "Cruelty," "secrecy," "inevitability of death," "unnecessary suffering," and other such categories have become associated with poison, but the "reasons" usually cited as the sufficient source of the prohibition on poison owe their *success* to a political context in which certain features of poison are given a particular meaning that stresses the inability to defend against (by other technological means) an easily available weapon of destruction, a very effective weapon of the weak.

Once rooted, the poison taboo is reinforced in the international realm by the appeal to civilization and civilized conduct. Poison is chastised as a weapon typical of savages and barbarians—the most civilized nations, it is claimed, refrain from using these weapons. Recall the words of T. J. Lawrence that the poison taboo at the Hague was "handed down immemorially among all peoples having any degree of civilization." For warfare to remain accepted as the proper way to contest power in international politics, the very idea of technologically unsophisticated peoples possessing indefensible methods of destruction had to be delegitimized. "A stupid despot may constrain his slaves with iron chains; but a true politician binds them even more strongly by the chain of their own ideas."[52] Conversely, warfare itself needed to be legitimized. Thus, at the same time that it denigrates poison as a "disgrace," Silinius' memorable phrase legitimizes the "iron" of the spear and sword. The standard of civilization was a powerful legitimizing inducement for nations eager to be included in the family of nations.[53]

The classic reason given for the abhorrence of poison—that it renders death inevitable—is nonetheless important in understanding the way warfare is culturally constituted. The meaning of warfare implicit in the standard understanding of the poison taboo is that war is a social contest rather than a no-holds-barred drive to extermination. Even if the occurrence of war seems to reflect an ever-present contest of power in social life, the form of war is not invariable. Mere killing is generally a means of war, rarely an end in itself; extermination campaigns and genocide are the rare exception rather than the rule. War is a contest of power, and the point of battle is to defeat the opponents' ability to resist according to a legitimated means of adjudicating what counts as power—a means that usually falls short of sheer physical annihilation. As Elaine Scarry points out in her thoughtful exploration of the meaning of war, the conclusion of most wars requires a form of social agreement, a form of institutionalized settlement of relations of domination that goes beyond mere extermination of all opponents.[54]

To the extent that the strength of the poison taboo can be attributed to a repugnance for rendering death in battle inevitable, it reflects the prevalent historical treatment of war as a political practice impregnated with social norms rather than devoid of them. If killing were the sole and necessary objective of all wars, the means to that end would not matter and a poison taboo would be unheard of. The success of the prohibition of poison, then, underscores the social features of the institution of war and its emphasis on notions such as honor. In short, Clausewitz's dictum that war is an extension of politics by other means is usually correct, excepting the relatively rare cases of absolute or total war.

The preceding argument further suggests that the political success and robustness of a prohibition on poison—as opposed to comparable aversions we surely have to other weapons that cause horrendous suffering—depends historically on the fact that war as a carefully circumscribed institution of the dominant requires expensive, elaborate, and technologically advanced means of warfare to be accepted as natural means for contesting "strength" and as unavoidable facts of life in international politics. That is, those exclusive means are legitimated that play to the strengths of established relations of domination, whether patriarchal or intergovernmental. War is rarely all-out slaughter but is rather a contest, a "rivalry in arms" in Gentili's telling words. Easily available "equalizers" that could upset the system without a fair physical fight on the dominant powers' own terms most therefore be delegitimized.[55] Johannes Felden in 1635 defended the use of poison *against the powerful*, and it was against just such notions that the discourse prohibiting poison was arrayed.[56]

The success of this ritualization of war is striking, especially considering that the chief means by which the West has judged the degree of civility of other cultures is precisely in terms of their level of technological achievement.[57] To delegitimize poison and poisoned weapons is to delegitimize a technological feat of unsurpassed efficiency, a value that is otherwise taken as the hallmark of civilization in the modern technological world. The otherwise self-sustaining logic of limitless technological innovation undermines itself when it is too successful—that is, when no technological counter can be found to a ruthlessly efficient and accessible means of killing which threatends to undermine other currencies of domination.

The virtual unanimity with which poison is unquestioningly associated with categories such as "barbarity," "cruelty," and "unnecessary suffering" testifies to the enormous success of this delegitimation process. Typical of this understanding is the statement that "savages use poisoned weapons; but civilized mankind has expelled them from its warfare . . . The secrecy and cruelty associated with death by poison, and the danger that innocent people may be made to suffer along with or instead of foes, will serve to account for the deep-seated abhorrence of such a method of destruction."[58]

To be sure, poison is cruel and barbarous but so are other weapons that are not so indelibly stamped with moral opprobrium. Neither an inherent quality of cruelty nor even a humanitarian concern for civilian suffering per se accounts for the successful proscription of poison as a practice of violence. Poison was perceived politically as a weapons technology that was too efficient and too readily available, and against which there was no defense. Moral categories gained hold only after poison was stigmatized as a weapon of technologically weak adversaries. To the extent that moral arguments of civilian discrimination and cruelty have come to justify the prohibition on poison and to associate poison with biological warfare, the particular social purposes of the ban have been forgotten. As Nietzsche forcefully observes, it is precisely such processes of forgetting that are crucial in the dominion of moral interpretations.[59] The common belief that the poison taboo dates from time immemorial imparts a veneer of unbroken continuity to the effectiveness of the taboo which in turn reinforces its moral power.

The task remains to determine how much the codification of the prohibition on poison at the Hague owes to these arguments from cruelty and civilian suffering. Guggenheim argues that the reports of the Hague Conference of 1899 indicate that Article 23(a) must be limited to acts of secret poisoning which indiscriminately endanger combatants and the civilian population. This interpretation would suggest that the taboo on poison had not yet become an absolute discourse and that rationales were still required to justify a prohibition. There is simply no foundation for this interpretation, however, for the records of the conference indicate merely that this article was included to respond to the formulation of Article 13(a) of Brussels.[60]

Although the moral interpretation of poison as something particularly heinous is a relatively recent political construction in European civilization, the notion had become so robust by the end of the nineteenth century that a prohibition on poison no longer required a moral justification. Moreover, the dominion of this interpretation has become so successful that the use of poison as a potential technology of war has largely gone out of practice. The original purposes of the ban have been forgotten. The ban on poison has become absolute; any use of poison, even against soldiers in the field, is prohibited. To put this phenomenon in sharper relief, we need only recall Lawrence's statement on the futility of weapons limitations, noting how it seems to forget that poison is a technology of war: "The attempts which have been made to forbid the introduction of new inventions into warfare, or prevent the use of instruments that cause destruction on a large scale, are doomed to failure. Man always has improved his weapons, and always will as long as he has need for them at all."[61]

As we saw in the Chapter 1, there is a general belief that only insignificant and ineffective weapons can be restrained. Typical of this widespread conviction is M. W. Royse's statement that "a weapon will be restricted in inverse proportion, more or less, to its effectiveness; that the more efficient a weapon or method of warfare the less likelihood there is of its being restricted in action by the rules of war."[62]

So prevalent is this truism that it has actually been invoked to explain the ban on poison. Despite the clear implications of Grotius's tract, one of his interpreters has read the accepted wisdom of weapons bans backwards into that essay and has quite incorrectly surmised that the ban "probably reflected the inefficiency of poison as a weapon."[63] Even William O'Brien, in one of the most historically sensitive treatments of the CW ban, which spends considerable effort analyzing the possible links between the CW norm and the prohibition against poison, overlooks poison by stating that chemical and biological warfare come closest to providing examples of totally outlawed means of warfare.[64]

The findings of this chapter belie such propositions, for poison can be thought of as precisely the kind of efficient instrument of destruction that Royse and O'Brien have in mind when dismissing the possibility of effective weapons bans. It has, however, come to be seen as a weapon indelibly associated with cruelty and unnecessary suffering, and has been the subject of spectacularly successful efforts to ban its use. "Necessary suffering," by implication, would seem to accrue from methods of violence which are the purview of the dominant or which can be countered technologically (in other words, by those who possess advanced technological and industrial capabilities). Peasants could not own the horses and armor of knights, and contemporary individuals cannot make warships or tanks—only the state can.

The domination of this moral interpretation of poison has rested upon and served a particular understanding of warfare as a contest of a particular kind of force among the powerful. Its acceptance has served an ordering function in defining a hierarchy of legitimate societal actors established through practices deemed appropriate to the realm of politics and war. Its success can be measured by the degree to which the burden of moral obloquy rests on those who would undermine the legitimacy of this practice of warfare—whereas so many ways of killing are numbingly accepted as unavoidable, a special moral disgust is reserved for poison.

The delegitimation of poison in international warfare is necessarily bound up with its ban within the realm of society. Criminal codes have sometimes made special distinctions for killing with poison, reserving particular punishments for poisoners. A statute of 1531 issued by Henry VII ordered "poisoners to be boiled to death."[65] As Foucault has observed, the purpose of such modes of criminal punishment is "to bring into play, as its extreme point, the dissymmetry between the subject who has dared to violate the law and the all-powerful sovereign who displays his strength."[66] The disciplinary mechanisms within society and those regulating warfare are both arrayed toward the configuration of sovereign power.

Absolute Beginnings

We can now turn to an examination of the mechanisms by which gas weapons were branded as unacceptable technologies of war, and the extent to which we can account for the obloquy of chemical weapons by a relationship to poison and the poison taboo. As delegates from around the world gathered at the Hague in July 1899, they decided to divide up the proposals for weapons limitations into different commissions and subcommissions for consideration. The second subcommission of the first commission considered the subject of limiting explosives. In the first two meetings, the delegates failed to reach agreement on an acceptable formula for limiting new explosives, rejecting means such as caliber, firing rate, length, and velocity. At the third meeting, the president of the commission, Jonkheer van Karnebeck, asked the Russian delegate whether he wished to frame any further propositions regarding limitations on the use of new explosives. The minutes of the proceedings indicate that Captain Scheine answered in the negative, but "his Government has instructed him to make a proposition concerning the prohibition of the putting into use of any new kind of explosive, the invention of which seems possible. It is a question of prohibiting the use of projectiles loaded with explosives which spread asphyxiating and deleterious gases."[67]

Some clarification was needed as to what Scheine meant by his proposal to ban this type of explosive shell. Two of the delegates observed "that in this case the use of all projectiles charged with explosives ought to be forbidden, since they all contain more or less injurious gases." As a result, the president, "with the consent of Mr. Scheine, defines the proposition to the effect that the prohibition shall relate solely to projectiles whose *purpose* is to spread asphyxiating gases and not those whose explosion *incidentally* produces these gases."[68]

Chemical weapons were considered an issue of international concern, then, before they had actually been developed as a feasible means of war. Ideas and plans for such weapons had occasionally surfaced during this period, but they had not yet become a reality for making modern war. A proposal for a chlorine gas shell was made to the U.S. Secretary of War in 1862, but there is no evidence that this suggestion was ever seriously considered.[69]

At the time of the Hague Conference then, the weapons under discussion were primarily understood as a new type of explosive which might be restricted, rather than a toxic weapon that was automatically and unproblematically subject to the customary prohibitions on poison. The records of the conference proceedings notably lack explicit links between poisonous weapons and gas shells. The lack becomes all the more obvious when we recognize that such interagreement links were made with respect to other weapons.

For example, not only did delegates at the Hague Conferences consider the relevance of general prohibitions to more specific ones, but they undertook discussions to restrict new weapons with great awareness of the possible relevance of existing prohibitions for new technologies. The absence of explicit references of the possible relevance of Article 23(a) to gas weapons, then, strongly suggests that the crucial and initial institutionalized prohibition on modern chemical weapons was not achieved by the unproblematic application of customary restraints on poison which is usually supposed. As another study has concluded: "Strong argument can be made that the conferences at the Hague did not actually intend to encompass the use of chemical-biological agents in warfare within the prohibitions of Article 23(a). . . . It would be strange to think that the parties intended gas to fall under the more general prohibition of poison if they felt obliged to provide for it specifically in another regulation."[70]

If we return to the minutes of the conference, we find that the immediate response to Scheine's proposal, from Captain Mahan of the United States, was to deny that such weapons were to be equated with poison. In Mahan's words:

the use of projectiles of the kind in question can not be considered as being a means which is prohibited on the same ground as the poisoning of waters. Such projectiles might even be considered as more humane than those which kill or cripple in a much more cruel manner, by tearing the body with pieces of metal. Supposing that projectiles of this kind should be invented, their use may produce decisive results. Moreover, it would involve neither useless cruelty nor bad faith, as exists in the case of poisoning waters. In his opinion, the use of those projectiles ought therefore to be considered as a lawful means of waging war.[71]

Scheine himself countered by equating such explosives with poison, arguing that "as it is the task of the Conference to limit the means of destruction, it is logical to prohibit new means, especially when, like the one in question, they are barbarous in character and are, in his opinion, equivalent to the poisoning of a river." However, the president of the subcommission, Jonkheer van Karnebeck, responded that although poisoning rivers is indeed treacherous, "asphyxiating projectiles no more have this character than ordinary ones." One other delegate sided with Scheine but offered a different rationale for prohibiting such explosive shells: "If directed against a besieged city, they would perhaps hit more harmless inhabitants than the ordinary projectiles." Following immediately upon this argument, the president asked whether the governments "could consent to prohibiting the use of projectiles charged with explosives and the express purpose of which is to spread asphyxiating gases." After France, Austria-Hungary, Sweden, Norway, Japan, the Netherlands, Denmark, Italy, Turkey, and Germany responded positively, Mahan responded "nay" and expanded upon his opposition:

1. The objection that a warlike device is barbarous has always been made against new weapons, which have nevertheless eventually been adopted. . . . It does not seem demonstrated to him that projectiles filled with asphyxiating gases are inhuman and uselessly cruel devices, and that they would not produce a decisive result.

2. He is the representative of a nation which is actuated by a keen desire

to render war more humane, but which may be called upon to make war, and it is therefore necessary not to deprive one's self, by means of hastily adopted resolutions of means which might later on be usefully employed.[72]

After a brief comment by the delegate from Siam, who asked whether such gas weapons might not be more humane than explosives, the matter was dropped, and the committee turned to dealing with torpedoes. When put to the vote before the subcommittee and the full committee, the proposal to ban asphyxiating shells was adopted with near unanimity; the United States cast the sole negative vote. At the final conference, the matter was again passed, with the opposition of only the United States and Britain.[73] At least one member of the committee perceived a connection between poison and explosive shells that emitted gas, and one delegate voiced the opinion that such shells were more cruel than bullets. It is interesting to note, however, that the proper designation of the novel category of asphyxiating shells and its relation to prohibitions on poison was actively debated rather than merely assumed. Moreover, it does not appear that such linkages were crucial to passing the Hague Declaration concerning asphyxiating shells which provided such a crucial step in the contemporary chemical weapons taboo. Finally, a revealing lacuna of discussion concerned the cruelty and barbarity of poison, within a debate which spiritedly contested the relative cruelty of explosive and gaseous shells.

The first gas weapons were not treated primarily as poison and thus were not subjected to by-now traditional restraints. Neither were they treated as exotic products of chemistry, as further evidenced by the treatment of unforeseen military technologies at the Hague. At the conference of 1899, the question of the use of "new means of destruction, which might have the tendency to come into vogue, such as those depending upon electricity or chemistry," was put aside for future consideration, despite the efforts of the Russian delegate, who favored prohibition because "the means of destruction at present employed were quite sufficient."[74] Interesting here is that asphyxiating shells at this juncture were not even associated with these chemical means or "chemical warfare," let alone poison.

The yet-to-be-invented asphyxiating shells were seen as a type of explosive, the special danger of which lay in the possibility of shelling civilian populations. This association seems crucial in understanding the efforts to prohibit this possible weapon. The rationale of civilian discrimination was the last to be voiced before the preliminary vote on gas shells, and it met no counterarguments. Moreover, the head of the U.S. delegation, A. D. White, suggests in his memoirs that the crucial argument for prohibiting gas was that it might be used against towns and civilians. As he states, Mahan's objections to banning gas were answered, "as it seemed to me, with force—that asphyxiating bombs might be used against towns for the destruction of vast numbers of noncombatants, including women and children, while torpedoes at sea are used only against the military and naval forces of the enemy."[75]

This evidence would seem to justify the conclusion that the first gas weapons came to be stigmatized at the Hague because of their association not so much with poison but with the destruction of innocents, a foundational concept in just-war doctrine.[76] I do not deny, of course, that the association with restraints on poison may have influenced the early development of ideas concerning what we would now recognize as chemical weapons. Several experimental ideas of using chemicals in warfare were proposed in Britain during the course of the nineteenth century, though most were rejected in the same manner as other impracticable proposals. In 1846 the British government rejected a plan to employ sulfur dioxide from burning ships in part because it believed that such a method would not be in keeping with the laws of warfare (the other reason being that a monopoly on such means could not be maintained). A decade later, in the Crimean War, the War Department again rejected such means, citing effects "so horrible that no honorable combatant" could use them. Also rejected was an idea to use shells filled with cyanide, reasoning that it was comparable to poisoning the enemy's water supply.[77]

A vitally important relationship certainly existed between the bans on poison and chemical weapons but this association was not the enabling discourse for the initial institutionalization of the chemical weapons taboo. To the extent that the chemical weapons taboo has been buttressed by its association with the poison taboo, this coupling represents an exemplary example of the genealogical operation of a moral institution insofar as the purposes and contexts of the bans are not simply identical. The poison taboo was a ban on a weapon of the weak; the Hague Declaration was an invitation to self-restraint among the strong.

The connection between historical restraints on poison and on the category of chemical weapons—though often assumed in analysis and very prevalent in practice—has not always been unproblematically present or maintained. The prohibition of chemical weapons requires a constitution and definition of the proscribed category, the boundaries of which are not simply self-evident. If chemical weapons are usually associated with traditional restraints on poison, there have been notable ruptures in the naturalizing operation of that discourse. We have already seen that explicit connections were not dominant at the Hague. In Chapter 4, I further show that explaining the CW taboo in terms of traditional restraints on poison does not accord very well with the vociferous arguments made in support of the humanitarian desirability of chemical weapons during and after World War I. Many proponents argued during this period—and some have argued since—that chemical weapons are the most humane of weapons, but no such arguments have even been countenanced with respect to poison. In short, the definition of chemical weapons is not an unproblematic construction that allows us to claim human beings have a uniquely inherent aversion to "them." That the link between poison and chemical weapons is not as self-evident as appears at first blush becomes particularly apparent with the debate over nonlethal chemical weapons that is analyzed in subsequent chapters.

To the extent that the CW taboo has been fortified by its association with restraints on poison, then, the previous account of the poison taboo itself shows this process to be a Russian doll of genealogical reinterpretations. The prohibitionary norms have grown to encompass the protection of civilians and soldiers in mass armies as well as the dominion of sovereigns.

What the first chemical weapons shared with poison was that both weapons had been subject to a ban of absolute character. It became possible to think of these weapons as nefarious technologies of warfare, any use of which was intrinsically immoral, regardless of whether they were used against civilians or only against soldiers in the field.

The Discipline of Civilization

Although the Hague ban was absolute, it was not unreservedly universal. Strictly speaking, the Hague Declaration established a discriminatory regime, insofar as its language stipulated that the ban against asphyxiating shells was "only binding on the Contracting Powers in the case of war between two or more of them." Furthermore, the declaration stated that "it shall cease to be binding from the time when, in a war between the Contracting Powers, one of the belligerents shall be joined by a non-Contracting Power." Those contracting powers were the nations that would count as the members of an emerging society of civilized states. That is, one of the qualifications of a civilized nation was to partake in the regulation of warfare that began among the European society of states in the mid–nineteenth century.[78]

The growing awareness of a standard of civilization during this period is noteworthy in several respects. First, part of the larger historical explanation for the origins of the chemical weapons taboo lies in the emergence during this period of concentrated and organized attacks on the institution of warfare as immoral and uncivilized. It was still generally believed at this time that war was natural and inevitable, but the novel sound of voices of protest led to efforts, most notably the Hague Conferences, to ameliorate warfare.[79]

Second, the raising of a standard of civilization in connection with the CW taboo recalls earlier weapons bans in history. In particular, the Second Lateran Council decree of 1139 outlawed the use of the crossbow, but only against Christians; against heathens, the crossbow was deemed an entirely appropriate weapon.[80] This tendency to permit the use of otherwise outlawed weapons against an alien "Other" has been observed by Robert O'Connell, who compares the savagery of interspecific competition to the circumscribed rituals of intraspecific competition.[81]

To some extent, the contractual language of the Hague implicates the origins of the CW taboo in such exclusionary practices. There is even evidence of an ancestral precursor that goes back to 1456. During the Turkish siege of Belgrade, the Hungarians used burning rags that had been dipped in "mysterious liquor" and produced a suffocating smoke. In words that echo those of the Lateran Council, an observer of the affair wrote that "it was a bad business. Christians must never use so murderous a method against other Christians. Still, it is quite in place against Turks and similar miscreants."[82] Similarly, Brechtel in 1591 noted that some writers recommended the use of such means against Turks, though he wondered whether such advocacy meant they might not be used against Christians also.[83]

In light of the exclusionary nature of such moral protests, it is intriguing that there was no suggestion during the Hague Conferences that the use of asphyxiating shells was to be regarded as legitimate against "uncivilized" nations. Although in strict legal terms, the declaration amounts to a no-use pledge among signatories only, there seems to have been no active establishment by those present that this contractual language simultaneously legitimized and positively sanctioned certain uses of asphyxiating shells (for example, against nonparticipants) against those outside the ken of the civilized family of nations.[84] Rather, the contractual language of the prohibition was a legitimizing inducement to join the society of civilized states, an invitation to self-discipline.

In addition, the declaration gave no explicit positive sanction to the use of asphyxiating shells by a contracting power in retaliation for their first use by another contracting power. Thus, whereas the Geneva Protocol of 1925 amounted to a "no first-use" pledge, owing to the right-of-retaliation reservations many nations attached to their signatures (see Chapter 4), the Hague Declaration and negotiations leading to it indicated no such explicit understanding. To the extent that a contracting power could legally use asphyxiating shells against another, it implicitly could only do so by resorting to the right of reprisal, which as a general tenet of international law is invoked as a form of law enforcement. In any case, the full import of these interpretive practices would still have to await the actual development and occurrence of chemical warfare.

The actual attainment of this potentially unique prohibition can be attributed significantly to the fact that no such weapons had yet been developed. Most important is the fact that this historical situation permitted the circumvention of the amoral monopoly that often accompanies the exclusive possession of a novel method of warfare. That is, the historical record demonstrates that moral qualms about the use of novel technologies of destruction issue most prominently (if not surprisingly) from unsuspecting and unprepared victims upon whom the weapons are initially inflicted. Moral objections may persist once the monopoly is lost and the initial victim incorporates the new weapon (as with the crossbow), but the overwhelming tendency is for such moral concerns to wither as the possibilities of technology are embraced by more than one party. With asphyxiating shells, this was not to be the case. Excepting the position of the United States, then, the moral protests that would accompany a future first use of such weapons would not simply mimic the usual cry of the unsuspecting victim. Rather, it would constitute a violation of a code of mutually acceptable conduct among the club of civilized nations—powerful and weak, technological sophisticate and innocent alike.

The significance of this feature of the prohibition is that such a ban can not be readily dismissed as the simple cries of the loser in the technological contest of war. The unique character of the effort at the Hague to institutionalize a prohibition against the entire category of weapons known as asphyxiating shells thus assumes far more importance than is usually acknowledged in the chemical weapons literature. Insofar as asphyxiating shells had been singled out as a weapon at the Hague, they could potentially play a symbolic role in the constitution or undermining of a common identity among the great powers as civilized nations. To the extent that this identity was secured, a violation of the standards of civilization from within the family of nations (the use of asphyxiating shells) would incur a painful process of having to castigate and constitute as savage part of oneself, an unsettling of the very identity of the civilized. It is "we" who would have failed our own test of civilized conduct in failing to resist the temptations of technology. As Michael Adas has shown, the chief means by which this common identity of a superior civilization was secured by mostly European nations was by the level of technological achievement—what set "civilized" nations apart was their technological superiority over backward and thus uncivilized areas.[85]

The mere fact of an initial and contested agreement in the form of the Hague Declaration cannot in and of itself, however, be taken as synonymous with a robust international norm, anymore than it can be taken as indicating an ultimately effective normative restraint on behavior. Nonetheless, the Hague Conferences did witness the emergence of an institutionalized international norm against asphyxiating shells. Even U.S. delegate Mahan, in reporting on the conference discussions on the prohibition to the U.S. commission, felt the need to explain in depth the U.S. opposition to the ban, insofar "as a certain disposition has been observed to attach odium to the view adopted by this Commission in this matter."[86]

Moreover, although the United States was the sole nation to reject the Hague Declaration on asphyxiating shells at both conferences, the leaders of that country were to become the chief proponents of a prohibition on gas weapons in the aftermath of World War I.[87] Insofar as it is claimed that the usual pattern for a new weapon is for it to be the target of cries of moral indignation and then to be accepted as legitimate, it seems curious indeed that the U.S. position on CW would have followed an opposite course: gas was initially treated as a legitimate weapon of warfare and was only later regarded as morally dubious. The sources of the original U.S. opposition may very well give us insight into factors that today could serve to erode the dominant and current perception of CW. Certainly we need to understand this opposition in order to fully appreciate the significance of the later U.S. acceptance of this norm.

Limiting War or Banning Weapons?

The rationales articulated by U.S. delegates at the Hague against the declaration on asphyxiating shells were echoed against the effort to make absolute a ban on projectiles from balloons. In suggesting that the ban on balloons be limited to five years, U.S. delegate Captain Crozier characterized his argument as a humanitarian one, although the definition of what contributes to humanitarian ends had undergone a radical transformation from his earlier justification of a ban on such methods. As he stated:

It seems to me difficult to justify by a humanitarian motive the prohibition of the use of balloons for the hurling of projectiles or other explosive materials. We are without experience in the use of arms whose employment we propose to prohibit forever. Granting that practical means of using balloons can be invented, who can say that such an invention will not be of a kind to make its use possible at a critical point on the field of battle, at a critical moment of the conflict, under conditions so defined and concentrated that it would decide the victory, and thus partake of the quality possessed by all perfected arms of localizing at important points the destruction of life and property and of sparing the sufferings of all who are not at the precise spot where the result is decided. Such use tends to diminish the evils of war and to support the humanitarian considerations which we have in view. I do not know of machines thus efficient and thus humanitarian, in the incomplete stage of development in which aerostation now is; but is it desirable to shut the door to their possible introduction among the permitted arms?[88]

This statement by Crozier stands in stark opposition to his earlier claim at the conference that the requirements of humanity dictate that such means be prohibited. Nevertheless, it does accurately reflect the position taken by the U.S. delegation at the Hague Conferences. The refusal of the United States to sign the declaration on asphyxiating shells and its successful efforts to limit the prohibition on balloons to five years were grounded in the original instructions to the U.S. delegates that issued from Secretary of State Hay.[89] According to those instructions,

The second, third, and fourth articles [of the Russian circular proposing subjects for consideration], relating to the non-employment of firearms, explosives, and other destructive agents, the restricted use of existing instruments of destruction, and the prohibition of certain contrivances employed in naval warfare, seem lacking in practicability, and the discussion of these propositions would probably prove provocative of divergence rather than unanimity of views. It is doubtful if wars are to be diminished by rendering them less destructive, for it is the plain lesson of history that the periods of peace have been longer protracted as the cost and destructiveness of war have increased. The expediency of restraining the inventive genius of our people in the direction of devising means of defense is by no means clear, and, considering the temptations to which men and nations may be exposed in a time of conflict, it is doubtful if an international agreement to this end would prove effective. The dissent of a single powerful nation might render it altogether nugatory. The delegates are, therefore, enjoined not to give the weight of their influence to the promotion of projects the realization of which is so uncertain.[90]

The U.S. delegation carried out these instructions dutifully and, it appears, with some conviction. As the final report from the delegates to Secretary of State Hay stated: "the American Commission approached the subject of the limitation of invention with much doubt. They had been justly reminded in their instructions of the fact that by the progress of invention as applied to the agencies of war, the frequency, and indeed the exhausting character of war had been as a rule diminished rather than increased."[91]

This position is of course not an unfamiliar one to students of international relations, echoing as it does a classic realist stance of "*si vis pacem, pere bellum*"—if you want peace prepare for war. In a similar spirit Prime Minister Lord Salisbury of Britain had originally answered Russian proposals for a disarmament conference with the sentiment that Britain was anxious for peace, but the perfection, costliness, and horror of modern weapons served as a "serious deterrent" to war.[92]

And yet it should be noted that this position amounts to more than a simple expression of the classical realist conception of war as an ever-present possibility in the anarchic states system. To be sure, this aspect of realist thought was expressed well enough by Hague delegate Mahan, who maintained that "until it is demonstrable that no evil exists, or threatens the world, which cannot be obviated without recourse to force, the obligation to readiness must remain; and, where evil is mighty and defiant, the obligation to use force—that is, war—arises."[93]

The idea that wars can be managed, shortened, or rendered more infrequent, however, is not the same as the idea that they can ultimately be eliminated from the realm of international politics. The latter is one of the prime tenets of liberal approaches to international politics. For liberal scholars, great power war has become increasingly obsolescent.[94] It was the humanitarian discourse of shortening and eliminating wars—and thus reducing suffering—that was invoked in order to make the commitment to unlimited technological innovation appear at once natural, inevitable, and beneficent.[95] That is, the condition for making U.S. opposition to a ban on asphyxiating shells appear acceptable was to marry the logic of the pursuit of unlimited technological efficiency with the avoidance of war and the amelioration of suffering.

Seth Low, one of the delegates to the Hague Conference of 1899, aptly justified the U.S. position of not encouraging "any mere limitations on invention in relation to warfare" according to the "historic attitude" of the United States that:

Wars are much less frequent in these days than they used to be; they are also much shorter in duration. Although more destructive while they last, it cannot be questioned that, by reason of their infrequency and their shorter duration, the sum of human misery which war inflicts is much less great in recent than in earlier times. As the engines of war increase in destructiveness, they usually become more costly; that is to say, both more expensive to make and more expensive to use. The fearful costliness of modern war is one very great restraint upon a resort to it. This is, probably, one of the reasons why, in America, it has never been thought wise to try to prevent the free application of invention to the improvement of the weapons and engines of war.[96]

The Hague Conferences furnished a battleground for these two fundamental positions on the relationship among war, morality, and unlimited technological innovation. The opening speech of the conference of 1907, made by its president M. de Nelidow, stands in stark contrast to the U.S. position. Commenting upon the efforts of Dr. Lieber to alleviate some of the horrors of the American Civil War, he remarked that:

I heard the opinion expressed that it was absolutely wrong to seek to mitigate the horrors of war. "In order that wars may be short and rare," I was told, "the peoples waging it must feel its full weight so that they will seek to put an end to it as soon as possible and not desire to resume it." This idea, gentlemen, seems absolutely fallacious to me. The horrors of the struggles of ancient times and of the wars of the Middle Ages did not diminish either their duration or their frequency, whereas the mitigations introduced during the second half of the last century into the methods of warfare and the treatment of prisoners and wounded, as well as the whole series of humanitarian measures which have done honor to the First Peace Conference, and which are to be amplified by the labours of the Conference we are opening, have by no means contributed toward developing a taste for war. They have, on the contrary, disseminated a sentiment of international comity throughout the civilized world, and created a peaceful current which is revealed in the manifestation of approval with which public opinion receives and, as I hope, will continue to receive our labours.[97]

Similar arguments are vividly evident in the work of the primary documenter of the Hague Conferences, whose reflections continually invoke the "real world" with phrases such as "we live in a world of reality." As James Brown Scott stated:

It is frequently said that the amelioration of warfare does not produce practical good, that the more barbarous the proceedings the less danger there will be of a resort to war. If that were so the savage state of man should indeed be the ideal one. If that were so the brutality and license of the Thirty Years' War should be the halcyon period to which the reformer should turn his gaze. The poisoning of streams, the taking of towns by assault, the massacre of prisoners, the violation of the innocent, should therefore by looked upon with favour and not condemned. We know, however, that the mere fear of danger does not deter, just as we know that the fear of punishment does not prevent crime. . . . If the danger of war and the severity of warfare do not act as a deterrent to war, it is nevertheless humanitarian to free it from suffering as far as possible.[98]

No doubt the preceding sentiments are genuine, but the humanitarian position expressed by representatives of the United States seems rather more disingenuous. The chief concern was the enhancement of national power through technological innovation and the legitimation of advanced technology as the currency of domination, not the progressive humanitarian effect of increasingly destructive technology on warfare.[99] The more candid statement of Britain's Admiral Fisher lays bare the thinking behind the U.S. stance identified previously. He maintained at the Hague Conference of 1899 "that each country desires to equip itself with the best arms that it can procure; that such arms tend to shorten and to prevent wars; and that a restriction on the invention and construction of new types of arms *would place civilized peoples in a disadvantageous position in time of war with nations less civilized or with savage tribes.*"[100]

This discursive strategy of justifying the unrelenting technological innovation of armaments with the end of warfare and the role of weapons bans in disciplining "uncivilized nations" is of utmost importance for two reasons. First, we need to attend to the ways that just-war discourse may serve to legitimize war rather than restrict or eliminate it.[101] These Foucauldian implications of the CW discourse become especially relevant when the U.S. position at the Hague is compared to later U.S. efforts to ban chemical weapons after World War I and the renewed policy of prohibiting the "poor man's bomb" of the Third World.

Second, even as humanitarian norms serve as a mere justification for the pursuit of national material power, those norms simultaneously perform a delegitimizing function against war. This function is not involved in the simple and naked justification of war and war-preparedness as desirable and noble. The fact that the acquisition of the means of war must be justified according to a discourse that simultaneously delegitimizes war signals a significant historical shift in the normative acceptability of war (see Chapter 5). To the extent that contemporary scholars are right to claim that great-power conventional war among the advanced democracies is obsolescent, the accumulating effect of norms denigrating war might have made itself felt by trapping elites in their own discourse that captured a wide societal acceptance.

The moral protests that accompanied novel weapons in the past typically issued from a surprised and disadvantaged enemy. Unique in the history of such normative limitations was the anticipatory proscription of a whole category of weapons among a self-designated society of civilized nations. The effect of this ban could render any future introduction of such weapons the subject of a more general obloquy among the most powerful states, A violation of this norm by these nations could painfully negate their own common and supposedly superior standard of civilized identity.

Given the origins of the poison taboo, its subsequent grafting upon the institutionalized prohibition of a category first designated as asphyxiating shells and later as chemical weapons is particularly fascinating, for it involves a genealogical appropriation distanced from the original purposes of the poison prohibition. The poison taboo originated in securing the purview of social relations of authority and excluding an indefensible weapon from the contestation of power. Its extension to chemical weapons represents a different purpose of mutual self-denial by the dominant powers themselves as a marker of civilization, which meant eschewing a new possible generation of means of domination by the industrial state. The legacy of the initial manifestation of the chemical weapons taboo, then, is a coming together of a genealogical appropriation of the poison taboo and a rereading of an institutionalized prohibition formally produced for other reasons.

CHAPTER THREE

World War I

> As is so often the case, the unity of the word does not guarantee
> the unity of the thing.
>   —Nietzsche, *Human, All-Too-Human*

Interpretive practices at the Hague Conferences served to set asphyxiating shells apart from other weapons. If it is intelligible to suggest that a normative discourse emerged from the Hague, it is nonetheless to say little concerning its robustness. The initial test for the normative prohibition on gas weapons was, of course, World War I. The widespread use of gas weapons (including those technically proscribed by the Hague Declaration) on an enormous scale in World War I makes it seem difficult not to conclude in A. M. Prentiss's words that "the abortive gas rule of 1899 failed to survive its first crucial test."[1] It is but a small step to surmise that, since the international agreements prohibiting such weapons apparently were "completely abrogated," the nascent norm prohibiting asphyxiating shells had met with a premature end.[2] So the authors of a careful study on this question conclude that while "a dogmatic answer can hardly be given as to the reality of an international norm interdicting the use of gas in warfare. . . . On the face and in balance it would seem that the evidence shifts the scales toward a conclusion either that no such rule was ever in being, or that if it was it did not survive the war. If there was such a rule, it did nothing to restrain the use of gas."[3]

For these reasons, most studies of the norm prohibiting CW treat World War I cursorily if at all. Ignoring World War I would of course be expected of accounts that are suspicious of the existence of a customary norm prohibiting CW in the first place. But even studies more sympathetic to the existence of a norm proscribing chemical weapons have difficulty reconciling their position with the experience of World War I. One of the most spirited defenses of a customary norm prohibiting chemical weapons could find little more than the following to say on the subject: "During World War I, when the first large-scale use of chemical weapons occurred, there was already a widespread belief that such use was contrary to the law of war. This is indicated by the fact that both sides sought to justify their actions by claiming that they were using gas in reprisal."[4]

To be sure, a genealogical analysis would seem quite at home with the idea of discontinuity, that the Hague norm had died during World War I only to be resurrected in the postwar period. But if this is a good reason to be cautious about overplaying the significance of World War I for the normative discourse on CW, it does not constitute a reason to dismiss it altogether. Rather than resting with the question of whether gas weapons were used or not, I seek here to understand how certain actions are normalized or stigmatized through discursive practices and to identify which interpretations guided practice. How was the field of acceptable practice defined during the conflict? In what ways were chemical weapons (re)constituted as a category of weapons through various discursive practices? What resistance did these adaptations and reinterpretations of the norm encounter? Can we understand any of the practices of World War I as contributing to the resuscitation of a norm proscribing chemical weapons after the war?

In this spirit, I scrutinize the discontinuities and continuities of the emergent norm proscribing chemical weapons to identify which features of the new weapon assumed political importance, which may have been subject to processes of normalization, and which (if any) were able to endure the apparent limitless character of the war. The purpose of focusing on World War I is not to strain to establish a continuous norm from the Hague Conferences through the war and into the conferences of the 1920s but to analyze how practices and meanings may have been organized during the war to produce the conditions that made certain policies seem natural or inevitable, regrettable, or unthinkable. With these considerations in mind, then, I attempt to fill in some of the silence about the role of the chemical weapons norm in World War I. Did the use of gas weapons and the reactions to it (political, military, public) amount to war as usual, or were there peculiarities that may have precipitated a postwar reincarnation of the norm?

Interpretive Grafts: The Construction of a Category

One of the features of the use of gas in World War I that quickly came to be distinguished as significant was the kind of weapons that were in question. This issue became especially salient for Britain and Germany, the major participants in the struggle over the definition of the status of gas warfare. Indeed, the question of which side was responsible for violating the Hague Declaration not only figured prominently in propaganda during the war but was a sensitive issue in postwar writings.[5] Yet throughout the din of accusations, recriminations, and general controversy on this question, the significance of a more basic development has gone relatively unnoticed: the very act of disaggregating a whole category of gas weapons constituted an interpretive refinement of the norm given expression at the Hague. In order to discern more precisely the nature of that shift, we need to examine national policies for the development and use of gas warfare. The objective is not so much to adjudicate the question of which side violated the Hague Declaration but to determine if we can discern the interpretations that seem to have guided the development and use of gas weapons and the interpretations that were (re)produced by subsequent practices.

I consider relevant developments in all major belligerent countries, but I focus on Britain and Germany, since they played the most active part in the struggle over the status of gas warfare. I canvas from available sources the interpretations of gas weapons manifest in the practices of the major belligerents and the ways in which certain features were defined as relevant in the development and use of these new weapons.

Before the war, chemical weapons formed no part of the military preparations of any of the major belligerents. This was due to a variety of reasons, especially the lack of the necessary industrial-scale technology and adequate chemical industries.[6] These factors for the most part precluded the serious contemplation of such weapons. The following passage sums up the situation:

> The most one can say about gas and smoke is that by the eve of the war military awareness of chemicals had increased to the extent that some soldiers were willing to consider them and a very few, with a more innovating turn of mind, were even experimenting with various compounds. . . . There were no military stocks of gases, nor of gas shell, save for very limited supplies of tear-gas grenades and cartridges in French hands. The forerunners were scientific curiosities and the belligerents of August 1914 had no conception of the practicalities of chemical warfare.[7]

With the beginning of the war, however, preparations were undertaken in earnest. Gas appears to have first been used by Germany and France in the form of harassing agents, though its use was isolated, ineffective, and did not garner any attention. The German chlorine cylinder attack at Ypres on April 22, 1915, signaled the beginning of large-scale gas warfare that by the end of the war involved as much as one-third of artillery munitions of the belligerents.[8]

Germany

The beginnings of an earnest effort to develop gas warfare date from October 1914, when the German chief of the general staff, General Falkenhayn, called a meeting to discuss methods for generating smoke or fire and materials having lachrymatory and other irritating effects that would cause the enemy to break cover and end the deadlock in the trenches.[9] According to German sources, these efforts were undertaken in response to indications that the French were developing gas weapons.[10] The result was the first use of gas in the war, in the form of two different kinds of shells, in October 1914 (Ni-Schrapnel) and January 1915 (T-Stoff shell).[11] These weapons were not lethal; in fact, these irritants had such insignificant results that production quickly ceased.

While more definitive evidence is lacking, German postwar accounts assert that these countermeasures were regarded as permitted by international law since the French had first used such gas in shells.[12] The further claim that these shells were permitted because they contained nonlethal agents has attracted scant notice, even though it is a claim uncontradicted by other evidence. It is of some importance, however, for not only does it reveal a degree of relevance of the Hague norm in the development of gas warfare by the Germans, it also represents the first significant interpretive refinement of that norm. From the outset of the war, the German High Command seems to have interpreted the Hague Declaration as a narrow proscription applicable only to lethal gases from shells. Irritants were regarded as no more taboo than smoke or other such techniques.

The most important consideration in the turn to lethal gas does not seem to have been the restrictions imposed by the Hague Declaration, however, but the fact that Germany was experiencing a shortage of high explosives. To resolve this ammunition crisis, research turned to the development of lethal gas weapons that break the deadlock in the trenches. As the SIPRI study summarizes:

> At first the intention was to load the chemicals into artillery projectiles as was being done with irritant agents, but at the time the output of shell was small and in any case the Supreme Command doubted whether large-area effects could be obtained from them. These doubts were subsequently vindicated by the failure of the T-Stoff shelling at Bolimow. Professor Haber, who was in charge of the development work, then sug-

gested that the gas might be discharged at the enemy directly from cylinders emplaced in forward trenches, relying on the wind to blow the gas cloud towards the enemy.[13]

One of the chemists involved, Otto Hahn, recalls that he objected that such means would violate the Hague prohibition. Haber argued in response that the French had begun gas warfare; moreover, such methods could save many lives by ending the war more quickly.[14] The last hurdle for the preparations led by Haber was to secure formal acceptance by the German Supreme Command. Chief of the German general staff, General Erich von Falkenhayn,

> while considering gas "unchivalrous", nevertheless hoped it would lead to a decisive solution in the West. The experts assured Falkenhayn that chlorine from cylinders was not a breach of Hague II and that there was no risk of early retaliation. Haber was not consulted by Falkenhayn about the legal aspect and subsequently wrote: "Although he never asked for my opinion on the state of the law, he left me in no doubt that he accepted the limitations of international law which he intended fully to adhere to." . . . In the end Falkenhayn gave the go-ahead around the middle of January.[15]

The development of cylinders to deliver gas does not seem to have been dictated by the restrictions of the Hague Declaration but by more technical and logistical requirements. As Haber remarks, "in 1915 and for much of 1916 the shell shortage left the chemists with no choice and perforce they had to concentrate on the practical problems of generating gas clouds."[16] Still, it appears that the Germans were aware that such methods technically did not constitute an abrogation of the Hague Declaration, which only prohibited *asphyxiating shells*. This interpretation played on two aspects of the defined prohibition—what counted as an "asphyxiating or deleterious" gas, and the distinction between shells and other means. One German postwar account maintained that the chlorine used in the cylinder attack at Ypres was no more lethal than French gas already used in February 1915—the Germans were simply able to achieve a greater concentration of gas with greater effect.[17]

The interpretation of gas delivered by cylinders as permissible under the Hague injunction may have been for the most part a convenient coincidence. The conjunction of technological developments and the first use of lethal shells by the French at Verdun—the significance of which will be discussed in more detail later—permitted this rhetorical position of German military decision makers. Although it may be that the development and use of chlorine gas from cylinders was pursued on the understanding that it did not conflict with the letter of the Hague prohibition, the idea of using cylinders demonstrates that the Germans "were prepared to ignore the moral issue posed by the Hague Conventions."[18] The postwar account of Major Geyer concedes that the Germans were willing to abrogate the spirit, at least, of the Hague Declaration. He suggests that the legal objections to the use of chlorine gas from cylinders bent to the pressure of military promise.[19] Similarly, General Berthold von Deimling was willing to pursue the possibility of victory despite the scruples that he, like any respectable soldier, had "poisoning the enemy like rats." According to Deimling, personal scruples must be silent, for "war is necessity and knows no law."[20]

Germany's willingness to cross the moral boundary of the Hague is also attested to by its readiness to engage the next stage of gas warfare—lethal shells. German accounts contend that the Germans were not the first to use lethal shells; according to the Germans, the French use of phosgene shells in 1916 was the first technical abrogation of the Hague Declaration.[21] This was the first time that shells had been used, the "sole object" of which was the diffusion of lethal gas.[22] The German response with lethal shells was so quick, however, that we cannot rule out Haber's conclusion that the decision to use them had likely already been made, regardless of the French actions.

Although there is some evidence, then, that an evolving understanding of the Hague norm played a role in the CW decisions of the German High Command, the significance of these normative concerns must be balanced with the repeated invocations by German authorities of the doctrine of *Kriegsraison*. The continual enunciation of this doctrine by military theorists and practitioners alike justified the resort to any and every means in warfare in order to defeat the enemy as quickly as possible.[23] This doctrine of "military necessity" formed the core of the manual outlining the rules of war issued by the German general staff for the instruction of German officers. As stated in the war book of the German general staff:

> In the matter of making an end of the enemy's forces by violence it is an incontestable and self-evident rule that the right of killing and annihilation in regard to the hostile combatants is inherent in the war power and its organs, that all means which modern inventions afford, including the fullest, most dangerous, and most massive means of destruction, may be utilized; these last, just because they attain the object of war as quickly as possible, are on that account to be regarded as indispensable and, when closely considered, the most human.[24]

These rules do not expressly address asphyxiating shells or other means of waging chemical warfare, for they had not yet been developed for the German war effort. In any case, the manual does not indicate much faith in written international agreements such as the Hague Conventions. Still, there is a profession of adherence to rules of civilized warfare that had developed among the standing armies of the states of European-Christian culture, limitations that grew out of "chivalrous feelings, Christian thought, higher civilization and, by no means least of all, the recognition of one's own advantage."[25] These limitations, which "are actually observed by the armies of all civilized States," distinguish the European states from "uncivilized and barbarous peoples . . . who are without the knowledge of civilized warfare."[26] They include rules regarding the capture and treatment of prisoners of war, who were not to be executed or ransomed as in past ages but protected against ill-treatment, permitted to write and receive letters, and so on. Feigned surrender, misuse of the Red Cross, and mistreatment of the sick and wounded are prohibited, as is the abuse of civilian populations of the enemy. Significantly, although the doctrine of *Kriegsraison* permits the use of every means of war without which the object of war cannot be obtained, it nonetheless excludes "the use of poison both individually and collectively (such as poisoning of streams and food supplies) [and] the propagation of infectious diseases."[27]

German considerations of the acceptability of gas revolved around the Hague Declaration and not customary restraints on poison. In the end, regardless of whether German professions of innocence regarding violations of the Hague norm indicate post-hoc justification rather than motivation, this discursive strategy became politicized because asphyxiating gases had been the subject of a legal prohibition acceded to by the key belligerents in the war. In postwar works, some German writers maintained that the Hague norm still applied.[28] In the absence of the Hague Declaration, such debates would not have been conceivable, and the attempt by the Germans to interpret the Hague proscription against "asphyxiating or deleterious gases" as banning only lethal and not irritant gases would have been a non-starter.

As expressed in official communiqués and newspaper articles during the war, Germans publicly justified their use of gas in several ways. Before the chlorine cylinder attack at Ypres, the Germans accused the Allies of using asphyxiating projectiles.[29] It is not certain that these allegations were carefully calculated to justify their future use of gas, because they began several days after the orders for the attack had actually been given and nearly four months after the original decision had been made to employ lethal gas.[30] Perhaps there was apprehension on the part of the Germans as to the acceptability of the cylinder attacks, but it seems more likely that the accusations were designed as counters in the propaganda battle against the British.[31]

The day after chlorine released from cylinders had actually been used, German radio broadcasts argued that this use of gas clouds was not a violation of the Hague, for that agreement only prohibited "the use of *projectiles*, the sole object of which is the diffusion of asphyxiating or deleterious gases."[32] Official British opinion seemed to concur that the cylinders were not a technical abrogation of the treaty, although the British certainly felt that the Germans had violated the spirit of the agreement.

Articles in leading newspapers that followed Ypres went further, however, arguing that the use of "a few shells which spread death in the air" was no more inhumane than the employment of "hundreds of guns and howitzers . . . in order to destroy and break to atoms everything living," a practice that made life in the trenches "a terrible hell."[33] It is unclear whether the erroneous references to gas shells (as opposed to cylinders) in the early press reports represented a propaganda effort by the Germans to conceal their new method, or if it was simply the result of ignorance on the part of the propaganda corps. In any case, these arguments and others to the effect that such weapons spared soldiers "the tortures and pains of death" publicly questioned the very integrity of the norm undertaken at the Hague, and reopened the wound inflicted by the United States at those conferences.[34] In this sense, the norm was being contested at its very core, and its original purposes and reasonableness were far from forgotten and unquestioned.

Britain

The normative interpretation of gas warfare embodied in the Hague Declaration figured prominently at several stages during the development of gas weaponry by the British. At the dawn of the conflict, numerous proposals for unusual weapons by various "cranks" led the secretary to the Committee of Imperial Defence (Maurice Hankey) to recommend the study of chemical warfare to the War Office in order to be ready to retaliate if the Germans should start it.[35] Spurred by a 1913 foreign press report of research in gases, inquiries from the War Office were made to the Foreign Office as to whether it was "permissible" under the Hague Declaration to employ preparations "giving rise to disagreeable fumes without causing permanent harm" and to introduce gas in high explosive shells. "In view of indications that the subject was being considered in other countries,"[36] the Foreign Office ruled that a shell "which contained a small portion of lachrymatory substance without asphyxiating or deleterious effect" was permissible by the wording of the conventions, "although contrary to its spirit."[37] In any case, it was decided that such a projectile was not to be used.[38] "Stink pots" and the use of two lachrymatory substances were investigated later but were abandoned in September 1914 as the War Office and the Admiralty prohibited the use of tear gas in shell.[39]

While the development of harassing agents was contemplated at this stage, investigation of more lethal gases was not. The War Office flatly rejected such suggestions in October 1914 as being barred by the terms of the Hague Declaration.[40] In short, British military and political leaders seem to have shared with their German counterparts a belief that while the spirit of the Hague might have prohibited the first use of all gases, the letter permitted at least the use of irritant lachrymatory gases. The British were more reticent to dash this spirit than were the Germans.[41]

Further efforts to provide irritant fillings for hand grenades or mechanically propelled bombs began early in December, 1914. A powerful lachrymator, ethyl iodoacetate, named SK, was adopted in part because its manufacture did not encroach upon materials needed for other military purposes. As chronicled by the official history of the Ministry of Munitions: "Early in March, 1915, it was suggested to General Headquarters, France, that 1000 S.K. grenades should be filled and stored in case the enemy should adopt similar methods; but it seems that no action was taken to effect supply until the German offensive of 22 April, after which schemes were immediately set on foot for making S.K. and filling it into grenades as a preliminary form of retaliation."[42] These emergency grenades were irritants because they were intended for close-range work in trenches shortly to be occupied by friendly troops. By January 1916, the General Staff decided that "annoyers" no longer had any military value, and they were accordingly withdrawn from service use.[43]

British preparations for gas warfare began in earnest as a reaction to the German cylinder gas attack at Ypres on April 22, 1915. Sir John French's request for means to retaliate in kind[44] was met the following day with Lord Kitchener's response that "the use of asphyxiating gases is, as you are aware, contrary to the rules and usages of war. Before we fall to the level of the degraded Germans I must submit the matter to the Government. These methods show to what depths of infamy our enemies will go in order to supplement their want of courage in facing our troops."[45]

On May 23, 1915, Sir John French asked for prompt supply of asphyxiating gases in addition to chemical grenades recently issued. He was then informed that cylinders of chlorine were being prepared and that experiments with other chemicals would take time.[46] It seems that chlorine cylinders were chosen as the preferred means of delivery (following German precedent) for essentially bureaucratic reasons. The alternative, gas shell, was outside the scope of the man in charge of preparations, Colonel Jackson, as they were the responsibility of the Director of Artillery.[47] Nonetheless, evidence suggests that this decision was not only made with a keen sensitivity to the Hague stipulations but that an interpretation of those injunctions developed along the lines of that professed by the Germans. Reporting on a cabinet meeting, Asquith wrote to George V that "some discussion took place on the recent resort by the enemy to the use of asphyxiating gases. As the gases are apparently stored in and drawn from cylinders, and not 'projectiles,' the employment of them is not perhaps an infraction of the literal terms of the Hague Convention."[48]

On June 16, French set out his conclusions on the gas offensive, including the request that the use of cylinder gas should be supplemented as soon as possible by "gases of a more poisonous nature contained in bombs dropped from aircraft, and in shells thrown by guns and trench mortars."[49] The discussion of such matters occurred at a conference held at Boulogne on June 19 between Major-General Ivor Philipps (parliamentary military secretary to the Ministry of Munitions), Colonel Foulkes (head of the special brigade that conducted gas operations) and Colonel Cummins. While the request for aerial bombs was ignored, "it was laid down that gas used in shell might be as deadly as gas in cylinders," and steps were taken to make lachrymatory shells in view of some recent success of German lachrymators.[50] Foulkes notes that a ban was placed on the employment of what was thought to be the most dangerous chemical substance in existence (prussic acid gas) out of humanitarian motives—the ban was not lifted until July 1916. British authorization for actual use of lethal artillery shells appears to have been a direct result of German use of lethal substances in artillery shell on Verdun, April 10, 1916, and, as Foulkes has noted, this Cabinet sanction was withheld for several weeks.[51] Foulkes himself was very critical of the Cabinet's decision not to employ chemicals that were more lethal than that used by the Germans.[52]

British decisions regarding devices to be used against the Germans distinguished clearly between lethal and neutralizing weapons.[53] The British used lethal gas weapons only in response to German use of chlorine clouds. Similarly, they resorted to lethal shells only after the Germans employed them. Both courses of action reveal a high degree of normative restraint in the use of gas. The fact that the British approved the development of lethal shells but did not use them until after the

Germans suggests, not only that their use of gas (versus the Germans') was entirely in accord with the stipulations of the Hague Declaration until that accord was violated, but that the use was largely dictated by those restraints.[54] In words that contain much truth (despite his own proclivities towards the use of chemical weapons), Churchill argued that "we were confined to a limited sphere of International Law until Germany forced us to take reprisals in the matter of poisonous gases."[55]

The operation of this restraint was evident in the War Committee's response to General Smuts' request for gas to use in German East Africa: "Hitherto the War Committee have not sanctioned the use of gas against any enemy force who has not already employed it. If this ruling is to govern this case the answer is simple."[56] The decision not to employ gas in this case was taken for largely technical reasons, however, and by January 21, 1917, the Cabinet authorized a first-use of gas shell against the Turks in Egypt. According to the minutes of the meeting:

> The War Cabinet, having regard to the atrocities perpetrated on the subject races by the Turks and their maltreatment of Allied prisoners during the present war, felt no hesitation in reversing the decisions—not to use gas against Turks unless the latter employed it first—which was reached at the time of the Gallipoli expedition. The War Cabinet, therefore, decided that:
> Gas shell could be used against the Turks.[57]

While gas was provided for several theaters in the Middle East, the British appear only to have used it against the Turks during the second Battle of Gaza in April 1917.[58]

In the end, even as restraints were being eroded, an axis around which the vexing political decisions turned was not simply the cruelty or inhumanity of gas warfare compared to other weapons but the issue of their legality. The distinctions that framed the development and use of gas weapons by the British during the war were for the most part reproduced in official discourse. The protests—or more accurately, the lack thereof—launched by the belligerents during the course of the war seem to confirm the general belief that only certain kinds of gas warfare were proscribed by the letter of the Hague Declaration.

The initial reception of gas warfare in the Allied press is remarkable for its unremarkableness—most of the first reports from the front on the use of gas (most of them false) did not confer an exceptional moral status to this weapon.[59] Language describing the employment of gas as "diabolical," "horrible," or even "cruel" was largely absent at first; to the extent that any special mention was made of the weapon, it was the accusation that the German use contravened international law (the Hague Declaration).[60] That is, the first reaction to gas was not galvanized so much by a sense that it was a devilish contrivance worse than the bayonet or explosive shell but that it was a method that violated the laws of civilized warfare as stipulated by the Hague Declaration.[61] But even these charges concerning gas warfare were largely overshadowed by other events. The controversy over treatment of prisoners of war garnered far more attention in the press and in Parliament during the spring of 1915, and, with the sinking of the Lusitania in May 1915, gas was further removed from a position of singular public concern.

Commenting on the unremarkable reception of the German use of gas at Ypres on April 22, 1915, the author of a survey of the atrocity propaganda of the war observes that "the general silence on the subject during the week following April 22 seemed to indicate that gas was not to be accounted as an atrocity."[62] Although various press reports suggested that Germany had violated the Hague Declaration, the lack of official protest by the Allies indicates a belief by British political leaders and the military that the German gas attack at Ypres did not in fact technically violate the Hague Declaration.[63] The ban only proscribed *shells the sole object of which was the diffusion of asphyxiating gas*.[64] Lectures given to the British military in 1926 concurred that Germany "can legitimately argue that when she first used gas in April, 1915, she did not break the letter" of the Hague Declaration.[65] This much was admitted at the time in an article by the London *Times*'s military correspondent in the week following the Ypres attack. Despite the press reports from the front that Germans had used asphyxiating bombs and shells, the inconspicuously placed column admitted that it was not clear that shells had been used at all, and that the letter of the declaration had not been violated.[66] It was, however, certainly agreed in Britain—and even in Germany—that Germany broke the spirit of the agreement.

Of course, more sensational press reports about the horrific sufferings of gassed soldiers appeared in the Allied press, and these reports focused on the immoral nature of the Germans for using such a diabolical weapon.[67] As Brown has noted, however, charges of the inhumanity of gas soon ceased as the Allies prepared to retaliate with their own. By mid-1917, a news blackout on gas had been imposed by Britain and France, motivated by a desire to mitigate the U.S. public's dread of entering the European war. In the following year, gas was heralded as a triumph of superior Allied industry, and thus "gas propaganda had run the policy gamut."[68] Discourse emphasizing the cruel and inhumane features of gas warfare thus had a meteoric existence—a spate of rather memorable depictions of horrible suffering which quickly diminished, although the images lingered for some years after the war in other forms, notably popular fiction.

To summarize: the statement that the Hague norm did nothing to restrain the use of gas is overdrawn, for the British with great deliberation lived up to their obligations under the Hague Declaration in their war against Germany.[69] Moreover, gas weapons had carved out political space in the debate over who bore responsibility for violating the Hague Declaration. The initial employment of gas warfare had invited its share of moral excoriation, a phenomenon characteristic of the introduction of most novel means of destruction. The reception of chemical weapons bore an additional element, however. In the eyes of British political and military leaders, the obloquy for using gas weapons resulted not simply from the unsurpassed cruelty they supposedly entailed compared to other contrivances of industrial warfare, but from the fact that their first use constituted an unpardonable breach of the spirit of international law.

France

The French (like the Russians) concentrated their first efforts at gas warfare on artillery-delivered munitions because they considered the cylinder method pioneered by the Germans to be too cumbersome. Although their efforts were sporadic, the French may have been innovators in one respect: they decided in July 1914 to use chemical shells as soon as practicable. At this point, however, the shells consisted of "militarily useless" tear gas.[70] The first use of gas by the French was apparently initiated by a conscripted policeman who introduced tear-gas grenades that had been used by Paris police for about three years.[71]

Considerations of the relative morality or legality of various methods of delivering gas played a role at several stages in the development of gas weapons for the French. A French circular captured by the Germans (dated February 21, 1915) described the tear-gas cartridges and grenades they were developing, and pointed out that in small quantities the chemical was not "deleterious."[72] Moreover, according to the director of the French chemical services, the Germans' use of gas at Ypres was a flagrant violation of the Hague Declaration and the inaugural act of the gas war.[73] The distinction between lethal and irritant gases (however delivered) was important to the French, and postwar accounts maintain that the use of irritant gases did not constitute a violation of the Hague Declaration.[74]

The distinction between lethal and nonlethal shells also seems to have figured significantly in the decision to formally authorize toxic shells. This occurred only after enquiries had been made by French officials as to their permissibility, for the French authorities still felt bound in some measure by the Hague Declaration.[75] Like the British, the French at first banned the use of shells containing phosgene and prussic acid, both of which were in stock at the end of 1915, and only permitted the employment of the former at the end of February 1916, when the situation at Verdun appeared critical. The ban on prussic acid was withdrawn later, and the agent first used by the French at Somme July 1, 1916.[76] Sensitive to the significance of using lethal gas in shells, the director of the French chemical services argued in 1919 that these shells had been held in reserve until the Germans used gas shells with a toxicity comparable to phosgene.[77] Although the evidence of postwar writings must be treated with caution, this position is not wholly implausible. The shells in question contained a lachrymatory irritant, but the K-Stoff shell could be regarded as "in fact the first German step towards lethal chemical shells, for, as the agent was rather volatile and well over twice as poisonous as chlorine, lethal dosages were much more likely to be experienced from its field concentrations than from the earlier irritant agents."[78]

It is at least conceivable that the French, like the British, felt obliged to refrain from the use of lethal shells until they believed the Hague Declaration had been formally breached by the Germans. More important for subsequent developments, the experience of World War I demonstrated that the lethality of chemical weapons depended as much upon the concentration of the agents as their inherent toxicity, a qualification that generated interminable arguments about who really first used "asphyxiating and deleterious gases" and waged lethal chemical warfare.

Finally, the French press greeted gas weapons with even less fanfare than the British press. The first gas attacks were generally depicted as just more of many instances of atrocious German conduct in the war. To the extent that the press counted gas as an atrocity, it was not because it was a cruel new weapon so much as because it violated the Hague Declaration.[79]

United States

Before April 1917, the United States paid little attention to gas warfare.[80] No preparations whatever were made during the two years between the introduction of gas and the U.S. entry into war.[81] Definite steps toward establishing a Chemical Warfare Service were taken only in August 1917, three months after U.S. troops left for France.[82] The army, for its part, did not seem to believe that gas was a problem and simply ignored it. The secretary of war's Annual Report for 1917, for example, acknowledged the tremendous impact of science on the European war, referring specifically to the introduction of airplanes and the submarine, but did not mention gas.[83]

When the United States entered the war, preparations initially focused mostly on defensive operations. Production of gas weapons got a late start, with only one chemical facility devoted to war gases fully operational by August 1918.[84] Use of gas by the United States was limited to several projectile attacks by the 1st Gas Regiment starting in June 1918.[85] Some U.S. forces hesitated to employ gas, mostly because of their unwillingness to use something with which they had no prior experience. The U.S. response to gas was an ambivalent one; some of those involved had become enthusiastic supporters of gas, while others had not.[86]

The question of the role of normative concerns with respect to U.S. gas warfare is moot insofar as that country did not enter the war until well after gas had become widely employed by the other major belligerents. The question of the use of toxic agents was simply never much of a political, public, or military issue; the use of gas was for the most part resignedly accepted as an unavoidable fact of the war.[87] President Wilson did not seem to have particular sensitivity toward the use of gas and delegated all gas warfare decisions to the War Department.[88] The War Department did feel a need to justify the adoption of gas, arguing that "the use of such methods by the enemy forces the United States to retaliate with similar measures."[89] To the extent that there was an identifiable moral distaste for gas, it perhaps lay with General Pershing, who observed of Germany's use of gas that "the impression was that the Germans had now thrown every consideration of humanity to the winds."[90] The chief of the U.S. Chemical Warfare Service during the war believed that lachrymatory substances were not illegal. In a reference to suffocating cartridges used by French police before World War I, Clarence West (with his co-author) states that their employment did not contravene the Hague as they did not entail death.[91]

The Role of the Hague Norm

The salience of the question concerning the legitimacy of gas warfare was largely attributable to the fact that asphyxiating shells had been outlawed by the "civilized" nations of the world at the Hague. To the extent that the reception of gas weapons differed from the usual reaction to a novel instrument of war it was due to the existence of a preemptory agreement of international law not to employ gas shells.[92] Notably, considerations regarding the acceptability of gas turned upon interpretations of the Hague Declaration rather than the acceptability of using poison. Gas warfare during World War I had not simply been subsumed within the same category as poison. On the contrary, its acceptability depended much more upon how various means measured up to the prohibition enacted at the Hague: did irritant agents, choking smokes, or lethal agents delivered by means other than shells violate the declaration? No one argued whether poison was acceptable or not; debate centered on the various means of employing gas, with the Germans even arguing that a ban on gas warfare was inhumane.

To the extent that the legitimacy of gas was controversial, we need to emphasize that it was its use against combatants that was politicized. By contrast, the use of other new devastating machines of war, such as the submarine, tank, and airplane, against military targets was never questioned; in the case of the submarine, for instance, only its use against merchant shipping and unprotected civilians incurred accusations of atrocity.

Furthermore, the contention that the norm died in the trenches of the war misses the significant development that no belligerent believed that the use of irritant gases was proscribed by the letter of international law, whereas the employment of lethal gases was forbidden at least in spirit. Even more important, British efforts at gas warfare were significantly restrained by the nascent chemical weapons norm, and their use of gas weapons was undertaken only in reaction to German use. The British introduced gas weapons against the Germans only as permitted by the declaration as they understood it. Moreover, while the norm does not appear to have been decisively important in Germany's preparations and use of chemical weapons, it clearly was relevant at the early stages in the development of gas weapons by the Germans. The Russians, for their part, were completely unprepared for gas warfare, for the tsarist chief of staff was against the use of gases.[93]

It is conceivable that none of the belligerents believed themselves to be the first technically to violate the Hague Declaration. From a strict legal viewpoint, the Hague Declaration was not actually violated insofar as it ceased to be in effect for World War I once nonsignatories joined the conflict. Although the Germans and probably the French were likely ready and willing to sacrifice the nascent norm under pressing military circumstances, the intra- and postwar controversy over who violated the Hague was more than a mere propaganda battle. The confusion over which weapons (and therefore which side) violated the Hague norm illustrates the enormous difficulty of identifying certain categories of chemical weapons in the fog of warfare.

In short, to argue simply that the Hague Declaration did nothing to restrain the use of gas[94] obscures the at times significant role various understandings of it played in the development, production and use of gas weapons. To claim a role for the norm, however, is not to ignore the multifarious interpretations given to the Hague norm or the fact that the

Germans questioned its very intent and function. Nor is it to overlook the absence of significant efforts during the course of the war to reestablish the validity of the norm once it had been breached. The British and Germans sporadically justified their use of gas weapons in the language of legitimate right of reprisal, which implies an attempt to enforce the norm and end the practice of gas warfare. Both sides apparently understood their use of gas predominantly as retaliation, however—escalation designed to deny an advantage to the enemy with no attempt to reinforce the prohibition. These factors indicate a norm that was far from robust. And yet, if these discontinuities and challenges to the norm threatened to invalidate it, the taboo was also strengthened by certain continuities in interpretation which were bolstered by practice.

Ironic Continuities

In comparison to the questions of who used gas weapons first and what kind of weapons were used, the question of *how* gas weapons were used was of decidedly secondary importance during the war and in subsequent treatments of gas warfare in the literature. If this situation is not particularly surprising—insofar as the answers to the former questions determine who bears the responsibility and obloquy for violating the Hague Declaration—it is also a point of no small significance for understanding the sources of the taboo.

Given the horrors of destruction conducted during World War I—the slaughter by machine guns, the widespread use of gas weapons, the introduction of the tank and airplane, attacks on civilians such as the submarine sinking of the Lusitania, and so on—it is striking that chemical weapons were not specifically targeted at civilians. Whereas much has been made of the belligerents' abstention from CW in World War II, the significance of this form of non-use in World War I has drawn scant attention. We might ask how much normative concerns account for this behavior (as opposed to, say, purely operational constraints). More to the point of this book, we can ask what form the normative interpretations concerning chemical weapons took and how we can account for them. Which features of chemical weapons were decisive in the definition of their status? Do these practices lead us to an understanding of the interpretation of gas weapons that arose following the war?

The Threat to Civilians

When the War Office was approached on October 16, 1914, with the suggestion to drop bombs filled with aqueous hydrocyanic acid from planes, it responded that this use violated the Hague Declaration. As mentioned previously Sir John French's request for aircraft gas bombs was ignored. Experiments with hydrogen cyanide–filled shells to be dropped from the air ended in 1916, for there were no planes with sufficient carrying capacity. Moreover, the Ministry of Munitions had no confidence in the bombs or their contents. In March 1918, Churchill (then minister of munitions) urged military authorities to take advantage of the opportunities for gas attacks on a large scale on the western front. In particular, he floated the idea of dropping gas bombs on targets close behind the front, claiming that it would demoralize the Germans and cause them to put on their respirators every time they heard a plane: "The objections to the proposal were not on grounds of retaliation, which would have been immediate, but because the RFC (soon to become the RAF) could not guarantee to deliver a bomb within 200 m of a given target. Hence there would be wasteful dispersion of the gas and the likelihood of injuring or killing noncombatants in such raids."[95]

As chronicled by Foulkes, acceptable battle plans for gas were formulated on the understanding that the only suitable locales were those with no civil populations.[96] Carrying that logic to an extreme, a proposal was made by Foulkes himself to expand gas use by shelling enemy's rear areas for days to force back civil populations before gas shell bombardment of enemy positions would commence. The plan was accepted in principle by general headquarters but was preempted by a German attack on the area.[97] One of several fanciful schemes suggested later in the war (1917 or so) was "to attack with barges filled with gas the Germans in occupation of important points on the Belgian coast; but this operation was deemed inexpedient owing to the obvious danger to the civil population and the risk of infringing Dutch neutrality by the drift of gas over the frontier."[98] In summary, then, although logistical constraints may have played a role in preventing the use of gas from the air, the desire to avoid civilian populations was the chief inhibition for the British.[99]

The policy of the United States reflected similar reluctance. Pershing rejected a suggestion by Colonel Fries that the Allies deliver gas by airplane but added that "while our aviators were not allowed to initiate such warfare, we were not unprepared to retaliate if it came to that."[100] S. J. Auld corroborates the existence of such preparations by claiming that the United States "devised, manufactured, and filled" bombs, each containing one ton of mustard gas to be used against Metz.[101] By 1918, plans had been developed which called for unrestricted bombing, including the possibility of gas bombing. Given the existence of these plans, Quester has argued that the gas bombing of German cities would have proceeded had the war lasted just a few weeks longer.[102] If this were indeed the case, the ending of the war before such use would have represented a chance occurrence of singular importance in the genealogical development of the chemical weapons norm. There is, however, "no indication that a decision was ever made to initiate strategic gas bombing."[103] The French, too, considered gas from planes, but abandoned the idea in the face of reluctance to use gas against civilians, according to V. Lefebure, liaison between the British Special Brigade and the French.[104]

On the German side, the idea of delivering gas bombs by zeppelins had its advocates early in the war, but they were vetoed by Falkenhayn. The plans were revived with the successful German raids on London in 1917. Again, however, the plans were vetoed, this time by Ludendorff, on the grounds that they would lead to immediate reprisal raids on the towns of the Saar and the Palatinate.[105] This evidence supplements the belief by the chief of the U.S. Chemical Warfare Service that "there was absolutely no reason for not so using gas, except that the German was afraid. In the early days of the use of gas he did not have enough gas, nor had he developed the use of aeroplanes to the point where it would have seemed advisable. When, however, he had the aeroplanes the war had not only begun to go against him, but he had become particularly fearful of gas and of aeroplane bombing."[106]

Despite the avoidance of intentional attacks on civilians during the conflict, there were at least five thousand noncombatant victims of gas warfare, including over a hundred dead.[107] These incidents not only went unpublicized at the time but subsequently garnered scant attention. Brown has reasonably conjectured that this official silence may be the product of the belligerents tacitly agreeing "that a certain 'spill-over' of gas into towns was an inevitable accompaniment to its tactical use in a congested countryside"—gas clouds sometimes advanced ten miles behind the front lines.[108] Haber speculates that it may have served a further purpose for the British:

> As the Germans had involved the people of Northern France in chemical warfare, they might do the same in south-east England using gas-filled bombs instead of shells. The effect on civilian morale was unpredictable and the Home Office decided to ignore poison gas in the revised leaflet on Air Raid Precautions issued on 1 October 1917, though it warned the public not to breathe "the fumes" given off by bombs or buy respirators unless they had a War Office guarantee.[109]

Attitudes towards gas warfare against civilians, then, were characterized by two distinctive features: a policy of avoidance, and an official silence regarding use. Not incidentally, a well-publicized appeal by the

Red Cross for the abolition of gas warfare was prompted by a concern for the "unoffending population" behind combat areas.[110] An interpretive consensus among the belligerents had thus emerged which not only cast gas warfare as an unusual threat to civilian populations but also resulted in abstention from gas warfare against noncombatants.[111]

This development is all the more remarkable given that inhibitions against air attacks against cities with explosive bombs were subject to gradual erosion during the war. In January 1915, the kaiser gave orders that permitted the bombing of London, but the activity was expressly restricted to military shipyards, arsenals, docks, and, in general, military establishments. By July 20, the orders to bomb London itself were given, barring only buildings of historic interest.[112] The different attitudes towards bombing with gas and explosive bombs is underscored by the fact that even a British parliamentarian thought the German bombing of London was justified, insofar as London was a defended area and thus a legitimate target. As Lord Montague declared in the House of Lords on June 26, 1917, it was "absolute humbug to talk of London as being an undefended city. The Germans had a perfect right to raid London."[113]

How could fear of retaliation prove so prohibitive for gas weapons, but not for submarine attacks against civilians or for air strikes against cities with explosive bombs? What is the connection between the stigma against gas weapons and the fear of retaliation?

The inhibitions on using gas weapons against civilians arose not only from a distaste for using them against someone else's civilians but also from a reluctance to have them inflicted upon one's own population. This reaction particularly seems to have characterized the German attitude. To the extent that it is difficult to disentangle the moral inhibitions of using gas weapons against enemy populations from the fear of retaliation against one's own civilians, the common element in such interpretations was the perception that there was no defense against gas.

Undefendable Technology

Gas was far from alone in being the subject of sensational literature and art that attempted to articulate the shocking experiences of technological warfare ushered in by World War I. The utter bewilderment occasioned by other experiences, especially the senseless slaughter of the machine-gun and the shell-shock of relentless artillery barrages, contributed to a general loss of faith in the unquestionable superiority of a European civilization based on technological progress.

Those who depicted the cruelties of gas in fictional or biographical accounts did not argue that other methods were somehow enjoyable, they simply related how being attacked by gas was horrible, as did those who wrote of the miseries of shell-shock and other depravities in the trenches.[114] Moreover, the reaction to gas was not uniform: some accounts embellished vivid accounts of their fears, and others provided relatively indifferent or technical descriptions. For every memorable rendition of the horrors of chemical warfare such as Wilfred Owen's "Dulce et Decorum Est," there is an *All Quiet on the Western Front* where gas is utterly unremarkable among the plethora of horrors of trench warfare and where, indeed, other miseries are singled out as objects of special revulsion. In the case of Remarque's soldiers, tanks "more than anything embody for us the horrors of war."[115]

The concern over defense against gas was more sustained, less subject to swings of propaganda, and had a less ambiguous effect on the acceptability of gas than did arguments about its relative humanity. Gas was distinguished from weapons that depended on physical contact, such as bullets, shells, and bayonets, because it was feared as a weapon against which physical barriers such as hills, trenches, and buildings were not effective. Civilian populations, of course, were the defenseless target par excellence, which may account for the ready association of gas with the threat to innocent noncombatants.

If gas had been indelibly defined as a weapon that rendered all defenseless before it, the interpretation of it as an immoral weapon would perhaps have prevailed in the climate of World War I. This discourse did not dominate wartime thinking, but this feature was one axis upon which the legitimacy of the weapon most crucially depended. This aspect of gas weapons aroused indignation and dread and operated according to a logic similar to that behind the poison taboo: the horror of a weapon against which there was no defense. In contrast to the case of poison, however, the possibility of defenses against gas provided a powerful counter-discourse that threatened to normalize perceptions of gas weapons.

Commanders in the field were quick to realize the importance of dispelling the notion that gas was a weapon against which there was no defense. Unlike the hazards of other weapons, "protection against gas was linked with morale, chemical warfare was an unanticipated danger, and the novelty of gas necessarily caused apprehension if not fear. The troops' confidence must not be undermined by gas. If the men thought they were defenseless they might panic and retreat."[116]

The same thinking governed the policies of Allied governments towards their publics. In a passage that sheds more light on the cycle of propaganda noted earlier, James Morgan Read observes that:

The very idea of the enemy's using a new and powerful weapon was uncomfortable, indeed even terrifying, especially before it was known whether countermeasures or protective devices were available. . . . The full atrociousness of gas was played down by the press to avoid paralysing the public nerve. Gradually as the public learned of effective measures of protection and realized that the new weapon did not guarantee an irresistible attack or the greatly feared "break-through," the horrors of gas were stressed.[117]

Ironically then, gas could take its place in the pantheon of German atrocities only when it was recognized by British political leaders that its most truly terrifying possibility—a weapon against which there was no defense—was *not* to be realized!

An outstanding example of the logic that governed this discourse of defenselessness was one of the first German defenses of the use of gas, a 1915 article in the *Kölnische Zeitung*:

The basic idea of the Hague agreements was to prevent unnecessary cruelty and unnecessary killing when milder methods of putting the enemy out of action suffice and are possible. From this standpoint the letting loose of smoke clouds, which, in a gentle wind, move quite slowly towards the enemy, is not only permissible by international law, but is an extraordinarily mild method of war.

It has always been permissible to compel the enemy to evacuate positions by artificially flooding them. Those who were not indignant, or even surprised, when our enemies in Flanders summoned water as a weapon against us, have no cause to be indignant when we make air our ally and employ it to carry stunning gases against the enemy. What the Hague Convention desired to prevent was the destruction without chance of escape of human lives en masse, which would have been the case if shells with poisonous gas were rained down on a defenseless enemy who did not see them coming and was exposed to them irremediably.[118]

Although the contested association of this logic of defenselessness set gas weapons as a category apart, there were some parallels with at least one other weapon. The initial characterization of the flamethrower as a particularly abominable weapon dissipated soon after its appearance, for the reason that "owing to its very limited radius of action and the visibility of the flame, the chances of escape are greater than where the instruments used are projectiles or shells."[119] Similarly, as soldiers became more familiar with the use of gas and defenses against it, many of the initial inhibitions ebbed and gas became increasingly—though grudgingly—accepted as another unavoidable technology of modern warfare that one may as well get used to.[120] The intrinsic qualities of gas or flame were less galvanizing than the possibility of avoiding inevitable death.

Of course, not all parties involved were reconciled to this strategy of normalization. Ironically, those least amenable to it were those who had no first-hand experience. Soldiers exposed to gas in the field were—however reluctantly—those who were the most accustomed to this new element of the war. Among others, the well-known military strategist B. H. Liddell Hart was gassed in World War I and subsequently advocated the use of gas in future wars as more humane than the conventional weapons such as high explosives.[121] Soldiers and commentators not exposed to gas were evidently susceptible to the same kinds of fear of the unknown that had caused such apprehension among soldiers when gas was first introduced.

In the end, the attitudes toward gas weapons were ambiguous. As Haber explains: "No one who experienced gas forgot it: it may not have harmed their bodies, but it left an indelible stain on their minds. However,—and this is a significant point—to some, chemical warfare was just a bothersome incident of the war, to others it was the focal point of their fears then and later."[122] Similarly, the authors of the first volume of the SIPRI study have convincingly argued:

> The facts of the matter are that some people felt gas to be an important weapon; that they were able to find ways of demonstrating its importance sufficiently convincingly for the initiation of large development, procurement and deployment programmes; and that by the end of the war gas had become a standard weapon, if not a universally popular one. Few people doubted that it would be used again in some future war, and because its technical and military possibilities had clearly not been exhausted it became a weapon to be taken seriously.[123]

If we put these fears and sense of moral outrage in historical relief, they can be seen in one sense as strikingly similar to the fear of the unknown that accompanied the introduction of novel weapons of the past. And yet, we have seen in this section some grounds by which gas weapons were set apart from other weapons. The perception that gas was a weapon against which there was no defense makes intelligible both the normative disdain for using them against enemy civilians and the fear of retaliation against one's own population. Yet there was nothing that indelibly and inevitably stamped gas weapons as indiscriminate killers of the defenseless. On one hand, the availability of technological means of defense had a normalizing effect on the acceptability of gas weapons. On the other hand, the fact that civilian populations were spared from the introduction of gas weapons provided fertile soil for vivid and terrifying imaginings of the future of gas warfare. If the experience of gas weapons during World War I was therefore ambiguous, the struggle over the definition of its status was to be politically contested in the postwar years.

The most judicious assessments of the reception of gas warfare have concluded that gas was not a universally reviled weapon at the close of World War I. As Brown has argued, "gas warfare was never singled out by the American public as a unique evil of the war in Europe," for "gas was only one of the many horrors of war," sharing the headlines with other German atrocity stories and the sinking of the Lusitania.[124] We are not, however, inevitably led to the conclusion that gas was treated *the same way* as other weapons have been in the past or as other weapons were during World War I. This chapter has demonstrated that there were in fact unique characteristics of the reception of gas as a tool of warfare.

Gas was the subject of considerable controversy even when it was used only against combatants. The submarine, tank, and airplane, by contrast, did not generate the same concern. This politicization of the weapon can largely be attributed to the fact that international law had proscribed the use of shells that diffused "asphyxiating or deleterious gases." The Hague Declaration itself approached the form of an absolute norm in the sense that it made no distinction between the use of asphyxiating shells against combatants and noncombatants.

Although an attempt was made to distinguish between lethal and irritant gases, this convergent reinterpretation of the Hague Declaration at the level of political and military leadership was not mirrored in public discourse. The distinction between lethal and irritant gases, and between shells and cylinders, was largely lost upon the public. This interpretive feature of gas weapons thus signaled a potential fracture line in a public discourse that treated all gases in warfare as belonging to an undifferentiated category. In short, the definition of the category of acceptable methods of employing gas was very contested, quite unlike the continued unacceptability of the use of poison or germs.[125]

Of particular significance is the finding that the association of gas warfare with the threat to innocent civilians (begun at the Hague) was reinforced during World War I. Whereas the distinction between lethal and irritant gases posed a potential discontinuity with the Hague norm, the association of gas with the death of defenseless innocents represents a most important interpretive continuity reinforced rather silently through political and military practice. Moreover, this interpretation indicated an important consensus of restraint across the otherwise violent expanses of slaughter during the war.

Although the definition of chemical weapons as an undefendable device was by no means universally accepted, its invocation raises certain parallels with the logic behind the banning of poison in Renaissance Europe. Indeed, gas warfare was readily coupled with poison and derided with similar rationales as "poison gas." This seemingly natural association was nonetheless at times interrupted, and gas weapons were not always and simply ostracized as a violation of international norms prohibiting poison. Nor was the logic of protest against chemical weapons always isomorphic with that of poison, as the disjuncture with the notion of defenselessness demonstrates. The controversy over the use of chemical weapons turned additionally and more specifically on the Hague Declaration prohibiting asphyxiating shells. Apparently in response to suggestions by the British secretary of state that the German use of gas was illegal as a violation of Article 23(a) of the Hague proscribing poison and poisoned weapons, it was countered in legal notes for the War Office:

It would be special pleading to ignore the Declaration and rely on the gases coming under Article 23 of the Hague Rules as poison, for asphyxiating and *deleterious* gases are provided for apart . . . We shall only make ourselves ridiculous if we try to stretch the meaning of "poison." The universally accepted view of the meaning of Art. 23 (a) is that it forbids poisoning drink or food, leaving poison about, deliberately spreading germs of disease, putting poison on outside of bullets, shells, or cutting weapons.[126]

The special status of chemical weapons is such a genealogical intrigue because it was the one novel weapon introduced in World War I for which defenses were potentially and actually effective. If gas weapons had been used against civilians during the war, the experience might have prepared the way for grudging acceptance of such a practice as yet another inevitability of warfare. Since chemical weapons were not intentionally used against civilians, however, even greater power accrued to this crucial identification of chemical weapons as weapons before which all were defenseless. Conversely, the normalizing process of gas weapons—which derived from the availability of technological means of defense—was less prominent.[127]

Conspicuously absent in the later years of the grinding conflict was the naturalizing discourse casting these weapons as humane in that they would help shorten the conflict. Such justifications, so prominent at the Hague and at the outset of the war, seem to have met their match with the bewildering shock of relentless destruction that was World War I. Indeed, unquestioned faith in the beneficence of technological progress was radically challenged by the disillusioning experience of the war.

The Interwar Period

Every new effective weapon has met with outcry against it as being an inhumane device. The more effective the new weapon, the greater the outcry. The same opposition that the use of gas is now meeting was encountered by bows and arrows, rifles, machine guns, and high-explosive shells, but each in turn has been accepted because they were effective. All history shows that in time of war any effective weapons available will be used.
—American Legion Report on Geneva Protocol, 1926

The only means of abolishing chemical warfare is to abolish the idea that it is possible to make war by such means.
—General Kalafatovitch, Geneva Conference, 1925

The decade after World War I spawned a series of international efforts to proscribe CW, most notably the Washington Naval Conference of 1922, negotiations at Geneva in 1925, and meetings of the Disarmament Conference of the League of Nations in the early 1930s. Although this period was in some respects the golden age of efforts to outlaw CW (at least before 1992), the Washington Treaty did not officially come into effect, the U.S. Senate failed to ratify the Geneva Protocol of 1925, and no agreement resulted from the Disarmament Conference, leaving the normative status of chemical weapons in a somewhat ambiguous institutional state.

The chemical weapons literature testifies to the chronology of developments, policies, and moods of the interwar period which were influential in the tide of events regarding CW.[1] This chapter adds to the existing literature by tracing depictions of chemical weapons, identifying their deployment, and assessing the implications of these operations for the development of a normative discourse concerning CW. What was portrayed as natural, inevitable, impossible, or unthinkable in the aftermath of World War I? In what ways were gas weapons constituted as unacceptable? What sources were available for these discursive strategies, and of what were they the product?

To pursue these interrogations, I focus upon two events: the 1921–1922 Conference on the Limitation of Armament held at Washington, and the Conference for the Supervision of the International Trade in Arms and Ammunition and in Implements of War held at Geneva in 1925. Developments surrounding the contemplated and actual use of chemical weapons in the interwar period are considered in the next chapter. I focus more heavily on the United States, for the paradoxical reason that this country was both the prime mover behind efforts to ban CW in this period and the chief opposition to those efforts; it was in the U.S. Senate that the Geneva Protocol met its stiffest challenge.

An Uncertain Read

In the immediate aftermath of the war, "those of the general public who could recall anything of the wartime publications on CW might have adopted any one of a number of assessments: gas as a humane weapon, gas as a terror weapon, gas as just another weapon as horrible as any other. . . . There was certainly no consensus of opinion, and during the Russian Civil War there appears to have been no outcry about the use of chemical weapons or their supply by the intervening powers."[2] In the 1920s, however, gas weapons became an item of public and government concern in Europe and the United States as the result of activity at the international level by organizations such as the Red Cross and League of Nations, and at the domestic level, by novelists, newspaper reports, military organizations, and chemical-industry lobby groups that generated alarmist forecasts of chemical warfare.[3]

The Permanent Advisory Commission on Military, Naval, and Air Questions of the League of Nations issued a report on gas warfare in October 1920. The commission, composed of representatives of the general staffs of the states members of the Council of the League, concluded that "the employment of gases is a fundamentally cruel method of carrying on war, *though not more so than certain other methods commonly employed*, provided that they are only employed against combatants. Their employment against noncombatants, however, must be regarded as barbarous and inexcusable."[4]

This report fairly represented the handling of gas weapons by the League of Nations during this period—there was disagreement over the nature of gas weapons and how they should be treated, but there was a frequent association of such means with the threat to civilians.[5] The treatment of gas warfare at the international level both reflected and rein-forced some of the major themes of gas propaganda in the United States and Europe, such as future projections of gas warfare in which whole cities would be destroyed with a few gas bombs.

In the United States, the overzealous lobbying efforts of a Chemical Warfare Service (CWS) fighting for survival and the massive publicity campaigns of a chemical industry seeking chemical tariffs combined to create an almost constant stream of gas propaganda. These efforts warned of the dangers the United States would face without a large chemical industry and at first stressed the experience of Germany in the last war and impending German "monstrosities of the future."[6] While the association of the dangers of gas with the Germans receded as the decade progressed, a continual theme of the propaganda emphasized the availability of new and enormously destructive chemicals, as in the headline proclaiming "War's Newest and Deadliest Weapon; 3 Drops of Poison Kill Any One They Touch."[7] Meanwhile, accidents at gas plants, the adoption of tear gas by police forces, and revelations about the gene-sis of Germany's wartime gas program kept gas in the news.[8]

In Europe, alarm accompanied the publication of similar reports about enormously destructive new chemicals; some of these reports originated in the U.S. propaganda efforts.[9] As in the United States, lobbyists ac-tively underscored the danger to Britain of permitting German suprem-acy in the dye industry,[10] and the public's attention on CW was main-tained by a number of issues, such as whether scientists should do secret CW work, industrial accidents, a controversy in France over the award-ing of a Nobel prize to Fritz Haber, and so on.[11]

The dissemination of these claims regarding CW generated all manner of opinions from a variety of sources. Some writers projected gas war-fare as a horrible and devastating inevitability of the future.[12] Other com-mentators, while agreeing that chemical warfare was inevitable, sug-gested that it was not substantially different from the introduction of new weapons in the past,[13] still others even argued that it offered the most humane method of warfare yet devised.[14] Still others felt that the prevention of gas warfare by international treaties and moral sanction was not out of the question.[15]

Little or no homogeneity of attitudes existed at the international level or even within different sectors of society, be it the general public, the military, or political elites.[16] It might be stretching matters to assert a groundswell of public pressure demanding the abolition of gas weapons, but all this attention nevertheless provided sufficient impetus to isolate gas weapons as the bête noire of postwar memories and to get them included on the agenda for a conference that was to be held in Washington, D.C., to address the looming prospect of a naval arms race between the great powers.[17]

In short, the fact that gas weapons were politicized enough to be discussed at the disarmament conference was due largely to the miscalculations of an overzealous chemical lobby. The strategy of emphasizing the dangers of chemical warfare in order to ensure the survival of the CWS and the profitability of the chemical industry had backfired, for it led to calls for the prohibition of gas warfare.[18] The power of the threats derived in part from the fact that they met little concerted opposition. The British government did not answer the exaggerated threats of gas attacks and was silent on the merits of defenses because it wished to avoid the political risks involved in any suggestion that it was advocating gas warfare.[19] Such political sensitivity testifies not only to the existence of the antigas stigma but to its indirect influence on developments during this period.

At the same time, the accidental nature of the overselling of the CW threat resonates with genealogical overtones important to this study. It has been forcefully argued that "to anyone who was prepared to consider the potentialities of CW dispassionately, it would have been clear that the chemical threat did not differ markedly from that posed by high-explosive weapons. Against well-equipped and well-disciplined troops, the chemical weapons of the time would never be overwhelming: if anything, their efficacy had declined since 1918."[20] Indeed, while reviewing the publication of the medical history of the war, the *Times'* medical correspondent concluded that "the horror of surprise and bewilderment" occasioned by the gas attack at Ypres "has been so far discounted that the alarmist statements often made about gas warfare in the future may be discounted also."[21] Moreover, some of the groups making alarmist claims of gas warfare were perfectly aware that "by no stretch of an informed imagination" could lewisite be seen as a "super-weapon," and that in no sense was a catastrophic capability for aerochemical warfare to be developed in the foreseeable future.[22] These developments led Brown to conclude that "propagandists were totally irresponsible in their exaggerations of new weapons developments."[23] Nonetheless, the scripting of scenarios of danger had successfully constructed a "shadow greater than the substance."[24]

In a book on U.S. foreign policy, David Campbell has shown how representations of "outside" threats participate in the on-going process of securing national identities for states.[25] These depictions of danger are not simply the response to objective conditions but involve the interpretive scripting of danger through political discourse. Similarly, Mary Douglas has investigated how danger and risk are politicized in society, arguing that they are cultural constructs.[26] The argument here parallels these formulations, for the reception of gas weapons in this period cannot be attributed simply to the objective threat they presented. Indeed, this prime puzzle of the period has not gone unnoticed. As Haber observes:

> While other weapons were being paraded on every conceivable occasion, poison gas disappeared. . . . Within a year of the Armistice not one of the former belligerents was in a position to manufacture poison gas on a large scale. . . . But out of sight did not mean out of mind. Poison gas, though there was hardly any after 1919, appeared more alarming than before, and the paradox of a non-existent weapon accompanied by growing public awareness of its potential threat calls for comment.[27]

The politicization of gas warfare in the early 1920s, then, was not so much the response to an objective condition as it was the inscription of scenarios of future danger that—given repeated and terrifying expression—found a receptive audience. This receptiveness was initially facilitated by the unpopularity of the Germans and their ready association with gas warfare of the past.[28] The more the inscription of danger turned toward future scenarios, however, the more the threat became disembodied from any particular foe and focused on the potential threat posed by the weapon itself.

The Washington Conference

On November 12, 1921, the Conference on the Limitation of Armament was convened in Washington, D.C., with the participation of the Great Powers: the United States, Britain, France, Italy, and Japan. The primary purpose of the conference was to work toward restrictions on the economically burdensome naval arms race between the great powers, with Far Eastern questions (such as the territorial integrity of China) also occupying a substantial portion of the deliberations.[29] As a decidedly tertiary consideration, the United States suggested in its invitations to other countries that "it may also be found advisable to formulate proposals by which, in the interest of humanity, the use of new agencies of warfare may be suitably controlled."[30] In response to a query by France as to what those "new agencies" would entail, Secretary of State Hughes responded by including gas, aircraft, and submarines.[31]

There was some question whether questions of land armament should have been included at all in the conference. Clearly, expectations regarding limitations on such means were virtually nonexistent; at the second meeting of the Committee on Limitation of Armament, Chairman Hughes was quite forthright that "any attempt to define a limit for military forces would be in vain," for it was well known "how established rules of international law had been blown to pieces" in the previous war.[32] Equally skeptical was Balfour of the British delegation, who believed "that there was no use in trying to limit the use of instruments in the hands of belligerents during the stress of warfare, when obedience to such regulations would only be rewarded by unfair advantage being taken of them by an unscrupulous enemy."[33]

Nevertheless, Hughes felt that the opinion of the civilized world should be acknowledged at the conference. Elihu Root, U.S. delegate, seems to have voiced prevailing opinion in agreeing with the prognosis that effective agreements on land armaments were unlikely while also concurring with Hughes that there might be some value to discussing such issues even without hope of an agreement:

> Whether the Committee succeeded or not in reaching a definite conclusion upon any matter connected with the limitation of land armament, sincere and practical consideration and discussion of the subject would itself greatly relieve the situation, and furnish the committee with a base from which some advance, not otherwise possible, might be made thereafter. The mere ascertaining of the obstacles in the way was itself a step in advance, changing vague and indefinite impressions, regarding matters to which they had not addressed their minds, into definite ascertainment of the particular reasons why a definite agreement could, or could not, be reached. This might bring many minds to a consideration of methods which would lead to future progress.[34]

Other members of the committee agreed that, as a nod to world opinion, these issues should at least be discussed.[35] They further agreed that the matter of land armaments should be referred to the Committee on Program and Procedure, in order to arrange subcommittees on "aeronautics, poison gases, and the laws of nations."[36] This move represented a continuation of the practice begun at the Hague of disaggregating gases from more general considerations of the laws of warfare and thus furthered the isolation of gas as a particular weapon of concern apart from other "conventional" weapons of war such as high explosives.

The submarine was the one other weapon besides gas which incurred a palpable measure of public distaste as a result of its use during the First World War. The issue of submarine warfare was framed in two opposing ways in committee deliberations. The first was to single out the weapon itself as inherently incompatible with acceptable standards of warfare and to seek to prohibit the use of that weapon. The second approach was to regard only certain uses—or misuses—of a weapon as the object of restraint. With but one exception, the latter view was accepted by the Committee members as the proper way with which to consider the question of submarine warfare.

The lone dissenting position was that of the British, whose delegate maintained that "the submarine can never be kept from bursting through the moral barrier which ought to limit its activities and that it will always yield to the temptation to make unrestricted use of all its powers."[37] In contrast, the French Government expressed the belief that "every method of warfare may or may not be employed in conformity with the laws of war, and that the inhuman and barbarous use made of the submarine by a belligerent in the late war is a reason for condemning that belligerent, but not for condemning the submarine."[38]

The French position prevailed in the committee. The Japanese delegate, for example, thought that "submarines in their legitimate employment were no more atrocious than poison gas or air bombs," and further, that "any weapon might become illegitimate if used without restriction."[39] The influential chairman of the committee, Charles Evans Hughes of the United States, concurred, adding that "unlimited warfare is not necessarily an attribute of the submarine alone."[40] Identical to the way in which other weapons were treated at the Hague Conferences, then, the predominant attitude towards submarines was ensconced within a value-neutral conception of technology which held that "it is possible to reconcile the use of submarines with the laws of humanity."[41] This understanding of the morally neutral character of technology made it possible to declare that the accusation of offending the laws of humanity "is brought against the men and *not against the instrument* that they made use of."[42] On the basis of this logic, the committee adopted a resolution to restrict *certain uses* of submarines in warfare according to the dictates of the laws of war.

Immediately following the adoption of this resolution on January 6, 1922, the committee turned to the question of gas warfare. The subcommittee appointed to consider gases in warfare, composed of members representing the five powers, had agreed "more or less unanimously" on its report, which was to inform the deliberations of the committee. In the judgment of the subcommittee, the total prohibition of all gases in warfare was impracticable, for the following reasons:

(1) No nation would dare agree to render itself unprepared for gas warfare if the possibility existed that an unscrupulous enemy might break an agreement for its own advantage;

(2) Given the emission of gases from conventional explosives, any attempt to forbid all use of gas in warfare would inevitably lead to confusion; and (3) Research and manufacture of gases of use in warfare was impossible to restrict.

The subcommittee's report did, however, entertain the possibility of attempting to limit the use of gas in the same way submarines had been handled. On the belief that "it is possible [but with greater difficulty] to confine the action of chemical warfare gases in the same manner as that of high explosives and other means of carrying on war," the subcommittee concluded that "the only limitation practicable is wholly to prohibit the use of gases against cities and other large bodies of noncombatants in the same manner as high explosives may be limited, but that there can be no limitation on their use against the armed forces of the enemy, ashore or afloat."[43] This judgment not only followed the approach taken by the committee with respect to submarines, but it agreed with the initial negotiating position of the United States with respect to gas. This position, as recommended by General Fries to the War Department general staff, was that "the only limitation that should be considered by the United States is the prohibition of its use against cities and non-combatants in exactly the same manner as the use of airplane bombs, high-explosive shells, or other weapons are prohibited."[44]

Pursuant to the recommendation cited above, the subcommittee reached a further conclusion that is of importance, for it eventually became a presumption for subsequent approaches to the question of limiting gas warfare. In the words of the members of the subcommittee, "the kinds of gases and their effects on human beings can not be taken as a basis for limitation."[45] In other words, no consideration was to be accorded the possibility of distinguishing between "nonpermissible" and "permissible" gases. In this sense, the alleged special humanitarian qualities of gas—whether one believed chemical weapons were more or less cruel—were bypassed as the pivotal criterion for basing restrictions on CW. In spite of the careful distinction between lethal and nonlethal gases observed by all of the belligerents in World War I, then, the legacy of that war seems to have been the practical impossibility of discerning between different gaseous agents in the fog of war.[46]

This reading is confirmed by the report of the general board of the Navy to the U.S. delegation. This document acknowledged that certain materials such as tear gases could be used without violating the principles of unnecessary suffering and avoidance of noncombatants, and that "other gases will, no doubt, be invented which could be so employed;

but there will be great difficulty in establishing a clear and definite de-marcation line between the lethal gases and those which produce unnec-essary suffering as distinguished from those gases which simply disable temporarily."[47] The rather inconspicuous acceptance of this conclusion by all parties at the Washington Conference removed the possibility of limiting gas warfare to nonlethal "knock-out" gases while prohibiting only lethal gases. All gases were to be considered as one whole, un-differentiated category, a category, similar to submarines, that for the subcommittee was neither inherently moral nor immoral.

If the subcommittee had not singled out gas as an inherently immoral weapon, delegates disagreed about whether poison gases nevertheless represented something qualitatively different from other categories of weapons:

> "The Subcommittee was divided on the question as to whether or not warfare gases form a method of warfare similar to other methods such as shrapnel, machine guns, rifle, bayonet, high explosives, airplane bombs, hand grenades and similar older methods."[48]

Although the subcommittee was divided, it chose to report that the American, British, and French members of the subcommittee, "who know gas, were emphatic that *chemical warfare gases form a method of wag-ing war similar to the older form.*"[49] This opinion is remarkable in that those who had actually experienced gas warfare were apparently prepared to regard it in more or less "conventional" terms, whereas those who had not had the opportunity to 'get used to' gas weapons were much less comfortable reconciling these new inventions to the traditional referents of war.

Defining Fears

The crucial importance of these developments are underscored if we ten-der the following counter-factual: if gas weapons had been used as a standard weapon against civilian populations during World War I, the special dread aroused by scenarios of future gas attacks on cities might have been less effective in galvanizing attitudes toward gas weapons as the bête noire of World War I. On balance, as we have seen, the actual experience of gas warfare itself tended toward a grudging conven-tionalizing of the weapon, whereas the absence of such direct engage-ment contributed to a continued sense of its strangeness and, ultimately, its unacceptability. This process has been noted for a variety of other weapons throughout the history of warfare:

In its early use, Greek fire certainly caused panic; it was regarded with extreme disfavour as an unknightly weapon, but steady troops soon grew accustomed to it. The same phenomenon was seen when gunpowder, a more terrible agent of destruction than Greek fire, came upon the scene. . . . Some early capitulations probably resulted from fear rather than damage—a few stone cannon balls falling inside a fortified place producing panic. As time went on, trained infantry stood firm under heavy fire from large guns and mortars, and every invention intended to make the use of infantry impossible has always failed in its purpose. Shrapnel, high-explosive, Flammenwerfer (that old friend), poison gas, rockets, aeroplane bombs, and all the paraphernalia of modern war have failed to shake the foot-soldier. He may be blown out of existence, but he stays where he is and this happens. The war of the future, it appears, with atomic bombs and bacterial warfare, is to be directed against the civilian population, who, it is anticipated, will capitulate.[50]

Fear, it seems, issues most forcefully from unfamiliarity, as taboo emerges from the unknown. Of course, not all soldiers accepted gas as just another weapon of war. Nevertheless, all of the veterans' organizations in the United States opposed the Geneva Protocol's ban on gas warfare. According to the official position of the American Legion, the ban on gas came from pacifists, not soldiers who generally regarded gas as an essential weapon: "It was the experience of hundreds of thousands engaged in the last war that gas was one of the most humane weapons of warfare and also the most effective in bringing any war to an end."[51]

Detractors to the humanitarian opposition to CW compared gas with explosives and other weapons. "Is gas warfare inhumane?" asked the author of an interwar report on CW. "Of course it is; all warfare is inhumane and barbarous." But, he continued: "Is gas warfare more inhumane and barbarous than other forms of warfare? Does it cause more suffering? Does it cause a larger proportion of deaths to casualties? Are the after effects of gas serious? In comparison with other means of warfare, gas warfare has something of which to boast. . . . Gas does not mutilate the body."[52]

Similarly, it was argued soon after the war that gas was not worse than being disemboweled by high explosives or bayonets, nor than having legs torn off or eyes gouged out—indeed, gas does none of these things.[53] Haldane argued that the sufferings caused by chlorine or phosgene "were utterly negligible compared with those produced by a good septic shell-wound."[54] In contrast, opponents of chemical weapons confined their case to the unobjectionable idea that exposure to gas was something other than a positive experience, and thus gas was not "humane"; they generally did not compare the relative cruelty of gas to other weapons—none of them argued that dismemberment by high explosives was less cruel. This has been a constant feature in the genealogy of the chemical weapons taboo up to the present time: those who have sought to legitimize chemical weapons have done so by appealing to the status of other (perhaps even more cruel) weapons that have already been accepted as unavoidable and legitimate: namely, "conventional weapons." The typical explanation for the chemical weapons taboo as resulting from the alleged uniquely horrific qualities of gas thus misleads: while that explanation implies that chemical arms are more horrible than other means, the prohibitionary discourse has been largely confined to gaining acceptance of the more circumscribed notion that chemical weapons are simply horrible. The plausibility of that discourse has depended on its isolation from discussion of the humanitarian qualities of other weapons. Indeed the constant reminder that the uses of so many other horribly cruel implements of war have been accepted as unavoidable routine procedure undercuts the moral basis of the chemical weapons taboo. To make the comparative contention that chemical weapons are more horrible than other weapons actually exposes the anomalous status of the prohibition.

In the end, the fact that many soldiers who experienced gas warfare actually opposed its prohibition undercuts current wisdom regarding the sources of the CW taboo. The thought has been expressed often that "the western abhorrence of chemical weapons results from our own experience of them in World War I."[55] Thus, it is argued, "those who did not share in that experience may not feel our moral compunction not to use chemical weapons."[56] A Nietzschean interpretation reveals that this position represents the teleological imposition of an essentialist misreading of events, which posits the actual encounter with CW as the logical impetus to its prohibition due to a natural and inevitable horror based on the intrinsic qualities of gas weapons. The CW story according to this view is a simple and tidy one: chemical weapons have been proscribed because they were tried out during World War I and all those involved were morally repulsed by the objective characteristics of these weapons—thus, whoever else might use them would have the same experience.

The opposite may have in fact been the case: the exposure to gas may have tended over the course of the war to erode any special horror towards CW, whereas it was precisely policymakers' and civilians' lack of real exposure to chemical weapons that explains their revulsion.[57] The chemical weapons taboo issued from a fear of the unknown. As Nietzsche remarked, "Being moral means being highly accessible to fear. Fear is the power by which the community is preserved."[58] This phenomenon was not missed by General Fries who—with some disdain—blamed the gas hysteria on ignorance: "Gas has unfortunately, among those who are unacquainted with it, the power of ghost stories over the imagination."[59] The CW taboo was not *produced* by the qualities of gas as experienced in World War I so much as non-events undergirded the construction of an interpretation that proved more powerful than the events themselves. "The greatest events—they are not our loudest but our stillest hours," Nietzsche reminds us.[60]

Another common explanation of the taboo is that the legacy of distaste from World War I issues from assessments that gas weapons were not militarily useful. Such claims are not sustainable and often result from a mistaken logical jump that since chemical weapons were not "decisive" (that is, war-winning) they were therefore not "useful." Few weapons indeed have been "decisive" in the history of warfare,[61] but this does not mean that they have no utility; nor was such a lack of decisiveness enough to prevent continued use of even marginal prototypes of modern weapons. The first firearms "were far from being as effective as might be supposed," and bows were regarded as more formidable and reliable weapons for hundreds of years after the introduction of firearms.[62] Mishaps with firearms were prevalent, and charges seemed as apt to explode in the face of the shooter as hit the target. Partington notes that as late as 1563 German gunners had a motto, "Das Treffen is nicht allweg Kunst / Es liegt meistteils an Gottes gunst" (the shot doesn't always proceed apace, it depends mostly on God's grace).[63]

Still, early firearms were not thereby rejected because of their marginal utility and accidents, features that remind us of the mishaps with early gas weapons. The first gas weapons posed comparable liabilities, but they were roundly regarded after World War I as being very useful in certain circumstances despite their limitations. In Britain, for example, the influential report of the Committee on Chemical Warfare Organization (the Holland Committee) stated "That gas is a legitimate weapon in war, the Committee have no shadow of doubt," and the members took it as a "foregone conclusion" that gas "will be used in the future" because no successful weapon has "ever been abandoned by Nations fighting for existence."[64] In either case, then, there is no comfort in the thought that the exposure to gas warfare will inevitably lead to its rejection in and of itself.

To return to the consideration of gas warfare at the Washington Conference, we might expect the nations of the world to deal with gas the way they dealt with submarines.[65] The subcommittee's report represented the deliberations of a selected group of experts, and, ostensibly, it was to provide reasoned and informed judgments upon which the committee's members would base their own opinions. In fact, however, the recommendations of this report received scant attention—testimony to the remarkable influence of Chairman Hughes in shaping the direction of the committee's treatment of gas warfare. After reading the report of the subcommittee, Hughes bypassed opening discussion and immediately proceeded to read the report of the advisory committee of the American delegation.

This advisory committee was composed of various public officials and private citizens, a composition that served to justify its claim that it represented the "conscience of the American people."[66] In the words of Frederic Brown, the report of this committee "was as emotional as the technical Subcommittee report had been rational," and consisted of a "collection of exaggerations and misstatements."[67] The most significant of these was the ready (and by now familiar) equation of the future use of gas with the destruction of "undefended and thickly populated cities." Accepting the notion that gas had to be treated as an undifferentiated category, the committee asserted that "there can be no actual restraint of the use by combatants of this new agency of warfare, if it is permitted in any guise."[68] Based on this reasoning, and without consideration of the counter-arguments that favored the use of gas, the committee resolved that "chemical warfare, including the use of gases, whether toxic or nontoxic, should be prohibited by international agreement, and should be classed with such unfair methods of warfare as poisoning wells, introducing germs of disease, and other methods that are abhorrent in modern warfare."[69]

Here, then, was an active attempt to define gas weapons as akin to poison and biological warfare, despite a recognition that some agents were "nontoxic." Chairman Hughes then read another report, signed by General Pershing, which stated that "chemical warfare should be abolished among nations, as abhorrent to civilization. It is a cruel, unfair and improper use of science. It is fraught with the gravest danger to noncombatants and demoralizes the better instincts of humanity."[70]

Hughes continued to push the deliberations of the committee in this direction, citing as a justification a putative "difference of opinion among experts" (one notes, however, that a "more or less" unanimous negative opinion regarding a prohibition prevailed among the subcommittee of "experts"). Hughes then read a report by the general board of the U.S. Navy. This report also recommended a ban on chemical weapons to guard against the possibility that many "innocent persons may deliberately be made the objects of gas attack by unscrupulous belligerents."[71]

Foregoing any deliberation on the issue, and departing from the practice with respect to other subjects of the conference (such as submarines and aircraft), Hughes disregarded the findings of the subcommittee and immediately proposed a resolution to prohibit the use of gas in warfare. A French suggestion to adjourn was rebuffed, and Elihu Root presented a resolution on behalf of the United States which, he claimed, offered "the most extraordinary consensus of opinion that one could well find upon any international subject." This claim was manifestly false—even within this very conference, as we have seen, there was anything but a consensus of opinion regarding the possible limitations on gas warfare.

This extraordinary and rather single-handed effort to prohibit gas weapons reflected Hughes's conviction that "the close of the Great War found old rules in need of reconsideration and new conditions crying for new rules," namely, "the peril of great populations placed at the mercy of new instruments of warfare."[72] Had Hughes confronted stiff opposition to this proposal, however, he appears to have been quite prepared to accept the same kind of limitations on gas as on other weapons: "if it should be found to be impracticable to prohibit the use of poison gas, it would still seem to be possible to restrain its use against cities and other large bodies of non-combatants as the experts, who were opposed to its prohibition, suggested."[73]

The resolution was accepted by the delegates at the Washington Conference largely because they believed the prohibition was nothing new, for it merely reiterated the provisions of Article 171 of the Versailles Treaty, which in turn were understood to have been based upon previous declarations that had been violated—namely the Hague Declaration.[74] Moreover, the delegates accepted that the resolution would not prevent nations from engaging in preparations for gas warfare to avoid being caught off guard in a future conflict. For these reasons, the declaration was not perceived as terribly important, a perception that overrode the discordance over gas weapons and ultimately secured agreement.[75]

Once again, a crucial defining moment in the development of the chemical weapons taboo was the result of rather fortuitous circumstances. In this case, ambiguous moral concerns were translated into an international prohibition—however tenuously—thanks to the existence of a previous institutionalization of the norm. The norm had for the first time provided its own self-sustaining rationale in the form of its ancestral lineage.

Genuine abhorrence of gas weapons did play more than a passive role in facilitating this reinstitutionalization of the norm. Britain, for its part, was initially opposed to the treaty but acceded to it because its leaders believed that government opposition to it would be difficult.[76] In the end, however, it would be straining matters to characterize Article 5 of the Washington Treaty as the product of a rational moral consensus on the nature and appropriate treatment of gas weapons. In genealogical fashion, the institutional embodiment of the CW taboo enacted in Washington was the result of the imposition of one reading of events over another alternative interpretation, as enacted by the active suppression and deft chairmanship of U.S. Secretary of State Hughes.

New Sources

The Washington Treaty marked an important move from attempts to limit certain uses of a new weapon to a blanket prohibition on any use: this development was not replicated with other weapons, not even submarines, which were part of the same treaty with gas weapons. In the preamble to the Treaty Relating to the Use of Submarines and Noxious Gases in Warfare, the signatory powers of the Washington Conference: "desiring to make more effective the rules adopted by civilized nations for the protection of the lives of neutrals and noncombatants at sea in time of war, and to prevent the use in war of noxious gases and chemicals, have determined to conclude a Treaty to this effect."[77] This statement reflects a subtle yet important difference in the treatment of submarines and noxious gases. No mention is made of submarines per se; there is only an affirmation of the general precept of the law of war that the lives of noncombatants and neutrals are to be protected. Contrary to the recommendations of the subcommittee that gas be treated in an exactly parallel fashion—that is, only its misuse against civilian populations should be forbidden—gas had nevertheless been singled out as an inherently undesirable weapon, regardless of against whom it was employed.

The first four articles of the treaty set down the rules to govern legitimate and illegitimate uses of submarines in warfare, according to principles of noncombatant immunity. Article 5, by contrast, is a blanket prohibition on the use of gas, the language of which was derived from the Hague Declarations of 1899 and 1907, and, in particular, Article 171 of the Treaty of Versailles. There is a noteworthy shift, however, from the phrasing of Article 171 of Versailles to that of the Washington Treaty. In a clause that seeks to buttress the authority of the taboo, the former treaty makes an appeal to previous legal prohibitions: "The use of asphyxiating, poisonous or other gases and all analogous liquids, materials or devices being prohibited" already, their manufacture in Germany was to be forbidden. In the Washington Treaty, this clause becomes the fol-

lowing: "The use of asphyxiating, poisonous or other gases and all analogous liquids, material or devices, having been justly condemned by the
general opinion of the civilized world and a prohibition of such use having been declared in treaties to which a majority of the civilized Powers
are parties."

Two significant points about the form of the gas prohibition at Washington must be noted. First, an institutional ancestry had become an additional source that was drawn upon by postwar advocates and framers
of a ban on gas. The putative justification for including prohibitions on
the manufacture of gas weapons in the peace treaties was the existence
of a previous ban, namely, the Hague Declaration.[78] Basing Article 5 of
the Washington Treaty explicitly upon the Hague Declaration and Article 171 of Versailles, however, obscured fundamental gaps and discontinuities in that legacy with an implied venerable institutional tradition.
On one level, the Washington Treaty was a blanket prohibition on any
use of any gases, and was therefore a considerable departure from the
Hague's more limited ban on asphyxiating shells. The same can be said
of the phrase in Versailles 171 that all gases were already prohibited, an
assumption that from a legal standpoint was by no means established.
Furthermore, the invocation of Versailles papered over the fact that Article 171 (and comparable articles in the other peace treaties) was essentially designed to limit German rearmament rather than to reaffirm a
more universal obligation of all parties to a tenet of international law.[79]
In short, the appeal to an institutional tradition disguised significant genealogical changes in interpretation, the existence of a contested history,
and the origins of those institutions (especially the anti-German character of Versailles) that were now invoked as a noble and universal heri-
tage.

Besides this ancestral and self-referential institutional support, the
framers of the Treaty of Washington explicitly drew upon a second
source that they could claim as their own: public opinion. Upon what
basis did this treaty declare that it was representing world opinion? This
clause resembles very closely the contention of the advisory committee
that "the conscience of the American people has been profoundly
shocked by the savage use of scientific discoveries for destruction rather
than for construction" and that it was the committee's duty to represent
this conscience by seeking a prohibition of all uses of gas warfare.[80] The
committee supported this claim by citing the results of a poll of U.S.
public opinion on issues that were on the agenda at Washington, a poll
that it had organized. It was reported that 366,795 respondents favored
the abolition of chemical weapons, whereas only 19 favored their "reten-
tion and restriction in use."[81]

Despite the committee's citing of the poll, however, its rather grandiose claim to be responding to public opinion was misleading insofar as that support was passive and receptive rather than an active pressure. Like the efforts of the U.S. delegation as a whole, this invocation of authority was based more on "the assumed strength of the power of public opinion" than any palpable groundswell of pressure from domestic opinion.[82] In the words of Thomas Buckley, the members of the committee "saw themselves not as a conduit but as representing each in his or her own way American public opinion. The administration used the committee to influence both foreign delegates and American opinion." As Buckley adds, "Harding and Hughes both followed, ignored and led public opinion at different times before, during and after the conference."[83]

In a similar manner, the framers of the treaty cited world opinion as their authority for Article 5, even while they in fact were hoping to generate it by institutionalizing a focal point for that opinion—creating the treaty itself. This production of public sentiment emerged as the primary purpose of the treaty even more clearly in the ratification hearings of the U.S. Senate.

The Construction of Opinion

If many of the issues regarding chemical weapons were glossed over at the Washington Arms Conference, their potential to resurface was realized with a vengeance during the U.S. Senate ratification hearings of the Washington Treaty. In particular, Senator James Wadsworth (N.Y.) argued that there was a great deal of misunderstanding regarding chemical weapons as a result of the Washington proceedings. His opening statement contains several important considerations:

> I know full well that there is a very strong and widespread sentiment, not only in this country but in other countries, against what is known as chemical warfare, and I notice that the first paragraph of this article refers to its use as having been "justly condemned" by the general opinion of the civilized world. In my judgment, a large number of people very much misunderstand the actual results of chemical warfare.[84]

Wadsworth took issue with the assumption that the prohibition of gas warfare is a "just" condemnation, offering evidence for why he thought otherwise. Citing statistics that a soldier who suffered from a gas attack was only one-twelfth as likely to die as a soldier who had been injured by explosives, bullets, and bayonets, Wadsworth provided empirical testimony that gas offered a more humane method of warfare than other means accepted as legitimate:

> Which is more cruel, a high-explosive shell which tears off a man's arm and blinds him and condemns him for the rest of his poor life to stagger down the pathway toward the grave, never free from suffering, or a gas wound which mutilates not at all and from which the medical records now show the soldier, in a comparatively short time and in an overwhelming majority of cases, entirely recovers? If we are to draw the line of demarcation as between a more cruel weapon and a less cruel weapon, frankly I can not see why it should be drawn in favour of the high-explosive shell and against the gas.[85]

The outcome of the debate over the relative humanity of gas versus other weapons was by no means decisive, but ratification of the treaty was secured by recourse to another line of justification. Senator Henry Cabot (Mass.) Lodge argued that regardless of whether or not Wadsworth's "humanity" arguments were sound,

> it seems to me just as well to get rid of methods of killing men, and to limit them as much as possible. The only way you can ever reach it is by the effect of public opinion. That is all that this clause [Article 5] is intended to effect. . . . This clause in this treaty is not expected to prevent the use of poison gases at the present. It is expected to do something toward crystallizing the public opinion of the world against it, and trying to make that public opinion more effective.[86]

This rationale of creating public opinion echoed the sentiment that prevailed at the Washington Conference, where it had been argued that agreement on the treaty was desirable in order to "do something to bring home to the consciences of mankind that poison gas was not a form of warfare which civilized nations could tolerate."[87] Even more explicitly, U.S. delegate Elihu Root expressed his belief that:

> the opinion of the people of civilized nations had tremendous force and exercised a powerful influence on the condition of the belligerents. . . . The public opinion of mankind was not the opinion of scientific and well-informed men, but of ill-informed men who formed opinions on simple and direct issues. If the public could be confused, public opinion was ineffective; but if the public was clear on the fundamentals of a question, then the opinion of mankind was something which no nation could afford to ignore or defy.

The purpose of the proposed treaty, according to Root, was thus "to put into such simple form the subject which had so stirred the feelings of a great part of the civilized world that the man in the street and the man on the farm could understand it."[88]

Upon the conclusion of Lodge's speech in the Senate, the vote on the Washington Treaty was summarily held and the treaty approved by a 72 to 0 vote. The treaty never officially went into effect, however, because France did not ratify it; the French opposed provisions relating to submarines. The Treaty therefore came to be regarded as a "dead letter" by 1925, but Article 5 was nevertheless of utmost importance in the development of the chemical weapons taboo, for its interpretations of gas weapons served directly as the basis for the more successful Geneva Protocol.

The delegates to the Washington Conference had been at least temporarily successful in "changing vague and indefinite impressions" into a "definite ascertainment of the particular reasons" why an agreement on chemical weapons could or could not be reached, as Root had originally envisioned. Those reasons did not primarily consist of a consensus on the issue of the humanity of gas weapons so much as a conviction that declaratory weapons limitations were of little consequence. The significant changes in the institutional expression of the norm commanded less notice than did the assumption that it was only an international agreement that could be violated in future warfare. In this negative way the existence of a previous institutionalized legacy of the chemical weapons norm tipped the scales in favor of a new prohibition, providing its own self-justificatory rationale. In the process, a particular interpretation of gas warfare—one characterized by "hysteria, misconceptions, and misinformation" rather than the unanimous deliberations of a subcommittee of experts—prevailed and was imbued with an institutional imprimatur.

The Geneva Protocol

The subject of gas warfare made its next international appearance at the 1925 Geneva conference, which convened under the auspices of the League of Nations to discuss the international trade in armaments. Here, too, the issue of gas weaponry was a decidedly tertiary concern. Indeed, it was decided early on that the raison d'être of the conference—to restrict or prohibit the export of means of warfare—was of little consequence for gas weapons. As Colonel Lohner of Switzerland stated in response to a U.S. proposal to restrict exports of means for gas warfare, it "is almost always impossible in practice to prohibit the export of these materials and implements of warfare."[89] The efforts of the conference turned instead to codifying the condemnation of chemical warfare and "laying down definite rules as to its application."

There was some debate regarding the competence of the conference to engage even in this circumscribed activity. Chairman Sosnkowski of Poland noted that the conference was convened for international trade in arms and "was not competent and did not possess the necessary powers to take any decisions in regard to the prohibition of chemical warfare."[90] The issue was referred to two committees that were to render their judgments to the conference. The Military, Naval, and Air Technical Committee recommended that the whole question be taken up at a future conference, while the legal committee was unable to reach agreement on the question of gas weapons. Nonetheless, many delegates felt strongly that they must not allow the opportunity to pass without affirming existing international statements on the matter. The Swiss delegation noted that while "a Conference to establish provision for the control of the trade in arms is certainly not the proper body to proclaim new principles of international law in regard to war," it is

> perfectly entitled to base its action on the recognized rules of international law when drawing up agreements; it can, consequently, refer in express terms to the binding force of these principles. The delegations of the various States have signed agreements expressly mentioning asphyxiating gases and have therefore given us evidence of the firm resolve of their Governments to put an end to the ravages of chemical warfare.
>
> The other States which are not bound by the Hague Convention of 1907 prohibiting the use of "poison or poisoned weapons" and "arms, projectiles or material calculated to cause unnecessary suffering" would, indeed, only be accepting an interpretation, in regard to a definite point, of a rule which a large number of them even now consider as binding.
>
> Finally, seeing that this prohibition "is binding on the conscience and practice of nations," as is very justly stated in the general report, we have before us, I think, everything required to enable us to proclaim the existence of a principle of international law.[91]

Several delegates explicitly invoked the existence of the Hague Declaration, Treaty of Versailles, and Washington Treaty as evidence that the use of poisonous and similar gases was at the time forbidden by the law and conscience of humankind. "A codification of this principle in a universal convention must constitute an additional guarantee and therefore a fresh advance," which, according to General de Marinis of Italy, amounted "to asking the States of the whole world to accede to Article V of the Treaty concluded at Washington on February 6ᵗʰ, 1922."[92] Agreeing that "there has been absolute unanimity that the use of asphyxiating gases in warfare is barbarous and should be condemned by every civilized nation," Theodore Burton of the United States proposed that the conference prepare a resolution based on Article 5 of the Washington Treaty of 1922.[93]

After a variety of statements in support of such efforts—including comments by the Italian, British, Canadian, and French delegates that those who had experienced gas in the last war realized what terrible engines of destruction they were, and the citation of fictional stories by China's delegate telling of the destruction of whole cities by twenty bombs—the proposal to establish a protocol embodying Article 5 of Treaty of Washington or some similar formula was adopted by vote.[94]

Once a draft of the protocol had been returned to the conference, discussion again ensued on the status of gas warfare. Delegate Komarnicki of Poland argued:

> From the legal point of view, however, it did not seem possible as yet to regard gases as weapons prohibited by International Law. Article V of the Washington Convention (which the speaker read) declared that the use of gases had been justly condemned by the general opinion of the civilized world. This was simply a moral condemnation and an attempt to embody the prohibition in International Law. . . . Notwithstanding, it might be desirable that the Contracting Parties should undertake on the one hand to regard the use of gases as prohibited under International Law, and on the other hand to secure the adherence of the other States to this new attitude.[95]

The delegate from Hungary replied that the question had in fact been settled by international law, notwithstanding the fact that the Washington Treaty was not yet in force. He argued that all states party to the Treaty of Versailles, by virtue of Article 171, were expressly prohibited from using such weapons, an incorrect argument that was not accepted by relevant parties. The U.S. delegation, for example, was of the opinion that "efforts to prohibit the use of this arm in future wars have resulted in several treaties on the subject, but have not yet resulted in all Powers represented at this conference being bound by ratified treaty obligations prohibiting the use of asphyxiating gas as a means of warfare."[96]

In the end, the general report to the conference recommended that a resolution be included which recognized gas warfare as justly condemned, and that every effort should be made for a convention prescribing export prohibition and dealing with chemical (and biological) weapons in general. The agreement reached at Geneva was thus understood to be a confirmation of already existing international law, however ambiguous that law appeared in strict legal terms. In short, the invocation of an institutional tradition was the definitive source that made the Geneva Protocol possible.

As was seen with the Washington Conference, positioning debates over gas warfare at the level of their institutional/ legal status had the effect of foreclosing more substantive and potentially disruptive deliberations over the origins and reasonableness of these legal strictures. For example, the Hungarian delegate noted that making defensive measures accessible to everyone, including noncombatants, would make gas warfare ineffective, as "no one would continue to use a weapon against which his adversary possessed effective means of defending himself."[97] This kind of suggestion cut sharply against the notion that gas weapons posed an undefendable threat, and, although they could be employed to mobilize support for efforts to deny the usability of such weapons, they were generally ignored. It is important to understand in the construction of an interpretation of gas weapons that, unlike nuclear weapons or poison, a characteristic of gas weapons was that effective defenses against them were practicable and available. "Thus attitudes towards gas, though firmly held, were based on incomplete reasoning in that they took no account of defence and the contribution it could make to blunting the weapon."[98]

The process of institutionalizing the taboo against chemical weapons at Geneva was nonetheless buttressed by the association of gas with poison, as well as by the inclusion of biological weapons in the prohibition. The latter represented a significant institutional innovation in the legal prohibition that went well beyond existing international agreements that the protocol was merely supposed to reiterate. In the end, then, the delegates agreed to a "Protocol for the Prohibition of the Use in War of Asphyxiating, Poisonous or Other Gases, and of Bacteriological Methods of Warfare," which included the following stipulations:

> Whereas the use in war of asphyxiating, poisonous or other gases, and of all analogous liquids, materials or devices, has been justly condemned by the general opinion of the civilised world; and
>
> Whereas the prohibition of such use has been declared in Treaties to which the majority of Powers of the world are Parties; and
>
> To the end that this prohibition shall be universally accepted as part of International Law, binding alike the conscience and the practice of nations;
>
> Declare:
>
> That the High Contracting Parties, so far as they are not already Parties to Treaties prohibiting such use, accept this prohibition, agree to extend this

prohibition to the use of bacteriological methods of warfare and agree to be bound as between themselves according to the terms of this declaration.

Resistance to the Protocol

The agreement of the delegates at Geneva to universalize the Washington ban on gas weapons generated another cycle of intense lobbying efforts by the CWS and U.S. chemical industry. This propaganda made the protocol seem more important than even its authors believed it to be. By all accounts, the deliberations on gas warfare were understood as only a transitory measure, perhaps until a future conference on gas warfare could be organized. Virulent opposition to the accord, however, raised its political profile—at least for a brief period of time—even as it was being defeated in the United States.

These efforts culminated in the opposition to the protocol in the U.S. Senate. Reiterating many of the arguments he made while opposing Article 5 of the Washington Treaty a few years earlier, Senator Wadsworth led the charge in 1926 based on the conviction that "we shall never be able to prevent in war the use of a weapon which is militarily effective." For Wadsworth,

> compared with other weapons used in warfare, gas is the least cruel, not only in its effect at the time of its use but in its after effects. If we are to base our action upon relative cruelty of weapons, we would better go to the high-explosive shell and attempt to draw a convention which would prevent nations using it, for if we compare the effects of high explosives, bullets, and shrapnel on the one side with the effects of gas upon the other we can not help reaching the conclusion that gas, while an extraordinarily effective weapon from the military standpoint, is the least cruel of the lot.[99]

Wadsworth cited casualty figures, questionnaires sent to 3,500 physicians, and the effectiveness of gas masks as evidence that gas very clearly was "the most humane of all weapons used in the last war."[100] Unlike the ratification debates of the Washington Conference and the deliberations at the Geneva Conference, the ratification hearings for the protocol in the United States were not primarily focused on the legal status of gas warfare. Rather, a number of different concerns were voiced pro and con.

The operation of the tenet that "no nation will refrain from using an effective weapon" was much in evidence among opponents of the protocol. In response to a query about bacteriological warfare and poisoning wells, Senator David Reed argued that even these methods could not be prevented, claiming that he had seen examples of such practices during the war. In addition, the idea resurfaced that gas would shorten war because it was so effective. Senator Lawrence Tyson (Tenn.) thought it extraordinary to stop gas warfare when the use of torpedoes is allowed, which he thought to be the most inhumane of weapons. Saying he could not understand why anyone wanted the protocol, he explained that his "idea about war is to make it effective, to go in and whip the enemy as soon as we can with every single power and efficient weapon that we can." Moreover, he noted that all of the veterans' organizations were opposed to the protocol—and they are the ones who ought to know about war.[101]

These arguments dispel the frequently voiced notion that the chemical weapons taboo must reflect a belief in the ineffectiveness of such means, insofar as weapons bans are allegedly only attained for militarily ineffective means. Precisely the opposite belief was in full display during this period: far from disparaging the military utility of chemical weapons, many policymakers and military personnel regarded them as potentially very valuable weapons. Many military assessments of gas warfare in the interwar period concluded that the weapons would be effective in certain operations. Even though the United States did not ratify the Geneva Protocol, most other important nations did, and thus one of the most notable weapons bans in history was attained on a weapon that was widely regarded as having military utility despite limitations.

On the crucial issue of the effect of gas on those who encountered it, Senator Hiram Bingham (Conn.) provided a most revealing account. He said that when he went to the front he was afraid of gas because, whereas they all knew very well how bayonets and bullets and explosives worked, gas "was something I did not understand and could not see." He intimated, however, that his ignorance was later dispelled—in his mind, those who had looked into the matter more than anyone else and who realized the horrors of war were those who opposed the treaty.[102]

Of the several arguments made that gas was a humane weapon, the position of Senator Joseph Ransdell (La.) is of particular interest. He voiced the belief that gas warfare should not be limited because if a potent lethal gas could be discovered which could be poured on great cities from flying machines, destroying every man, woman, and child, then fear would deter countries from going to war: "The surest means of preventing war would be the development of such a weapon as that— one that would make it infinitely more horrible than now."[103]

Ransdell's words provide one of the few instances of this period when the logic of general deterrence emerged in the context of gas warfare.[104] At the Hague Conferences, the argument was made by the U.S. delegation that the ever-increasing lethality of weapons innovations would decrease the occurrence and duration of war. Not until after World War I, however, did the specter of gas warfare emerge to be specifically invoked as a candidate for the job of eliminating war more generally.[105]

The significance of this is that the inscription of danger to civilians— and not just greater slaughter on the battlefield—was for the first time invoked as a morally desirable state of affairs, insofar as such gas capabilities could portend the very end of warfare. This invocation is juxtaposed with the remarkable absence of the "threat to civilians" argument at the Senate hearings on the protocol, an argument that in the past had proven so crucial in facilitating efforts to proscribe gas weapons.[106] Indeed, support of any kind for the protocol was barely audible, as the voices of opposition overwhelmed the two lone senators who spoke in favor of the treaty.[107] The civilian argument had not only been completely overshadowed but had been turned on its head during U.S. Senate ratification debates on the protocol.

In contrast to 1922, the issue that defined the acceptability of the Geneva prohibition in 1927 was how legal prohibitions would affect preparations for gas warfare. Senator Borah argued that the protocol had no effect on preparations, whereas Wadsworth questioned the worth of pledging fidelity to the world while preparing soldiers to use gas. Would these preparations not indicate very clearly that the United States had no confidence in the strength of the treaty when the test came? And if not, why sign it? As Borah argued, "We indulge in a hypocritical gesture or else we invite calamity to the Republic; one or the other."[108]

The issue of the effect of a ban on readiness surfaced as the successful focal point for opponents of legal prohibition on gas warfare in 1926–1927. Despite protestations to the contrary by the protocol's advocates, this concern was not wholly unjustified. After the conclusion of the Washington Treaty, the U.S. War Department ordered that the manufacture of poison gas for the army be discontinued and that research on gas warfare be limited to what was necessary for defensive purposes.[109] Indeed, preparations were scaled down so much that the army did not have the capability to employ gas warfare by 1927.[110] In Britain, gas measures were relegated to a secondary position and training was cut down based on the understanding that the Washington Treaty permitted only defensive research.[111] Even the very weak institutionalization of a prohibitionary norm against chemical weapons embodied in the Washington Treaty (recall that it never officially came into effect) therefore had a palpable impact on actual CW policies, for the treaty was a ready excuse to reduce gas preparations.

The success of the protocol's opponents and their ability to frame the discussion in terms of preparedness owed much to the absence of any organized strategy by the Coolidge administration to secure passage of the treaty.[112] Proponents of the protocol seem to have assumed that there would be little difficulty ratifying the treaty given the near-unanimity with which the Washington Treaty had been ratified by the Senate just a few years earlier. By the time they realized their mistake, it was too late to mobilize support for the Senate's assent. The administration did not invest additional political energy to ratify the protocol because it was already deemed a lost cause. The unwillingness to mobilize support after being caught by surprise can be taken as an indication that commitment to the norm was weak. As Rodney McElroy suggests, however, a proper account of this event should not overestimate the strength of the protocol's opponents but rather emphasize the absence of any coherent strategy for ratification.[113] In the end, the protocol was clearly headed for defeat if put to a vote in the Senate, and it was thus referred back to the Committee on Foreign Relations, where it languished until Truman removed it from consideration by the Senate in the late 1940s.

The opposition to the protocol in the United States should not deflect attention from the support for ratification in other countries—with the exception of the United States and Japan, the protocol was ratified by most of the major nations of the world within five years.[114] Many nations acceded to the protocol only after appending reservations to their ratifications to the effect that the protocol was binding only with respect to other parties to the protocol, and/or the protocol would cease to be binding with respect to enemy states whose armed forces or allies violated the prohibition.[115] Although the protocol had therefore greatly extended the international scope of the CW taboo, the reservations were generally regarded to have in effect rendered it a no-first-use pledge.

From the end of the 1920s on, Europe led efforts to extend the protocol's prohibition on the use of chemical weapons, primarily in the Preparatory Commission for the Conference of Disarmament at the League of Nations and within the actual Conference of Disarmament itself. These discussions were directed toward restrictions on preparations for chemical warfare, but the conference failed to produce any agreement.

Despite its failure, the conference did witness the emergence of an Anglo-French interpretation that the use of tear gases was prohibited by the Geneva Protocol. There had been ambiguity as to whether the protocol's prohibition on "asphyxiating, poisonous, or other gases, and of all analogous materials and devices," was intended to include nonlethal gases, but in December 1930 eleven other members of the Preparatory Commission agreed with the British and French that tear gases were proscribed. The United States was the sole dissenter, arguing that it was inconsistent to prohibit the use of gases in warfare that were permitted for domestic police purposes.[116] This issue remained a simmering point of controversy for the chemical weapons taboo.

Scripting Danger

Several themes of analytical significance emerge from the treatment of CW during this period. Above all, the continuing presence of fears of hypothesized gas attacks on civilians was the crucial enabling condition for gas to be depicted as unacceptable. In their absence, the prohibition on gas warfare seemed far less urgent. As I argued in Chapter 3, the unique prevalence of such associations with gas weapons was far from inevitable. Indeed, it could be considered as positively anomalous, considering the dominance of the view that the moral value of a weapon depends upon how it is used—recall the statement of Secretary of State Hughes himself that "unlimited warfare is not necessarily an attribute of the submarine alone." The power of these depictions of gas weapons is all the more striking considering how at odds they were with the actual practice of World War I. The restraint from using gas against civilian targets which was exhibited by all sides in the conflict was a rather concrete demonstration that "unlimited warfare is not necessarily an attribute of gas weapons alone." As the authors of one of the SIPRI studies concluded: "The chemical warfare conducted from 1915 to 1918 showed that it is possible—in some cases at least—to confine the effects of chemical weapons predominantly to the fighting forces. These weapons, *by their nature*, are, therefore, no more contrary to the principle of immunity of the civilian population than are conventional weapons."[117]

And yet, the dominant lesson grafted on the experience of the war was not that the distinction between combatants and noncombatants was in fact more stringently upheld with respect to gas than other weapons. In fact, the construction of an imagined danger proved far more galvanizing than even the soldier's ambiguous experience of actually confronting—and often surviving without mutilation—the danger itself.

A crucial reason for the effectiveness of the threat is that even some of the most vocal opponents of a prohibition on gas warfare participated in its construction. As we have seen, the fact that the Washington Conference included the issue of gas weapons at all is due in large part to the miscalculations of the gas lobby in the United States. The significance of this genealogical accident was that those who sought to establish a gas warfare constituency and capability drew upon and fomented the same dialogue of dread used by those who sought to prohibit gas weapons. Thus the gas lobby replicated the efforts of bodies such as the Red Cross, which explicitly exploited gas as a symbol of war in order to regulate the conduct of warfare.[118]

These claims of the enormous destructive power of future chemical weapons became difficult to reconcile with the other strategy of the propagandists to portray gas as the most humane weapon of war, or at least as just another weapon that would inevitably be used in the next conflict, like all other weapons innovations in the past.[119] By the time the Geneva Protocol was at issue, then, the same people who years before had warned of the catastrophic effects of future gas warfare on cities were claiming that such fears were unfounded.[120] In a moment of unsurpassed irony, the president of the American Chemical Society declared condescendingly that the widespread feeling against gas was the result of war hysteria and propaganda![121] From this point on, more sober assessments of gas warfare increasingly appeared.[122]

A third discursive strategy to legitimize CW can be discerned from the anti-prohibition propaganda of the period. These efforts coalesced around the attempt to emphasize the positive benefits flowing from the chemical industry and research based on war gases. General Amos Fries of the CWS led the charge as the service proclaimed the benefits of gas in eliminating rats, rattlesnakes, insects, and other pests; advocated the use of tear gas by police for riot control; and testified to the use of war gases to disinfect clothing to stop the spread of typhus.[123] These efforts knew few bounds, as the CWS and chemical industry not only promoted the use of chlorine to cure respiratory diseases and the common cold, but went so far as to claim that chlorine gas was curing more people suffering from respiratory diseases than were killed by German gas in 1915.[124]

This strategy of legitimizing gases is important because it is accomplished by accessing the dominant value-neutral conception of technology to naturalize the production of chemicals for use in warfare. To the extent it is successful, this discursive strategy downplays the novel moral situations raised by the possibility of widespread chemical warfare as yet another inevitable and unremarkable occurrence in the march of technology. Indeed, much of the lobbying against the Geneva Protocol came to be framed in the language of inevitability: CW was here to stay as an unavoidable feature of modern warfare.[125] Of course, it is easy in our modern technological temper to treat this kind of discourse as unquestionable common knowledge. The failure of the world's military establishments to embrace CW, however, testifies that it is not as unassailable as it may seem.

Increasingly, interpretations of chemical weapons played down their supposed catastrophic destructive capability. Claims appeared that high explosives represented more of a threat to cities than gas, and these revamped assessments gained a measure of public acceptance.[126] In a sense, however, the damage had been done, for an interpretation of gas weapons as an immoral horror that required unique political action had been frozen in institutional form. This is not to say that this interpretation was henceforth destined to dominate uncontested, nor to claim that it had an immediate and crucial impact on chemical weapons policies of all nations. Rather, the claim is only that this interpretation of chemical arms was given an international imprimatur and legal legacy against which opponents of gas bans would have to battle.

In the years immediately following World War I, the success of constructions of the gas warfare threat can be attributed to a significant degree to the easy coupling of gas to the unpopularity of the Germans—thus the prohibition against gas warfare in Article 171 of Versailles found an all-too receptive audience. Still, although this imposed legal stricture against gas weapons was originally grounded in anti-German sentiment, these motivations for a gas prohibition gradually gave way to a concern with the weapon itself. Indeed, at the Washington Conference, U.S. delegate Elihu Root privately explained that it was his resolutions to limit activities of *submarines* that were designed to "meet public opinion with regard to [the] horrors and lawlessness of the Germans."[127] Moreover, the Navy Board acknowledged in its report to the Washington Conference that the United States, far from attempting to gain an advantage over the Germans with a ban, "would undoubtedly give up a material advantage if gas warfare were abolished."[128] That is, adherence to the chemical weapons prohibition was against the self-interest of the United States.

While the emasculation of German military capabilities was unquestionably behind Article 171 of Versailles, anti-German sentiment alone does not adequately account for subsequent developments in the prohibitionary norm. This imposed prohibition was not, however, altogether irrelevant. On the contrary, what transpired was an ennobling reinterpretation of this particular institutional component of the taboo, employed toward more universal ends. In genealogical fashion, then, the power politics played out at Versailles came to underwrite and indirectly support both the Washington and Geneva prohibitions, insofar as their framers drew upon Article 171 as a source of universal international law: an imposed dictate of military and political discipline was vitally important in sustaining an international institutional embodiment of the anti-CW norm.

The fits and starts, reinterpretations and impositions, of this crucial period in the history of the CW taboo are legion. Article 171 of Versailles was imposed upon the Germans yet was cited as evidence of a universal legal norm proscribing the use of chemical weapons. The absolute form of the prohibition contained in Article 5 of the Washington Treaty would likely have disappeared in the face of opposition, but opposition was never mounted because the treaty was not seen as particularly important. That is, the belief that "no effective weapons can ever be the subject of restraint" actually worked in a perverse way to help secure the international prohibition of gas weapons. And even though Article 5 never came into effect, it was crucial in providing the basis—even the interpretive rationale—for agreement to the Geneva Protocol. Finally, having led the efforts to prohibit CW, the United States then provided the chief opposition by its failure to secure ratification of the treaty when an organized attempt to do so might well have been successful.

The genealogical temper of the chemical weapons taboo could not be more plain. As Alexander Nehamas has written, in showing that moral institutions exhibit a "contingent, complicated and motley character," "genealogy allows for chance occurrences and fortuitous connections, for mutations and for marriages, for violent expansions and intrusions."[129] In a remark that could very well be directed toward essentialist explanations of the CW taboo, Nehamas writes that the error of the non-genealogical analysis of moral institutions

> consists, first, in assuming that the dominant sense of a word, the accepted interpretation of a value, or the current function of an institution is naturally appropriate to it and never the product of earlier operations, of reversals, impositions, and appropriations. That is, their error consists in being ignorant of the specific historical and genealogical tangles that produce contingent structures we mistakenly consider given, solid, and extending without change into the future as well as into the past.[130]

The fate of the product of this tangled history—a particular interpretation of CW that had been given institutional and international sanction—awaited its trial in warfare, an event not long in coming.

Colonizing Chemical Warfare

Even the thought of a possibility can shake and transform us.
—Nietzsche, *Nachlass*

Much of the scholarly attention on chemical weapons has been directed toward explaining the absence of gas warfare in the major theaters of battle during World War II.[1] The stigma against chemical weapons has been identified as an important factor mitigating against the initiation of chemical warfare, and several studies address in detail the specific instances in which legal and moral restraints, combined with other factors such as deterrence, military culture, and unpreparedness, affected the behavior of each of the major belligerents with respect to the use of chemical weapons.[2]

These studies in some ways provided the starting point of this book. Taking as a given their conclusions that the norm was relevant, I have examined a complementary set of questions, seeking to explore how we arrived at the definition of chemical weapons as a special category and what has happened since. In this chapter, I illustrate how explanations for the non-use of chemical weapons during World War II are incomplete without an understanding of how that category was constituted apart from other weapons and how other factors retarding the use of these weapons came to have political salience in the normative context established by the norm. The taboo was not the all-determining "master-variable" that in isolation prevented the use of chemical weapons during World War II; it was a necessary if not sufficient condition that permitted the possibility of avoiding chemical warfare. In the absence of the context established by this international norm and the thresholds set thereby, World War II in all likelihood would have been a chemical war.

The task of this chapter, then, is to complement more comprehensive explanations for the non-use of chemical weapons in World War II with a detailed interpretive understanding of how gas was constituted as a peculiar category apart from other weapons. I therefore identify the features of the discourse and the departures, continuities, and innovations in the category of chemical weapons. The aim is to examine how the sources and features of the chemical weapons discourse politicized the use of these weapons to an unusual degree and thus operated to prevent their use. How and by what processes was the threshold instantiated, maintained, or eroded during the horrors of World War II?

By way of prologue, I examine a major breach of the Geneva Protocol in the immediate prewar period—the use of gas by the Italians in their war against Abyssinia in 1935–1936. This episode not only highlights how international norms can be reconstituted after their violation, but it also provides an opportunity to assess diachronically the status of the norm against the violations of World War I and the Iran-Iraq war.[3]

The Italo-Ethiopian War

On October 3, 1935, Italian armies invaded Abyssinia to consolidate their colonial holdings in East Africa. The first reports of the use of gas came in October, and the Italians apparently tried to drop mustard bombs together with explosives in November 1935.[4] Reports cited an experimental dropping of tear-gas grenades from airplanes against Ethiopian troops in the Takkaze Valley during December 1935.[5] These efforts and the experimental use of mustard-gas bombs by the end of the month appear to have been rather ineffectual. In January the Italians began to employ mustard-gas sprayers attached to aircraft, drenching soldiers, pastures, livestock, and civilians.[6] Organized resistance ended early in April 1936, and the use of chemical weapons has been regarded by some analysts as having played a prominent role in bringing quick victory to the Italians, though victory would have come to them in any case.

In light of the attention focused upon gas warfare during the interwar period, the public response to this actual case of the use of chemical weapons might seem rather muted. This relative silence was largely the result of the secrecy that surrounded the waging of CW: the Italians kept their use of gas a closely guarded secret through strict censorship and did not admit to having used chemical weapons (indeed, not until 1996 did the Italian government acknowledge the use of gas). Beginning in December 1935, reports of the use of chemical weapons came from medical personnel and newspaper correspondents in Ethiopia as well from allegations made by Ethiopian officials.[7] Even though these reports could not have taken informed governments by complete surprise, official recognition and confirmation of these reports in the international community was slow to materialize and only came to a head by April 1936.[8] Even then, the allegations that did surface failed to ignite the public imagination or catch widespread political attention, mostly because the use of gas only became an issue by the time the war was virtually over.[9]

The League of Nations' response to the invasion of Abyssinia provided some treatment of this incident as an issue of political importance, even though the league was not institutionally empowered to oversee the Geneva Protocol—a charge that the Italians used in defending themselves against allegations of violating the protocol. Still, because the league provided an international forum where allegations were leveled at Italy, the issue could not be ignored completely. Italy had signed the Geneva Protocol in 1925, and Ethiopia joined in 1935 in view of its conflict with Italy.

In December 1935, the emperor of Ethiopia charged that the Italians employed asphyxiating and poison gas, and protested that these "inhuman practices" were "in defiance and violation of . . . international undertakings."[10] Italy initially ignored the league's request to respond to these allegations, but in response to continued accusations, the Italian minister for foreign affairs eventually stated the oblique position that the observance of the laws of war had to be bilateral: "The Italian military authorities cannot do otherwise than punish every inhuman atrocity committed by its adversary in contempt of every principle of law and morality."[11]

As the league continued to push the issue further, the Italian government still did not admit it had used gas. Similarly, the Italian press was mute on the issue, only breaking the silence with an emphatic and blanket denial of the charges.[12] Eventually, the Italians did feel compelled to provide a rationalization for such action, a step that most observers have interpreted as an implicit admission that the allegations of waging CW were credible.[13] While repeating its assurances that it intended to comply with the provisions of the protocol, Italy argued that the protocol contained no provision excluding the right of reprisal "in punishment of such abominable atrocities as those committed by the Ethiopian forces (torture and decapitation of prisoners; emasculation of the wounded and killed; savagery towards, and the killing of non-combatants, systematic use of dum-dum bullets, etc.)."[14] This position was maintained by the Italians as long as CW and Ethiopia remained an issue.

The discourse on the use of chemical weapons during World War I provides a useful template to compare the status of the norm during the Abyssinian case. In consonance with past practices, the use of gas by Italy was excoriated whether it was used against soldiers or civilians; the absolute character of the norm was thus not subject to revision. The use of a particular weapon—and not simply how it was used—continued to be framed as a political issue. During league deliberations over the Italians' waging of CW, the Australian delegate observed that allegations had been made by both sides regarding infringement of conventions for the conduct of war. All of these charges were hideous, he said, "but there was one that stood out in its menace to humanity and civilization far above everything else, and that was the charge that poisonous and asphyxiating gases were being employed in war. If that charge proved true, it was impossible fully to realize what menace it constituted to every nation on earth."[15]

As in World War I, the initial employment of chemical weapons seems to have been a testing of the waters with nonlethal tear gas. Even before this actual use, the Italians had announced their intention to open the war with an air-delivered tear-gas attack on Addis Ababa.[16] Emperor Heile Selassie stated that gas had been employed generally only after the Italians became convinced after their probes that the international community would take no significant action in response.[17] Also similar to the World War I situations, the first official protest by Ethiopia was not lodged until Italy used more lethal chemical weapons (mustard gas), a short time after the use of nonlethal agents.[18]

In contrast to these continuities were the discursive practices of the accused party. During World War I the Germans explicitly defended the use of gas not simply as retaliation but as a method of warfare no less humane than explosives. The Italians, however, far from justifying gas as a humane weapon, would not even admit outright that they had employed chemical weapons. Indeed, rather than declaring that the chemical weapons taboo was an irrelevant and vacuous stricture of international law, the Italians actually upheld the Geneva Protocol as an authoritative expression of an international norm. In this sense, at least, the Italians' use of gas can be seen as less of a full frontal assault on the prohibitionary norm than the Germans' use in World War I.

This qualification is not meant to downplay the seriousness of the Italians' willingness to violate the prohibition; above all, the intentional use of gas against civilians represented the crossing of a tenuous threshold that had been upheld during World War I.[19] Still, the Italians admitted that the use of gas was a violation of an international norm. A violation is only a violation if there is something to violate.

This dictum has important consequences for the study of norms in international politics. Convincing demonstrations of the efficacy of norms suffer from the analytical shortcoming that the best empirical evidence for a particular norm may actually be no evidence at all. The deeper and more robust a norm, and the more profoundly it structures social practices, the less likely it is ever to be consciously invoked as a reason for action. Paradoxically, then, violations of norms often provide the most appropriate windows for analyzing their operation. A violation of a norm can be taken as evidence for a norm, as long as it is viewed as an anomaly that needs to be disciplined rather than standard procedure or the beginnings thereof. For this reason, an assessment of the role of norms in international politics must submit to an understanding of the meaning of discursive practices.[20]

Gas warfare before World War II, then, was not—at least, not yet—wholly accepted as an unquestioned and unremarkable standard procedure for the community of nations. The use of gas was controversial; the use of explosives, bayonets, and bullets was not. Moreover, debates over the humanity of gas warfare were conspicuous by their absence; it seems to have been generally accepted by all concerned that the use of gas was an extreme method of warfare.[21] Italy felt compelled to defend itself against charges that it had engaged in what was regarded as an aberrant practice.

Still, the question arises: given its blatant violation, what can be said about the robustness of the norm? One way to gauge the efficacy of norms, as discussed in previous chapters, is to assess how extreme a situation is required to justify its violation, in this case the use of chemical weapons. To use an analogy: the societal prohibition against murder is not generally regarded as having been invalidated in cases of killing in self-defense. The taboo against killing can be regarded as generally upheld even as it is violated from a strictly behavioral point of view so long as the crossing of the threshold is understood as an extreme exception accepted by others. On this score the chemical weapons norm does not fare well during this period. It amounted to far less than a powerful inhibition on the Italians, who certainly were not driven to use gas only as a desperate fight for their own survival. In this sense the norm was a very weak restraint on the Italians.

Assessing the overall robustness of a international norm in light of a violation also involves taking into account the effect of subsequent practices by others to reinforce or further erode the norm. Prohibitionary moral institutions are social—that is, shared—and not merely the property of any one individual actor, and their efficacy is contingent upon their continued and shared reproduction through social practices. This feature of norms points to a difficulty accommodating the role of norms within a positivist model of social science.[22] The question "how robust is the norm?" in effect is a demand for a prediction regarding the likely subsequent course of events without the advantage of hindsight. Rigorous predictions worth their name in the human sciences are a rare and perhaps stillborn breed, and such gauges are particularly difficult to come by with respect to social norms. Such intersubjective meanings are contingent human constructions whose status depends upon subsequent instantiation, or the lack thereof, through social practices. This is a central insight of interpretive social science and constructivist approaches to international politics.[23]

In this light, the designation of the chemical weapons taboo as strong or weak depends not just on Italy's practices but in large part upon whether the responses of the world community subsequently instantiated the norm as one that was crossed with mild or serious consequences, with little or great concern. The conclusions of one volume of the SIPRI study illustrate this analytical quandary:

> From the point of view of the customary norm, which is not only violated but also weakened by such practice, the most important point to note is that this case, seen in historical perspective, has been—and is generally recognized to have been—an outstanding exception. . . . In retrospect, *but only in retrospect*, the Ethiopian case seems to be more indicative of the strength of the law than of its weakness.[24]

Conferring such a status on the Italian use of chemical weapons thus merits caution, especially from the genealogical standpoint, given its aversion to the imposition of cloaked teleologies. It is vastly easier to define the Italian incident as an exception that proves the rule from the perspective of the post–World War II era than it would have been in 1936. Not all hindsight is 20–20, and we need to examine how this event was interpreted at the time and subsequently: Was this incident understood to indicate the first step toward the dissolution of the anti-gas regime and the inevitability of gas warfare, or was it read as having in any way served to reinforce or redirect the taboo against CW? Were these interpretations embodied in subsequent practices?

Harbinger of Disaster or the Colonizing of CW?

To the extent that the sufferings of the Abyssinians were understood as a harbinger of things to come, both the designation of this incident as a violation and the non-use of chemical weapons in World War II become all the more anomalous. For many, the Italians' use of gas was a concrete illustration of the dominant conviction—and fear—that gas would inevitably be used in warfare. The willingness to translate the Abyssinian experience to Europe was most evident in Anthony Eden's impassioned appeal for sanctions against Italy:

This protocol concerns the inhabitants of every great city in the world. It is for them a charter against extermination. If a convention such as this can be torn up, will not our peoples . . . ask, and ask with reason, what is the value of any international instrument to which our representatives put their name; how can we have confidence that our own folk, despite all solemnly signed protocols, will not be burned, blinded, done to death in agony hereafter?[25]

Drawing similar parallels, Germany's chief of chemical warfare argued in 1939 that, based on the Abyssinian war and World War I, chemical weapons would play an even larger role in future war. Germany would have to be fully prepared for CW since the protocol provided for no recourse against violators, as futile British efforts to sanction Italy proved.[26] This is not to say, however, that those who believed in (or at least feared) the inevitability of gas warfare did so with near-apocalyptic visions. Many voices took issue with the sensationalism of the "prophets of gloom," arguing that incendiary bombs represented a far greater threat to civilian populations than gas.[27]

There were competing interpretations of the implications of Italy's use of gas in Abyssinia, even within German military circles. Although the Italian campaign demonstrated for some observers the decisive effects CW could achieve, some believed that comparable results could not be expected against a modern army trained for gas warfare. Rather, the Italian case was taken to typify a new type of colonial war as practiced after World War I.[28] Carl Krauch, a director of Germany's chemical conglomerate IG-Farben, made the following revealing statement in 1939: "Chemistry is definitely the weapon of the poor man, but it can achieve decisive results only if it is used unexpectedly at the beginning of a war and to an extent considered completely impossible by the enemy."[29]

In the United States, Italy's employment of CW was not perceived as a stimulus to increased readiness because "the military denied that there were any lessons to be learned from the use of gas as a weapon of opportunity against a totally unprepared enemy in a colonial war."[30] Similarly, one author of the period argued that the experience of the Italo-Ethiopian war had shown that gas would be resorted to only if a belligerent had desperate reason and if enemy retaliation in kind were impossible.[31] Even British intelligence, while concluding of Italy "that in future war she would employ the gas weapon," added the proviso "unless special circumstances render such a course inadvisable."[32]

The dominant view of the inevitability of gas warfare was therefore marked by a rupture that resisted the universal conventionalizing of CW as standard procedure. This rupture was manifested in the demarcation of distinct zones of warfare—war among the "civilized" advanced industrialized countries was a different matter from conflicts involving other areas such as the colonies. As George Quester observes, a standard view of world affairs after Versailles was that the arenas of European war and colonial war might well have been separable.[33] And the use of chemical weapons might be less unacceptable in one area than another.[34]

It has been remarked that the Abyssinian case represents one incident in a post–World War I pattern of chemical warfare against ill-prepared, less-industrialized areas. These incidents could include the previously mentioned sanctioning of the use of chemical weapons by the British in Palestine, alleged uses by the British in frontier regions of India and Afghanistan, the use of gas by the Spanish and French in Morocco, and Japanese chemical and biological warfare against China in the 1930s.[35] The pattern implies a striking similarity between the chemical weapons taboo and moral restraints on other weapons in the past (see Chapter 2), namely, that banned weapons are often prohibited only among "civilized" peoples, while their use against uncivilized others is tolerated. Furthermore, these cases imply that a deterrence explanation can account for the use or non-use of chemical weapons: such weapons are only employed when an adversary cannot reply in kind.

While suggestive, the deterrence argument cannot by itself account for the pattern of chemical weapons use and non-use, for there have been many occasions when a chemically armed belligerent faced an unprepared adversary and lethal chemical weapons still were not employed. Such incidents include the Spanish civil war, several Soviet interventions in the 1930s, and a variety of colonial conflicts, not to mention a number of other notable examples during and after World War II such as Korea, Vietnam, Afghanistan, and so on.[36] Moreover, several of the cases of alleged use of chemical weapons occurred before the ratification of the protocol by the parties involved and before the adoption of retaliation-only policies by most countries in the interwar period. Proposals for British use of gas in India, for one, were vigorously opposed by the British Foreign Office as contrary to the British retaliation-only policy, which could not be reversed so soon after the condemnation of Germany for its initial use of gas in World War I.[37] Patterns of restraint by deterrence and an additional normative inhibition against any first use of gas are both in evidence, though neither phenomenon by itself accounts for all situations.

What can be said of this period, however, is that CW was a symbol of demarcation between war among the "civilized" and "uncivilized" nations. Differentiation in the actual conduct of the institution of war in different arenas has been noted by many authors. For John Mueller, major war—war among developed states—has been subject to a gradual obsolescence that has not occurred in other areas of the globe.[38] Francis Fukuyama has drawn a sharp distinction between the behavior of the Third World and the industrial democracies—the historical and post-historical parts of the world. He argues that the rules of the latter are different from those of the former, and that only in the historical world do the old rules of power politics continue to apply.[39] Likewise, Richard Rosecrance has drawn a distinction between trading states and territorial states, and James Goldgeier and Michael McFaul have conceptualized international politics as a tale of two worlds: the core—a society of states characterized by a set of shared norms—and the periphery, where military force is still a valued means for settling disputes.[40] Meanwhile, Michael Doyle's rediscovery of Kant's proposal for a perpetual peace has prompted a vigorous research agenda investigating the apparent finding that there is a peace among liberal democracies.[41]

Consonant with such depictions of the contemporary division of realms of violence in international affairs, the treatment of CW in some circles during the 1930s reflected the understanding that modern warfare between industrialized powers was a qualitatively different situation than war involving peripheral areas.[42] This understanding was largely a legacy of the norms of colonialism which demarcated the civilized parts of humanity from the primitive, savage, uncivilized. From such distinctions, Puchala and Hopkins assert: "it followed politically that inequality was an appropriate principle of international organization and that standards and modes of behavior displayed toward other international actors depended upon which category those others fell into. Toward the "uncivilized" it was reasonable to behave paternalistically, patronizingly, and dictatorially, and acceptable to behave brutally if the situation demanded."[43]

The universality of the chemical weapons taboo was therefore attenuated by its embeddedness in these more diffuse norms of international society. As the Italian press argued, the "Ethiopians have repeatedly shown she [sic] is not worthy of the rank of a civilized nation."[44] Chemical weapons signified this difference, serving as a potent symbol of prohibitive levels of modern destruction imbued with the possibility of a stand-off maintained at levels of destruction lower than what was technologically possible. The chemical weapons taboo remained embedded in the hierarchical ordering of international politics into the "civilized" and "uncivilized" arenas.

World War II

The non-use of chemical weapons during World War II has been explained by three basic clusters of factors: normative and legal constraints; the lack of adequate military interest in and preparation for the initiation of gas warfare; and deterrence or the fear of retaliation. The major scholarship concurs that neither arguments from deterrence nor claims about the alleged lack of utility of CW adequately explain the non-use of gas; furthermore, they have not dismissed the prohibitionary norm as irrelevant in this explanatory equation. As John Ellis van Courtland Moon's study summarizes, in addition to deterrence, "the unpreparedness of the major belligerents, the cultural and institutional inhibitions against the use of chemical weapons, and the mutual overestimation of the opponent's preparedness" all worked to prevent the employment of CW.[45]

The World War II literature has shown how some factors mattered more than others in different stages and aspects of the story. Most authors have dismissed the chemical weapons norm as relatively inconsequential in immediately affecting decisions not to wage CW. Thus, the authors of the SIPRI study have claimed that in particular decision-making contexts, "the dominant constraints of lack of military interest in CW, fear of retaliation and lack of material capability made the legal constraints on initiation virtually irrelevant."[46] Similarly, Brown has stated that "neither public opinion nor legal restriction were directly effective; but, on the other hand, lack of assimilation and fear of retaliation proved to be significant restraints."[47]

Even so, these authors recognize that the unpreparedness of the military is not an unproblematic variable and has to be explained. The SIPRI study, for instance, argues that unpreparedness was crucial, and "the reluctance to accept gas as a useful weapon stemmed at least as much—probably far more—from institutional pressures and psychological constraints as from rational considerations of its military utility."[48] Legal constraints were important "not because of any direct influence on the decision whether or not to initiate CW, but rather because of their influence in retarding acceptance of gas as a standard weapon of war, and hence in their contribution to the belligerents' overall unpreparedness to wage CW, and their leaders' unwillingness to authorize it."[49]

In parallel fashion, Brown has singled out fear of retaliation and unpreparedness as the most important restraints on the waging of CW, with the latter more fundamental. Still, he argues that "treaty prohibition, though imperfect, reinforced both public and military dislike and

fear of chemical warfare and provided a ready excuse for lack of substantive preparation."[50] It was "decades of conditioning to a second-
strike philosophy," he adds, that prevented preparedness.[51] Finally,
Jeffrey Legro identifies the anti-CW regime as the weakest of his troika
of explanatory factors, which also include deterrence and military culture. Still, he maintains that "we cannot prove that these norms did not
turn the military away from the poison cloud any more than it would
have on its own," and he argues that the prohibitionary norm was influential in dictating boundaries of acceptable conduct.[52]

It is a point of utmost analytical importance that the authors of the
most systematic analyses of World War II are unable to dismiss the role
of the stigma against using chemical weapons.[53] The reason that the prohibitionary norm against chemical weapons cannot be discounted is that
the chemical weapons taboo was a necessary condition for the avoidance
of chemical warfare in World War II. To say that the taboo is required to
understand the abstinence from CW is to raise the counter-factual proba-
bility that chemical warfare would have been waged in the absence of
the taboo.

For the most part, scholars have recognized that it is unsatisfactory to
isolate the lack of CW preparedness as an unexplained variable in explaining non-use. They acknowledge that this factor is fully understood
only by taking into account the stigma attached to the use of chemical
weapons. Nevertheless, these authors—like rationalist international relations theorists more generally—have been much more prone to take deterrence unproblematically, treating it as a discrete, independent variable.[54] This approach sidesteps altogether the crucial question of how *any*
use at all of chemical weapons as a category came to be defined in terms
of deterrence whereas other weapons did not. To posit the fear of retaliation as an unproblematic variable that prevented the waging of CW begs
the question. The objective of the previous chapters has been to show
that there was nothing inevitable about chemical weapons being defined
as "deterrent" weapons or about how that category itself was defined.
How could the fear of CW retaliation prove more prohibitive than the
fear of incendiary weapons in mass fire-bombing attacks or submarine
attacks on civilian ships, and why was even the limited use of nonlethal
gases proscribed?[55]

Arguments from deterrence require an understanding of their intimate
relationship with the chemical weapons stigma just as much as do arguments from unpreparedness. I do not argue that either the fear of retaliation or military resistance to CW is simply reducible to the normative
and legal dimensions of the chemical weapons taboo, but I do highlight
the context-effect of norms in social and political life. Although norms

may function instrumentally in cost-benefit decisions, they can also help define more broadly the context of understanding of a situation, within which the assigning of costs and benefits gains meaning in the first place.[56] I illustrate this feature of norms through an analysis of several representative developments during World War II.

Retaliatory Fears

A primary effect of the chemical weapons norm institutionalized in the Geneva Protocol was the development of retaliation-only policies and corresponding preparations that had the effect of further inhibiting the initiation of gas warfare.[57] The adoption of a no-first-use stance was particularly and explicitly made in the Allied countries.[58] What gave particular sanction to the no-first-use policy of individual countries during the war was the exchange of explicit declaratory pledges not to violate the chemical weapons norm and initiate gas warfare. In Britain and France, these pledges followed from a longstanding policy that, in light of their commitments to the Washington Treaty and Geneva Protocol, they would endeavor to obtain a guarantee from the enemy to refrain from the use of gas at the outset of a conflict.[59] A solemn Anglo-French Declaration made at the outset of hostilities pledged that bombings and use of submarines would be directed toward military targets only and would avoid civilians. In the same pledge, Britain and France also reaffirmed "their intention to abide by the terms of the Geneva Protocol of 1925 prohibiting the use in war of asphyxiating or poisonous or other gases and of bacteriological methods of warfare."[60] In response to a request for similar assurances, Germany stated that "the German Government will observe during the War the prohibitions which form the subject of the Geneva protocol of June 17, 1925 and which are mentioned in the note of Lord Halifax of September 3, 1939. She reserves complete freedom of action in the event that the provisions of the protocol are violated on the part of the enemy."[61]

The Soviets' declaratory policy had been set out some time earlier. In February 1938 Soviet War Commissar Voroshilov stated: "Ten years ago or more the Soviet Union signed a convention abolishing the use of poison gas and bacteriological warfare. To that we still adhere, but if our enemies use such methods against us, I tell you that we are prepared—fully prepared—to use them also and to use them against aggressors on their own soil."[62]

At the beginning of the war, the British circulated a note to Japan similar to that sent to Germans in September 1939, and they received an affirmative but "evasive" response. According to one author, the United States remained silent on the matter because its leaders felt that there was little to be gained from an appeal to the protocol (since neither the United States nor Japan was a party to it).[63] Throughout the war, the Japanese had assumed that the United States would not wage CW, apparently based upon Roosevelt's unalterable opposition to gas warfare.

More explicit Japanese commitments to refrain from CW were not forthcoming until January 1944, when the Japanese became alarmed by a *New York Times* article that suggested the United States might be considering using gas.[64] In messages relayed through the Swiss government and the apostolic delegate, the Japanese denied the use of gas "during the present conflict," and declared themselves "decided not to make use of it in the future on [the] supposition that troops of United Nations also abstain from using it." The United States responded by noting receipt of the statement and referring the Japanese to the president's statement of June 8, 1943.[65]

Many people continued to believe throughout the war that chemical weapons would be used, but in the Allied countries the belief was accompanied by the understanding that *someone else* would initiate their use in Europe or the Pacific.[66] This was not only a very tenuous assumption, but it required considerable dissonance to maintain. Several gas accidents had to be covered up, including one extraordinary instance involving a British officer notifying his German counterpart that a release of gas was accidental, an explanation the latter accepted.[67] Ignoring potentially inflammatory incidents and rhetoric is of course radically different from the situation during World War I, where chemical weapons incidents were manufactured for the propaganda value of accusing the enemy of yet another atrocity.[68]

Another phenomenon that cut against the grain of the unacceptability of any first use of chemical weapons was the use of gas by Japan in China.[69] To the extent that Allied decision makers were confident that reports of such use were true,[70] the use was deliberately ignored and for the most part regarded as distinct from the question of gas warfare between the industrialized belligerents in the major theaters of battle. It does appear that no such incidents took place after Roosevelt issued his warnings about the use of chemical weapons. Still, the limited tolerance of the use of gas can be understood as a continuation of the demarcation of realms of war seen in the Abyssinian case. China was not regarded as an equal member in the club of advanced civilized nations, for it had not yet emerged from the humiliating subjection of the unequal treaties that relegated it to neocolonial status.[71] The use of chemical weapons, while regrettable and formally taboo, was apparently less of an atrocity if confined to areas outside the core of civilized nations.

The restraint on using chemical weapons in the European theater was therefore maintained in spite of incidents that otherwise could easily have been taken as justification for initiation. Accepted in the United States, Britain, the Soviet Union, and France, this retaliation-only policy was not only in line with the Geneva Protocol but implied that chemical weapons might not even be used. It is unlikely this permissive situation would have arisen in the absence of the taboo.

In Germany, gas had been viewed much less as solely a weapon of retaliation. Still, by August 1940 the high command forbade all branches of the armed forces to use poison gas, and even the use of gas in retaliation was subject to Hitler's direct approval.[72] By the early years of the war, the "use of chemical warfare by Germany was contingent upon initiation of chemical warfare by the enemy, the *expectation* being that chemical warfare as such could possibly be avoided entirely."[73] This policy did not preclude, of course, the use of gas in extermination campaigns within occupied territories.

German restraint during this period issued in part from the implications of a belief that the advantages offered by the initiation of CW were not worth the costs to Germany of being stigmatized as the first to violate the international legal prohibition.[74] According to General Hermann Ochsner, head of the German chemical troops, the cost-sensitivity of the Germans to the anti-CW norm was particularly important in the first phase of the war when Germany was on the offensive and the war had not yet become a total war.[75] The use of a means of warfare that had become a symbol of unlimited war would preclude a more limited conflict.[76] The symbolic value of CW in this regard was particularly important in accounting for the failure of the Germans to use chemical weapons in the evacuation of Dunkirk, when they could have been very destructive. The Germans believed that the employment of CW against retreating allied troops at Dunkirk would have been regarded as particularly heinous and would have precluded the possibility of an early peace with Britain.[77]

Japan appears also to have accepted this retaliation-only understanding of CW, though later than the other belligerents. After employing gas against the Chinese, Japan reduced its CW preparedness in 1941–1942. Japanese troops were ordered specifically not to employ gas against Western Powers in 1941. According to Brown, any subsequent use of gas against the Chinese might have reflected poor command and control of lower units, as the imperial general staff specifically forbade the use of toxic agents by local commanders.[78] This decision was taken because of the legal obligations not to use chemical weapons, low production compared to the United States, and the fear of retaliation.[79] Interestingly, there was no deterrence through the establishment of a retaliatory capability, as the Japanese unilaterally reduced their offensive capability to deter. The Japanese position was based solely on the enemy's declaratory policy.[80]

By 1941, then, it is fair to say that longstanding (Allied) and emerging (German and Japanese) expectations of the belligerents that each would not initiate gas warfare had converged into a threshold that forestalled the use of chemical weapons. Thus, although there had been a mutual belief that chemical weapons would eventually be used, this assumption coexisted with a convergent disinclination by each of these belligerents to initiate gas warfare in their confrontations in Europe or the Pacific. While the former view amounts to business as usual, the possibility that a weapon might not be used as contained in adherence to a no-first-use policy represents a radical departure from the usual standardization of weapons. The no-first-use pledge embodied in the Geneva Protocol was the principal manifestation of the chemical weapons taboo during the war, and its absolute form was the primary way in which the treatment of chemical weapons can be distinguished from the treatment of other weapons over the course of the conflict.

Indeed, while the Geneva Protocol is often regarded as "only" a no-first-use pledge, this status was uniquely conferred upon the entire category of chemical weapons, and it constituted the background of intentions that operated as a prohibitionary threshold—the norm—holding out the hope that CW would not be waged. The ambivalence implied in the uneasy coexistence of these assumptions of inevitability and non-initiation was captured in a lecture to officers of the Soviet General Staff in 1941: "It is quite apparent that the enemy will, sooner or later, use vesicant agents in order to improve his lot if—during the course of the war—he gets into a difficult situation. That is so clear that it requires no proof. All the same, one still hopes everywhere that the enemy will 'perhaps' not use 'frightful chemistry'."[81]

This converging expectation was tenuous indeed, and was subject to constant second-guessing throughout the war. While this manifestation of the CW norm was therefore far from being unquestioned and robust, it is important to note the degree to which the assumption of retaliation-only departs from business as usual. The invention of new weapons technologies represents the introduction of new kinds or even levels of destruction. One could imagine a hypothetical scenario in which potential adversaries recognize that their temporary monopoly on a given weapon will eventually give way to mutual infliction of that weapon's violence, and therefore agree to hold constant the existing level of destruction by disavowing the new technology. This level of ritualization does not, of course, represent the greater part of the actual history of warfare and technology. It does come close, however, to depicting the situation sanctioned by the international institutionalization of the chemical weapons taboo. As a diplomat said in 1922, this taboo "means that in the next war each of us promises to wait until the other fellow uses gas until we do."[82] A crucial difference with chemical weapons was the institutionalized anticipation of these new weapons at the Hague which preempted the usually one-sided cycle of moral protests that accompanies the monopoly of a weapons invention (see Chapter 2).

The importance of this phenomenon is highlighted when the experience of chemical weapons is compared to that of other weapons in history. As J. R. Hale has chronicled, the introduction of the use of firearms in medieval Europe excited a variety of complaints, including arguments that firearms were "less effective than the old familiar weapons," that bows were more reliable and efficient than the more complicated firearms. "Most arguments," according to Hale, "were based on the assumption that firearms were devilish and their use blasphemous, that they were unchivalrous and that they caused too much suffering."[83] These reactions eerily echo the variety of resistances voiced against chemical weapons, defined as they have been in terms of considerations of military culture, humanity, and efficiency.

Still, firearms had their supporters. Some advocates of the new weapons argued that they actually reduced casualties in battle, again echoing the CW debate. More telling, however, was the fact that guns and cannons came to be extolled and admired as thrilling artifacts of a new age of scientific discovery. Roaring cannon were a "pleasure to behold," and as Hale relates, "When Giambelli's explosive-packed infernal machine killed some five hundred of the besiegers of Antwerp in 1585, the European reaction was one not of outraged sensibility but rather of grudging admiration."[84] Cities were proud of their guns, and cannon became a status symbol of national and civic politics.

In sharp contrast to the secrecy surrounding chemical weapons, "the appeal of guns was so strong," Hale notes, "and they slipped into men's consciousness by so many insidious routes, that opposition was partly disarmed by familiarity."[85] Guns were domesticated by giving them names, appearing on engravings everywhere, tooled as art, used for processions, a measurement of length, and so on. Early English renaissance drama shows guns took over from swords as a virility symbol, and this "service of gunpowder to imagery . . . meant that men met the gun in language as familiarly as in painting and sculpture, and this helped to reconcile them to meeting it in real life."[86]

Such legitimizing processes of familiarity had not occurred—not yet at any rate—with respect to chemical weapons. Indeed, official national commitments that castigated chemical weapons ensured quite the opposite effect, driving the new technology into a shadowy background of illegitimacy. The formal institutionalization in international law of the absolute moral rejection of an entire category of chemical weapons retarded the standardization of chemical arms in ways not experienced by past technologies.

Reinforcing the Threshold

Although there is no shortage of discursive material concerning the interpretations of chemical weapons during World War II, the public discourse is somewhat thinner than might be expected given the attention devoted to CW during the previous several decades. This relative silence is not simply due to the obvious lack of attention that any non-event would garner but is more importantly the result of the active suppression of statements concerning gas warfare at the highest political and military levels.

For the first several years of the war, Churchill was constrained from making public announcements that Britain would retaliate against German CW for fear that Germans would interpret this statement as a threat of British initiation of CW.[87] In a memo to the chiefs of staff committee, Churchill wrote: "It is important that nothing should appear in newspapers, or be spoken on the BBC, which suggests that we are making a fuss about anti-gas arrangements, because the enemy will only use this as part of his excuse, saying that we are about to use it on him."[88]

This caution seems prudent in light of a potentially disastrous incident in the early days of the war. The Germans suffered several mustard-gas casualties at a bridge in Poland as a result of an explosion on September 8, 1939. Britain vigorously denied German accusations that the mustard gas had been obtained from the United Kingdom. A British report countered that the German lies indicated "an intention on the part of Germany to use poison gas on the Western Front in contravention of the 1925 Geneva Protocol, to which they are signatories." Further, it recalled the German lie on April 17, 1915, that the British had used gas bombs the previous day, and how five days later the Germans launched the first gas attack.[89] Given their desire to avoid gas warfare, both sides most likely recognized the dangers of misinterpretation involved in using such occasions for propaganda purposes (especially after World War I), giving support to the preferred stance of studied silence.

The secrecy concerning chemical weapons was similar in Germany, where as early as August 1935 the high command had ordered all com-

mands to keep secret the possible use of gas while Germany was officially bound by the protocol.[90] This general silence regarding CW was
important insofar as it imbued with special authority declarations that
were forthcoming during the course of the war. The exchange of these
declarations was crucial, for they represented the active production of
the chemical weapons threshold through an intrawar discourse. The
threshold was not simply left as an unsaid assumption secretly held by
individual belligerents but had an actively international cast, mutually
constituted by all relevant parties. The chemical weapons taboo was an
international norm.

After hostilities began, one of the first instances that broke the silence
on CW occurred in July 1941 when the Soviets claimed, on the basis of
captured manual on offensive use of gas, that the Germans were getting
ready to use chemical weapons. Germany quickly responded via the official news agency that the manual was merely a training guide—as allowed by the protocol—and not an imminent plan. But, "if the Soviet
[sic] use the discovery of German instructions about gas as an excuse to
begin gas warfare, Germany will answer appropriately."[91]

Another incident took place in May 1942, when it was reported that
German military spokesmen had denied that Germany intended to use
gas offensively. They pointed out that only one-third of the civilian population had gas masks, that Germany could not long sustain gas warfare
on all fronts without dislocating her chemical industry vital for the war
effort, and that retaliation would be certain.[92] Despite the shared no-first-
use expectation communicated by this remarkable disclosure, unrestricted air warfare and Soviet fears that Germans were about to initiate
CW prompted a prominent declaration by Churchill that made the headlines in May 1942:

> The Soviet Government have expressed to us the view that the Germans,
> in the desperation of their assault, may make use of poison gas against the
> armies and peoples of Russia. We are, ourselves, firmly resolved not to
> use this odious weapon unless it is first used by the Germans. Knowing
> our Hun, however, we have not neglected to make preparations on a for-
> midable scale.
>
> I wish now to make it plain that we shall treat the unprovoked use of
> poison gas against our Russian ally exactly as if it were used against our-
> selves and if we are satisfied that this new outrage has been committed by
> Hitler, we will use our great and growing air superiority in the West to
> carry gas warfare on the largest possible scale far and wide upon the
> towns and cities of Germany. It is thus for Hitler to choose whether he
> wishes to add this additional horror to aerial warfare.[93]

While awaiting an official German reply, the *Times* correspondent quoted German military spokesmen to the effect that Hitler's declaration not to resort to gas still held good and had never been revoked. The same spokesmen admitted that gas had been used twice during the war already—once in Poland and later in Russia—but said that the German military authorities explicitly declared that a mistake had been made.[94] The official German reaction was less contrite, portraying Churchill as "mad with desperation" and accusing him of attempting to

> mask his foul intentions by trumping up the lie that it was really Germany which contemplated this crime against humanity. But should Mr. Churchill disregard this solemn warning, the British people would suffer a fearful revenge, because German industry is infinitely better equipped than the British for gas war. The German Army has made the most minute preparations, and all civilian gas masks have been overhauled only a few weeks ago.[95]

Shortly thereafter President Roosevelt reiterated his already well-known and adamant opposition to gas warfare, a position he had made public as early as 1937:

> Authoritative reports are reaching this Government of the use by Japanese armed forces in various localities of China of poisonous or noxious gases. I desire to make it unmistakably clear that if Japan persists in this inhumane form of warfare against China or against any other of the United Nations, such action will be regarded by this Government as though taken against the United States, and retaliation in kind and in full measure will be meted out. We shall be prepared to enforce complete retribution. Upon Japan will rest the responsibility.[96]

Another exchange took place in spring 1943 as the British government repeated Churchill's warning in the face of more Soviet fears of a German CW assault.[97] The German response emphasized that the earlier official declarations on CW were unequivocal and still binding. It added candidly that military circles in Germany would not dream of engaging in gas war, because it would be useless except perhaps in case of a grand-scale action preparatory to a German landing on English soil, and because only in the event of gas war being immediately effective and decisive would Germany escape retaliation in kind by the enemy.[98] Again, Roosevelt shortly stepped in with a commitment and warning:

> From time to time since the present war began there have been reports that one or more of the Axis powers are seriously contemplating the use

of poisonous or noxious gases or other inhumane devices of warfare. I have been loath to believe that any nation, even our present enemies, could or would be willing to loose upon mankind such terrible and inhumane weapons. . . .

The use of such weapons has been outlawed by the general opinion of civilized mankind. This country has not used them, and I hope that we never will be compelled to use them. I state categorically that we shall in no circumstances resort to the use of such weapons unless the first use of them is by our enemies.

. . . I want to make clear beyond all doubt to any of our enemies contemplating a resort to such desperate and barbarous methods that acts of this nature committed against any one of the United Nations will be regarded as having been committed against the United States itself and will be treated accordingly. We promise to perpetrators of such crimes full and swift retaliation in kind, and I feel obliged now to warn the Axis armies and the Axis peoples, in Europe and in Asia, that the terrible consequences of any use of these inhumane methods on their part will be brought down swiftly and surely upon their own heads. Any use of gas by any Axis power, therefore, will immediately be followed by the fullest possible retaliation upon munition centres, seaports, and other military objectives throughout the whole extent of the territory of such Axis country.[99]

As these statements reveal, the designation of chemical weapons as a threshold of utmost political and military importance was actively upheld throughout the course of the war. The "natural" course of events— the use of any and all useful weapons in intense warfare—was not left alone to carry forth its own logic but was retarded by these discursive practices. In the next section, three defining aspects of these statements are identified as being particularly relevant to understanding the distinctive features of the chemical weapons discourse.

Absolute

One continuing feature of the discourse during World War II was the absolute nature of the prohibition, carrying on the institutional legacy begun at the Hague. Efforts at restraining other means of warfare were made before and during the war, particularly the prevention of submarine and air warfare against civilian targets.[100] As underscored in the preceding statements, however, efforts to restrict chemical weapons were unique in that they sought to prevent any use of any type of the weapon—

including nonlethal gases against soldiers—and not solely a particularly heinous employment such as use against defenseless civilians. This was a crucial difference between efforts to restrain gas and other forms of warfare. Submarines and bombers could be used against legitimate targets, but any use of chemical weapons was forbidden.

The effect of this absolute prohibition was to raise the ante involved in crossing the threshold. Because no use of chemical weapons was acceptable, any use of them was taken to justify their unlimited use in response. The significance of this feature of the taboo was particularly important in the case of the Allied landings at Normandy. The D-Day invasion presented the Germans with an especially inviting opportunity to use chemical weapons, one that might have been decisive in repelling the landing and even in changing the course of the war, as both the Germans and Allies recognized.[101] The failure of the Germans to wage CW against the Allied landings is therefore especially important. Allied commanders were greatly relieved when no chemical weapons were used, recognizing that their employment likely would have cost them the beachhead.[102]

This failure to employ chemical weapons has been attributed to two primary factors: the fear of retaliation and inadequate offensive and defensive preparations.[103] Concerning the former, the Germans avoided what likely would have been a devastatingly effective chemical attack against the Allies' D-Day landings at Normandy in part because of fears that it would bring on Allied gas attacks against German cities.[104] They were likely correct, for though Britain was committed to use gas only in response to German initiation, it planned to "drench German cities with gas on the largest possible scale" in response to a German first use.[105]

All of the major belligerents assumed that chemical weapons could not be employed in a limited way, despite the obvious evidence to the contrary in China and the previous experience of World War I, where gas was not targeted at civilians. Their assumption is all the more anomalous given the dominance of the value-neutral view of technology, which is grounded upon the instrumentalist assumption that the employment of technology is limited to a means to independently-arrived at ends. The chemical weapons discourse thus worked to produce a particular accepted wisdom that framed chemical arms as absolute weapons of destruction, rather than weapons that, like any others, would be used as standard issue in consonance with specific and limited tactical, strategic, and political goals. The taboo against CW was constituted in a fundamentally different way from the usual just-war criteria of noncombatant immunity upon which other restraints were based. Even as restraints protecting civilians were shattered during the war, soldiers in the field and civilians alike were the beneficiaries of the absolute form of the CW taboo. Restraint defined in terms of abhorrence for the weapon itself, rather than for how it was used, constituted a qualitatively different threshold from that of other weapons.

Norms and Desperate Thresholds

The characterization of the chemical weapons taboo as an "absolute" one is meant in a particular sense and should not be taken to imply that CW would not have been initiated under any circumstances whatsoever. It is nonetheless remarkable that the British seriously considered the initiation of CW only on two occasions.[106] The first was as a measure to repel a possible German invasion. In June 1940, John Dill, chief of the imperial general staff, suggested that the war cabinet be asked to allow the armed forces "to anticipate the use of the gas by the enemy, by ourselves taking the initiative in our defence against invasion, even if Germany or Italy has not by that time started chemical warfare."[107] Dill was eventually to withdraw this suggestion in the face of stiff opposition from, among others, the director of home defence, who worried about "throwing away the incalculable moral advantage of keeping our pledges."[108] This position was echoed by Major-General Henderson, who argued in a remarkable statement that with the initiation of chemical warfare

> we throw away the incalculable moral strength we derive from keeping our pledged word for a tactical surprise. . . . Our corresponding loss would be greater not only abroad but in our own country too, as such a departure from our principles and traditions would have the most deplorable effects not only on our own people but even on the fighting services. Some of us would begin to wonder whether it really mattered which side won.[109]

This passage illustrates how the chemical weapons norm mattered as a gauge of identity. For many British, the use of this proscribed means would bring into question what kind of people they were. The British, in the eyes of those like Henderson, just did not do that kind of thing. If they did, it would be difficult to distinguish them morally from the enemy.

The first use of gas was authorized by the "Victor" Cabinet in an anti-invasion exercise, raising the question of whether advance authority should actually be given to initiate the use of gas in the actual event of a German invasion.[110] Although it is entirely possible and even likely that the British would have initiated the use of chemical weapons if the Germans invaded England, the chiefs of staff decided not to seek advance authority for even the retaliatory use of gas from the War Cabinet, recognizing that "the decision must continue to rest with the Cabinet who will be guided by the circumstances prevailing at the time."[111] Incredibly, even these dire British deliberations for the use of gas were couched in terms of the possibility of using chemical weapons in retaliation "*if gas is used by the enemy* in connection with an attempt at invasion."[112] That is, using CW in "retaliation" against the Germans seems to have been understood as retaliation against German use of chemical weapons during an invasion, rather than using gas as retaliation in a general sense against a German invasion. Remarkably, deliberations about gas could revolve around the retaliation-only assumption even in the context of a German landing on the British homeland.

A truly desperate situation was required to justify the initiation of CW.[113] Britain's deputy chief of air staff, while considering the initiation of CW in the event of an invasion and the implications of violating the Geneva Protocol, felt compelled to declare that "it is better to break our word than to lose the British Empire."[114] That the use of chemical weapons would even be an issue at this crucial juncture and would require justification—the very self-preservation of Britain versus the keeping of international commitments—is indicative of an extremely demanding threshold.

The establishment of such thresholds is a principle way norms work in social life. Prohibitionary norms rarely render violations impossible but instead make them unlikely by raising the threshold of what counts as a legitimate exception to the rule. Few people would feel the need to deliberate over the legitimacy of violating societal norms against murder in the event of a deadly attack on themselves—self-defence is a widely accepted exception to the injunction not to kill. The existence of such exceptions does not mean that the norm is otherwise not robust, however; it simply means that there is a very high threshold in accepting a violation as an exception, and those exceptions are not undertaken lightly. That chemical weapons could not be used without the additional justification of such extraordinary circumstances testifies to the workings and importance of the norm.

A second occasion that prompted Britain to seriously consider initiating CW was the launching of V-rockets on June 13, 1944, six days after the Normandy invasion. This case is particularly interesting because Britain realized at this point that its dominance of the skies made it superior to Germany in CW capability. Churchill repeatedly sought "cold-blooded calculations" on the merits of initiating CW against the Germans in retaliation for the V-1 attacks, though ultimately he was unable to overcome the opposition in the military. His July 6, 1944, memo to the service chiefs on this issue is particularly revealing and is worth quoting at length:

> I want you to think very seriously over this question of using poison gas. I would not use it unless it could be shown either that (a) it was life or death for us, or (b) that it would shorten the war by a year.
>
> It is absurd to consider morality on this topic when everybody used it in the last war without a word of complaint from the moralists or the Church. On the other hand, in the last war the bombing of open cities was regarded as forbidden. Now everybody does it as a matter of course. It is simply a question of fashion changing as she does between long and short skirts for women.
>
> I want a cold-blooded calculation made as to how it would pay us to use poison gas, by which I mean principally mustard. . . .
>
> Why have the Germans not used it? Not certainly out of moral scruples or affection for us . . . the only reason they have not used it against us is that they fear the retaliation. . . .
>
> Although one sees how unpleasant it is to receive poison gas attacks, from which nearly everyone recovers, it is useless to protest that an equal amount of HE will not inflict greater cruelties and sufferings on troops or civilians. One really must not be bound within silly conventions of the mind whether they be those that ruled in the last war or those in reverse which rule in this.
>
> If the bombardment of London really became a serious nuisance . . . I should be prepared to do *anything* that would hit the enemy in a murderous place. I may certainly have to ask you to support me in using poison gas. We could drench the cities of the Ruhr and many other cities in Germany in such a way that most of the population would be requiring constant medical attention. . . . I do not see why we should always have all the disadvantages of being the gentleman while they have all the advantages of being the cad. There are times when this may be so but not now.
>
> I quite agree it may be several weeks or even months before I shall ask you to drench Germany with poison gas, and if we do it, let us do it one hundred per cent. In the meanwhile, I want the matter studied in cold blood by sensible people and not by that particular set of psalm-singing uniformed defeatists which one runs across now here now there.[115]

In response, the joint planning staff issued their report on the massive use of chemical weapons, recommending against it. In particular, they singled out the difficulty of judging the effects of a chemical war on

British morale: "After nearly five years of war and five weeks' experience of the flying bombs, public morale in the areas affected is less resilient, and might react unfavourably at first if gas were now used, although the shock would diminish as the efficacy of the protective and remedial measure became apparent. The public at large might, however, be resentful of being subjected to gas attack if it felt that this could have been avoided."[116]

Similarly, the joint chiefs of staff met and concluded that while it was true that the Allies could drench German cities more so than they could ours, "There is no reason to believe that the German authorities would have any greater difficulty in holding down the cowed German population, if they were subjected to gas attack, than they have had during the past months of intensive high explosive and incendiary bombings. The same cannot be said for our own people, who are in no such inarticulate condition."[117]

A feature attributed to chemical weapons that was understood to distinguish them from other enormously destructive weapons was their supposed psychological value against civilian populations. The Allies were not alone in this untested belief: the Germans failed to wage CW on D-Day largely because they feared that even limited chemical retaliation against their cities could have a devastating effect on morale.[118] What is interesting—even ironic—is that this putative terror value was largely self-manufactured, deriving from the normative discourse of the interwar years. As the chief of Germany's chemical troops put it, large-scale attacks against civilian populations were planned because of their psychological effects, as "the stupid and hysterical earlier propaganda of the League of Nations has also influenced world opinion in this question in such a way that panic is inevitable."[119] The power of this understanding of chemical weapons is particularly intriguing given the failures of strategic bombing to achieve its supposed and much-touted capability to destroy morale.

This special dread of the possible effects of CW also derived in large measure from the fact that these were still novel instruments of war in terms of their use against civilians. The special apprehension and fear that issues from the confrontation with sheer novelty in human life (what gas proponents called "ignorance") still held in an almost anachronistic way with respect to CW because European civilians had still not yet been subjected to chemical attacks. Abstinence from civilian gas attacks during World War I and continued adherence to the taboo in Europe during World War II meant that chemical weapons were still an unknown quantity for these combatants, an "untried form of attack" as opposed to well-tried means such as high explosives and incendiaries.[120]

In Europe at least, gas was an old weapon still novel beyond its time. Unfamiliarity fed uncertainty, which in turn bred fear, enhancing the symbolic status of chemical weapons.

On the other side of the Atlantic, the moral inhibitions of the United States against initiating CW had relaxed in the last year of the war with the death of the staunchly antigas Roosevelt. Further, U.S. public opposition to the employment of CW against the Japanese had eroded, a development that stands as a warning against attributing greater power to the taboo than abstinence might otherwise suggest. Racist propaganda heated up against the Japanese, and the castigation of the Japanese as uncivilized barbarians drew support from their "sneak attack" at Pearl Harbor and their mistreatment of prisoners of war. The more such propaganda took root and defined the Japanese as utterly alien, the more acceptable became the use of gas against this "uncivilized" enemy. An article in the *New York Times* stated that evidence of Japanese atrocities against prisoners of war meant that "there will be less moral repugnance than ever before against the use of certain methods of warfare that we have hitherto refrained from using . . . Gas is generally greatly overrated by the lay mind as an effective military tactic; just as the lay mind wrongly ascribes to it alone a peculiar moral malignancy, which however, should also properly be shared by high explosives, tanks, etc."[121]

Headlines appeared proclaiming "We should gas Japan" and "You can cook 'em better with gas."[122] The appearance in U.S. newspapers of open calls for "gassing the Japs" indicated a degree of apparent public support and raises the question of whether the United States would have employed chemical weapons if the atomic bomb had not been developed and the war had not ended sooner. It is clear that the U.S. military did have plans for the employment of chemical weapons against Japan, and there were advocates for such use. While any answer must remain speculative, one author has concluded that gas still would not have been employed, for the restraints against use were too powerful.[123] Another author concludes that restraints would have eventually broken down by 1946 or 1947.[124] In genealogical fashion, the non-use of chemical weapons and the influence of the taboo in this case owe much to the contingencies of timing, insofar as the legacy of the CW stigma embodied in Roosevelt's opposition and subsequent unpreparedness lingered long enough to prevent the use of gas before the war was over. The threshold had held by raising a variety of barriers to an ebbing and perhaps rising tide that, given more time and other circumstances, could well have been overwhelmed.

For these reasons, the genealogical stance sensitizes us to the crucial play of circumstances. The maintenance of the taboo owes much to reasons other than simply moral inhibition; nevertheless it is the fact of abstinence itself—regardless of the reasons—that over time and in turn buttresses the normative resistance to CW.

It is nontheless remarkable that the United States did not employ gas against the Japanese even when the United States determined that it faced no significant threat of retaliation and when chemical weapons could contribute to the saving of American lives. Casualties among U.S. soldiers were expected to be extremely high in assaults against Japanese forces holed up in the caves and tunnels of the Pacific Islands. Tests conducted in 1945 led to a conclusion that "war gases, both persistent and nonpersistent, are effective against Japanese defensive positions of the types tested." General Wait of the Chemical Warfare Service was even more positive, arguing that "gas is the most promising of all weapons for overcoming cave defenses."[125] Especially when used in combination with other weapons, chemical weapons were regarded as potentially very useful.

Over and above considerations of military preparedness, then, the threshold against employing chemical weapons in World War II had obviously become much steeper than in World War I. Indeed, so high had the threshold become that gas would only have been used in utter desperation. As I mentioned earlier, the existence of prohibitionary social norms does not mean that they cannot be violated; and their violation does not necessarily mean the norms no longer exist or do not matter. Norms matter by raising the threshold of violations of social practices, sometimes so high that certain actions exceed the realm of intelligibility. The chemical weapons taboo did not have the latter unquestioned status, but, despite the harrowing destruction entailed in incendiary and atomic bombing raids, it was the use of gas—any use, even nonlethal gas against soldiers in the field—that was designated as the unparalleled desperate act in that most desperate of wars. The employment of chemical weapons required extraordinary justification that can be adequately understood only with an appreciation of the machinations from the Hague into the 1920s.

Defense

Considerations of defense demarcated chemical weapons from other weapons. Because defense against CW was possible, the lack of adequate defensive preparations was regarded as so unacceptably delinquent that gas could not be employed. This reasoning stands in stark contrast, of course, to other weapons such as explosives, incendiaries, and so forth, where the lack of means of defense provided anything but a rationale for their non-use. The assumption that "the bomber will always get through" did not prove robust in restraining city-busting attacks.[126]

This is what is so intriguing about the persistence of the chemical weapons taboo: unlike cases such as poison or nuclear weapons, chemical weapons are not so easily defined as weapons against which there is no defense. In those cases, the operation of the logic of deterrence—"I won't use them if you won't"—is less problematic. In the case of gas, however, the British in particular had a rather well-prepared civil defense network in case of gas attack, having issued 44 million masks by 1939, enough for every person.[127]

I mentioned earlier the view that the existence of a well-prepared enemy was often regarded as a reason not to initiate CW, since its effectiveness could be significantly reduced. Ironically, however, the lack of availability of defense against gas also often provided a compelling reason not to initiate CW. At the beginning of 1944, Hitler apparently told Romanian Marshal Antonescue that because of the lack of effective protective equipment for German civilians, the use of new gases could not be considered for the time being. If this situation were remedied, however, London and other cities would be attacked.[128] That is, considerations of defense came to forestall the use of gas because defense *was* actually possible. The possibility of defense translated into a requirement, and the lack thereof provided yet another extraordinary hurdle of justification that the proponents of gas had to surmount.

Unpreparing for Chemical Warfare

It was noted earlier that the lack of adequate offensive and defensive preparations for gas warfare is generally agreed to have been a primary reason why none of the major belligerents were willing to initiate CW. This negligence in turn has been attributed to a combination of factors, including military unwillingness to promote a weapon that was unpopular or did not fit mobile offensive strategies; the effects of international law; political, moral, and psychological opposition to gas; the resistance of military culture to a weapon it found unchivalrous; and so on. Certain inherent liabilities of chemical weapons were relevant in this regard (such as dependency on wind conditions, the extra logistical burden they required, etc.), but these issues alone cannot account for the decisiveness of the reluctance in preparing for CW. As one volume of the SIPRI study concludes: "Fear of retaliation may have been the ultimate constraint on initiation of CW during World War II, but unpreparedness, caused partly by the legal prohibition, partly by the shadow of possible retaliation against cities and by other deeper factors, was the operational constraint."[129]

It is here that the normative opposition to CW is given pride of place in explanations for the non-use of chemical weapons, it being generally agreed that moral and legal restraints were vital in preventing the assimilation of gas by military establishments. The conservatism of military cultures does not suffice to account for the failure of the Atlantic belligerents to assimilate chemical weapons, for such matters were not decided by military establishments alone. This is particularly the case of the U.S. experience, as Brown writes: "Due in significant measure to its awareness of the abhorrence with which the public viewed gas during the twenties and thirties, the Army never seriously pressed for gas warfare readiness; an Army desiring integration into the mainstream of American life would not burnish its image by meaningful support of a weapon so distasteful to the public."[130] Moreover, gas warfare policy was a presidential decision because of the politicizing effect of past international conferences and a genuine desire to limit unrestricted war.[131]

It is clear that normative opposition to CW—sanctioned in international law—is indispensable to understanding the lack of CW preparedness by the major belligerents of World War II and, ultimately, to explaining the non-use of chemical weapons during the conflict. In this section I seek to illustrate in thematic fashion the context-effects of this norm.

One way to illustrate this process is to examine how the prohibitionary norm influenced preparations by affecting allocation decisions. Most of the World War II accounts previously cited have noted that one of the factors inhibiting adequate CW preparations was the scarcity of resources in the pressing wartime economies. In Germany, the participants in the German military program testify to this effect: "Because of the most urgent tasks of German rearmament before the outbreak of the war in 1939 and the enormous expense of material required for conducting the war and the always insufficient number of personnel, the German preparations for chemical warfare were always more or less the stepchild of armament in peace time, and this was even more true in time of war."[132]

The crucial point to consider with respect to this phenomenon is that a particular interpretation of chemical weapons—one described in this study—tipped the scales in favor of other weapons in allocation decisions. If chemical arms were simply another unremarkable standard weapon to be used in combination with other weapons in situations where they were advantageous, the context of allocation decisions would have looked rather different. The fact that chemical weapons were not so regarded was to a significant degree attributable to the effects of their having been stigmatized in international law:

> Although the German High Command endeavoured to be prepared for all eventualities in the field of chemical warfare, and to be ready for effective retaliation against enemy use of chemical warfare, the objection on the basis of international law against initiating chemical warfare had always been duly taken into consideration. These objections were considered to be so predominant that in the general course of rearmament of the German Armed Forces the measures to be taken in the field of chemical warfare had never been considered as having any priority; on the contrary, requirements for chemical warfare were frequently and deliberately given a priority inferior to that allocated to requirements of others arms and services.[133]

Although some evidence suggests that such postwar accounts might overstate the adherence to the international legal prohibition at least in the German case, the point is not that the taboo by itself prevented the Germans from making decisions to launch chemical warfare.[134] But the fact that some preparations were in fact made does not demonstrate that the taboo did not matter either; after all, the Geneva Protocol did not proscribe preparations for CW or even ban many of its parties from the use of gas in retaliation.

The central issue here is that allocation priorities became another barrier to chemical weapon use, an impediment not encountered by other weapons, and they became a barrier largely by virtue of a weapons-specific taboo that delegitimized the weapon as a whole. By contrast, restrictions were usually sought by limiting how weapons were to be used, such as prohibiting the use of submarines against civilian shipping—which would not affect preparations for the weapon itself because the weapon could be legitimately employed for a variety of tasks. Thus, during Britain's deliberations over CW preparations before the war, the advocacy of full-scale capabilities by the Air Ministry and War Office gave way to the priorities established by the Treasury, for the reason that "it would be illogical to reduce our offensive or defensive capacity in more important directions in order to include an ideal scale of provision for a weapon which it is hoped will never be used. Gas provision is therefore a direction in which some risk may legitimately be taken."[135]

Similarly, the lack of adequate offensive preparation was especially vital in forestalling the U.S. use of gas against Japan in the last years of the war. A major reason for the crucial shortfall of CW capabilities was the unwillingness of theater commanders to use up valuable shipping space with equipment that was solely for retaliation against an enemy action that might never take place—that is, equipment that might never be used.[136]

It has often been remarked that chemical weapons were not a priority because there were alternatives available. The point is, however, that no one would have bothered searching for alternatives and for reasons not to employ chemical weapons if they had been an utterly unremarkable and unpoliticized weapon. Despite the expectation that someone else would use chemical weapons, the mutual no-initiation positions in effect amounted to something far different from the assumption that their use was inevitable. This difference becomes especially clear in juxtaposition to a truly unquestioned assumption that, say, high-explosive bombs would be used in the war. The assumption that gas might not be used, embodied in the Geneva Protocol, established a subtly different context for considerations of CW and provided the crucially enabling reasons why preparations could be permitted to lag.

The development of gas warfare capabilities, let alone their use, required an extra burden of proof that was not placed upon other weapons. In Germany, it was held that the production of gas on a large scale could be justified on military grounds only if a large-scale offensive use of poison gas were planned at the outset of a war, an eventuality that never happened.[137] At the beginning of the war, Germany had some 12,000 tons of chemical agents, 80 percent of which was mustard.[138] Compare this figure to the 7,600 tons of mustard gas Germany produced during World War I.[139] Assessments of what was sufficient to wage chemical warfare had apparently changed markedly. Similarly, the offensive use of gas was considered at several junctures by the Germans (such as against France after the defeat of Poland), but it was judged that the necessary superiority was not yet available for a decisive strike, and preparations were confined to a retaliatory capability.[140]

Another striking example of this phenomenon was the German decision not to employ gas against the Allied landing at Normandy. One of the major reasons given for German restraint in this situation was the assessment that offensive and defensive preparations for gas were not adequate, but what is interesting here is the definition of "adequate." At the time of the Normandy landing, Germany had a six-month supply of gas, including the Luftwaffe's half a million gas bombs and spray tanks which could be used by aircraft.[141] And yet, this store was not deemed sufficient to wage CW.

The upshot is that the criteria of sufficiency was not the same for chemical weapons as it was for other weapons. Invariably, "sufficient" preparations of gas were deemed unavailable, when by the standards of an unpoliticized weapon rather large amounts of such arms often were on hand. In part this anomaly issued from a belief that either one should have a enormous supply of chemical weapons or none at all—a chemical attack had to be massive in order to be effective. However, definitions of adequacy do not simply emerge from objective calculations, and before and during the war they were not immune to political considerations. In Britain, the chief of the air staff ordered that the operational requirements for CW be reviewed because they were based on what he believed to be a "purely arbitrary" assumption that 40–50 percent of the total bomber effort would have to be exerted in the form of gas for any employment of CW.[142]

In addition, because chemical weapons were not to be used and had not yet been used, assessments of their use were made by isolating the relative advantage their employment would bring with respect to other weapons. Thus, rather than simply being employed without question as a standard auxiliary to high explosives and incendiaries in bombing raids or to augment other weapons in battlefield operations, the use of chemical weapons had to be *decisive* (often in and of itself), not just *useful*, in order to justify their employment. By World War II, the burden of proof for the decisiveness of CW was incomparably—and as it turned out, prohibitively—high. This cost was partly the result of military assessments that gas warfare was not worth initiating unless it was decisive, because the net effect of the mutual employment of gas would just be a further logistical complication of the battlefield and the addition of extra burdens upon soldiers.[143] The same, of course, could be said of many weapons. The performance of the machine gun in the trench warfare of World War I particularly comes to mind. Machine guns greatly complicated military manoeuver on the battlefield, almost shutting it down while multiplying the slaughter, all to little or no end. No one suggested as a result that machine guns might not be used. In the case of CW, in contrast, the anticipatory nature of the Hague Declaration and continued ostracism of gas meant that as long as restraint continued to hold the tenuous belief could be maintained that these weapons might actually not be employed.

Throughout history the fact that few other weapons have proven to be so "decisive" as to turn around a war did not hinder their employment, especially in their early and often less effective forms.[144] Typical weapons today are regarded in unremarkable terms as meeting the standard of utility; indeed, the question is hardly ever brought up. Rarely, however, have such weapons met the criterion of decisiveness that is so often required of chemical weapons. Hale's observations on the introduction of the first firearms serves to make the point of comparison: "The effects of firearms were specific and dramatic: they raised problems of tactics, equipment, and supply; wars cost more, new methods of fortification had to be devised, but they had little effect on the fortunes of campaigns as a whole or on the balance of political power. . . . Firearms may have decided the issue of a single battle . . . but they cannot be said to have decided a war."[145]

What counts as "suitable," "adequate," "useful," or "decisive" is highly context-dependent, and, in the case of CW, such assessments were highly politicized. An extraordinary burden of proof was demanded of chemical weapons that not only required that they be decisive in any given battle, but that uninterrupted future supply could be counted upon.

What counted as suitable preparations was therefore different for gas than for other weapons. Thus, while the United States was no less prepared for CW than for mechanized warfare at the outbreak of the war, discussions on tanks and airplanes revolved solely around questions of quantity and methods of employment. Gas, however, as Brown points out, "was not evaluated in these terms," but rather was "consistently associated with a normative qualifying expression" by military and civilian leaders.[146] As in Germany, considerations concerning gas warfare revolved around the politically loaded terms of defense and retaliation rather than unquestioned assumptions of initiation and employment uncomplicated by extra justificatory burdens.[147]

Even though chemical weapons were regarded as effective and even potentially decisive in some circumstances, the usual criterion of utility was not enough to gain acceptance of the weapon. The accepted wisdom that "all useful weapons will be used in war" was therefore retarded, along with its corollary that "restraint matters only for useless weapons." In the context of an international prohibitory norm against CW, justifications for the use of chemical weapons required better reasons than the usual unsaid test of effectiveness and utility. Thus "the fundamental reason for non-use of chemical weapons almost certainly lay at a deeper level than military inexpediency."[148] The importation of moral criteria outside of technology's self-justificatory logic of efficiency meant that there was resistance to the technological determinism implied by the dominance of a test of means that becomes the end.[149]

As we have seen, the chemical weapons taboo established a different context for thinking about gas that multiplied the justificatory burden for CW, thus removing the use of these weapons further from other weapons as an unremarkable practice. In this way, Brown explains, the restraints embodied in treaty prohibition, "though imperfect, reinforced both public and military dislike and fear of chemical warfare and provided a ready excuse for lack of substantive preparation."[150] These factors constituted a threshold for justifying CW that raised the ante high enough that, in combination with the timing of the historical course of events, chemical arms were not employed as a battlefield weapon in the major theaters of Allied-Axis confrontation. As this chapter demonstrates, this non-event is not reducible to the objective physical features of the weapon alone but owes much to the normative discourse that institutionalized a prohibition on any use of this category of weapon.

CHAPTER SIX

A Weapon of the Weak

There are different views on this matter from different angles. You are living on a civilized continent. You are living on a peaceful continent.

— Tariq Aziz, Iraqi foreign minister, 1988

Between World War II and the Iran-Iraq War of the 1980s, a number of events detracted from, transformed, and bolstered the chemical weapons norm. Egypt's apparent use of chemical weapons in Yemen in the 1960s, controversy over the U.S. use of defoliants and tear gas in Vietnam, the "yellow rain" scandal in South East Asia, and allegations of Soviet CW in Afghanistan all seemed to indicate that the hold of the chemical weapons norm was becoming a tenuous one.

Nevertheless, there were indications that the norm was able to withstand these challenges. Indeed, the politicization of these events often kept the issue of the status of the chemical weapons taboo on the international agenda. The seeds of the multilateral negotiation process at the Geneva disarmament conferences, which eventually culminated in the Chemical Weapons Convention (CWC) of 1993, were sown largely in the fallout of Egypt's apparent use of chemical weapons in Yemen and the controversy over the use of herbicides and irritant chemical agents in Vietnam by the United States.[1] As a result of the latter, the Nixon administration moved to ratify the Geneva Protocol, and the Senate finally gave its consent for the president to ratify the protocol in 1975.[2] Moreover, with the Biological Weapons Convention of 1972, agreement was reached on the prohibition of the development, production, and stockpiling of bacteriological and toxin weapons.[3] Years later, on the heels of the end of the Cold War, the United States and the former Soviet Union agreed to dismantle their chemical weapons stockpiles. In September 1992, two decades of negotiations within the United Nations disarmament conferences finally produced the CWC, a far-reaching agreement signed by over 150 nations that extends the prohibition on the use of chemical weapons to a ban on their development, possession, and transfer.

This chapter focuses on a contained set of events that thrust the issue of CW back into the spotlight of world politics in the 1980s and 1990s and exemplify the important features of the contemporary chemical weapons discourse. The re-emergence of chemical warfare as a prominent issue in global politics during this period arose from the use of chemical weapons in the Iran-Iraq War and subsequent fears that chemical agents would be used by Iraq in the Gulf War of 1990–1991. These events spurred renewed efforts to prohibit CW, marked most notably by the Paris Conference of 1989 and agreement on the CWC which was opened for signature in January 1993. These wars and reactions to them concentrated the attention of the international community on CW in spectacular fashion, and they correspondingly provide a rich vein of discursive practices for examination of the contemporary meaning of the chemical weapons taboo.

Again in this chapter, I counterpoise a case of the use of chemical weapons with a subsequent case of non-use. The analysis of the Iran-Iraq War and the Gulf War is then followed by a treatment of the implications of the CWC. This chapter examines both the constitution of the chemical weapons discourse and how this normative formation affected the development and (non-)use of chemical weapons. The ensuing genealogical inquiry identifies changes in the discourse and their sources, and then assesses the implications of the interpretive continuities and transmutations for the robustness of the norm. I focus particular attention on postwar efforts to reinvigorate the norm, as well as on the effects of nuclear weapons on the interpretations of chemical weapons. Have nuclear weapons made chemical weapons seem less novel, and thus less terrible and more acceptable—as the historical cycle hypothesis would argue? Have they rendered chemical weapons obsolete and thus more amenable to moral compunction? Or do chemical weapons instead hold an allure by virtue of their stigma as a weapon of mass destruction akin to nuclear weapons?

The Iran-Iraq War

The use of chemical weapons during the Iran-Iraq War has been taken to indicate that the normative inhibitions against waging CW did nothing to restrain Iraq's use of chemical agents—that is, the chemical weapons taboo simply did not matter.[4] The logic of this line of thinking suggests that the Iran-Iraq War is best understood as a recurrence of the futility of normative restraints against CW as exemplified in World War I and the Italo-Ethiopian War. The argument developed here, however, is that the chemical weapons norm continued to serve as the signifier of a threshold of desperation during the 1980s, and therefore its role during this period more closely resembles the case of World War II, when chemical weapons were *not* used between the primary Allied and Axis powers. This counter-intuitive interpretation that the most recent case of chemical weapons' use closely resembles the most prominent case of non-use is clarified by a genealogical focus on the discourse and an understanding of the operation of norms in international society.

Preparations

Iranian political leaders seem to have accepted the international norm proscribing CW to the extent that Iran neither possessed chemical weapons nor had any means to produce its own when Iraq started to use such weapons. Iranian efforts at chemical warfare were undertaken only after being attacked by Iraqi chemical munitions, and they never reached anything near the level of those attained by Iraq. Some sources suggest that Iran did employ chemical weapons in desperate retaliation against Iraq, employing chemical mortar and artillery rounds by 1985. If this claim is true, these weapons were likely captured Iraqi munitions. By the cease-fire of August 20, 1988, Iran was beginning to produce its own mustard gas and nerve gas, according to some analysts.[5]

Iraq, by contrast, began research into the production of the irritant agent CS for riot control purposes in the late 1970s. Military-scale production of CW was started in the early 1980s. Production of mustard gas began in 1981; production of the nerve gases sarin and tabun did not start until 1984.[6] Although reliable information on Iraqi motivations and attitudes towards CW is scarce, one source has argued that the Iraqi program seems to have been undertaken "in response to reports that both Egyptian and Israeli forces were equipped with chemical weapons at the time of the October War [1973] and the threat posed by Iran and its Kurdish Rebels."[7]

Desperate Warnings

The bare fact of Iraqi use of chemical weapons would seem to indicate prima facie that the chemical weapons norm did not matter during the Iran-Iraq War. As is the case with the other wars previously examined however, a simple behavioral test of whether such weapons were used or not does not sufficiently capture the role of the norm in the Iran-Iraq War. The evidence indicates that Iraqi leaders did in fact feel constrained by the existence of a norm prohibiting CW, and only after the failure of the international community to demonstrate its commitment to the norm in the face of Iraq's initial testing of the waters did Iraq feel free to flout the chemical weapons taboo.

As several authors have now noted, Iraq's venture into chemical warfare was cautious and circumspect.[8] While Iraq was still on the offensive in the early years of the war, gas warfare was not employed. As Iraq started to suffer losses at the hands of Iranian human-wave attacks, its leaders began to sound out the ramifications of using gas in a variety of ways. In August 1982, Baghdad's Voice of the Masses Radio issued a thinly veiled threat to the Iranians by ominously stating that there was "a certain insecticide for every kind of insect."[9] In October, the Iraqi chargé d'affaires in Denmark stated that "Iraq will use a new secret weapon of mass destruction if the Iranians launch a major offensive on the border."[10] Lest these warnings were not taken seriously, Iraqi broadcasts to Iran repeated these threats "in the form of an ultimatum": "This is a very serious warning. If the aggressions by Khomeyni's forces continue, we shall use a weapon that will annihilate and leave no signs of the aggressive revolution guards and misled people. . . . Before using this new weapon, we issue our warning and advise families not to allow the regime to take their children to the fronts."[11]

Iraq further tested the waters by employing nonlethal tear gas as its first foray into chemical warfare.[12] In this way, as one author has argued, "even the seemingly unambiguous threshold of non-use of chemical weapons was finessed by the Iraqis through an initial use of non-lethal tear gas in the summer of 1982."[13] There was virtually no reaction by the international community to these probes, even though the Iranians had begun to make allegations that the Iraqis were using gas weapons as early as 1981.[14] The initial reports of tear gas only drew a comment from U.S. officials that they were confident that Iraq had no lethal CW capabilities.[15] Iraqi broadcasts countered that Iran's claims were not only false, but were made in order to "justify its [inhuman] act of using chemical weapons in war." Claiming that "Iraq has never, in no case and in no war, used nor will it use chemical weapons," these broadcasts warned Iran's leaders that if they committed the "wicked" act of using chemical weapons in the war, "Iraq will retaliate and will reply in kind."[16]

Iraq had joined the Geneva Protocol in 1931 with a right-of-retaliation reservation. The initial decision to introduce lethal chemical weapons and to unambiguously violate the taboo as institutionalized in the protocol appears to have been taken only as a last resort, a final defensive measure to thwart the Iranian "human wave" offensives of 1982 at a time when it appeared to Iraq that it was losing the war. Even then, Iraq's first use of lethal gas was a field trial of mustard gas, which "scarcely suggested a calculated attempt to maximize the surprise effect of introducing chemical weapons."[17] In December 1982, mustard gas was used more extensively to deal with human-wave and night attacks by the Iranians. After employing lethal chemical agents at Wal-Fajr 2 in July 1983, Iraq again warned Iran of the extensive use of chemical weapons. A September 1983 statement by the Iraqi high command stated that Iraq "was armed with modern weapons that (would) be used for the first time in war . . . not used in previous attacks for humanitarian reasons . . . if you execute the orders of Khomeini's regime . . . your death will be certain because this time we will use a weapon that will destroy any moving creature on the fronts."[18]

As these warnings attest, Iraq's "incremental and heavily circum-scribed" use of chemical weapons indicates that the decision to violate the norm prohibiting CW was not taken lightly by the Iraqis. In the words of one author: "Iraq did not employ lethal gas before it had indi-cated its intentions both by using tear gas first and by issuing continuous and persistent warnings about it so as to leave the door open for an Iranian retreat. When Iran failed to heed these warnings, Iraq employed this weapon only in vital segments of the front and only when it saw no other way to check the Iranian offensives."[19]

One indicator of the existence of a norm is the expectation of rebuke for deviating from existing practices.[20] Iraqi leaders felt constrained by the existence of a norm prohibiting CW and were apprehensive of the international reaction to its violation. While Iraq thus appeared vulner-able to efforts to enforce the norm, its leaders discovered that the taboo was not to have the robust backing that they were apparently willing to heed. This situation parallels very closely the Italian use of chemical weapons in Ethiopia: probes of nonlethal tear gas were undertaken to gauge the reaction of the international community, followed by the grad-ually expanding use of chemical weapons in the face of little opposition.

In response to Iraq's use of chemical weapons, Iran attempted to arouse world opinion. When its initial protests failed to mobilize a sig-nificant international reaction, Iran flew chemical warfare casualties to Western Europe, where doctors confirmed that the soldiers were victims of mustard gas. By the end of 1984, inspectors from the United Nations had established beyond doubt that there had been at least one Iraqi at-tack in which mustard gas had been used.[21] These efforts and a Red Cross statement did much to corroborate Iranian charges in the eyes of the outside world.[22]

On March 5, 1985, the U.S. State Department announced the government's conclusion that Iraq had been waging lethal CW. By March 26, U.S. Secretary of State George Schultz raised the issue with Iraq's foreign minister. The following day, the U.S. government announced its conclusion that Iraq had indeed been using chemical weapons and publicly condemned such use. An April 25 Security Council statement strongly condemned the use of chemical weapons in general terms but stopped short of specifically condemning Iraq, though it identified Iranian soldiers in the war against Iraq as the victims of CW.[23]

Despite the gradual emergence of a consensus that Iraq had indeed waged CW in violation of the Geneva Protocol, Iraq did not suffer formal condemnation and sanction.[24] In public media and U.S. congressional debates, the Cold War "Yellow Rain" controversy concerning allegations of CW in South East Asia and Afghanistan occupied at least as much attention on the CW front as accusations of Iraqi use of chemical weapons. Few members of the world community were anxious to see Iraq fall to Iran's Islamic Revolution. They were, therefore, more willing to tolerate CW if it repelled the Iranians.

If one indicator of the existence of a norm is the expectation of rebuke for violations, a further gauge of its strength is the extent to which violations are actually punished. According to this standard, much as in cases of previous violations, the chemical weapons taboo did not qualify as a robust universal norm. Even so, it is possible that the tepid initial international response to Iraq's use of chemical weapons may have had "some temporary success" in forestalling Iraqi chemical warfare.[25] Employing them sporadically when its forces came under intense military pressure, Iraq did not make extensive use of chemical weapons between March 1984 and Iran's Faw offensive early in 1986. Some analysts have speculated that this pause was the result of Iraqi anxiety about the international reaction. In the absence of convincing evidence, however, alternative explanations for this hesitation remain equally plausible.[26]

Iraq's resumption of extensive chemical warfare was only taken while Iraq, again, was on the defense, at Faw in 1986 and Basra in 1987. Eventually, Iraqi use of chemical agents progressed to the point that they began to use the weapons in offensive operations. In 1987, the Iraqis crossed the final threshold: they employed chemical weapons in attacks against civilians, first against Iranian Kurds, and then against their own Kurdish population.[27] A former director of Iraqi military intelligence claims that Saddam Hussein had decided early in 1988 to take the chemical war further with a chemical attack on Tehran, but the action was forestalled when the war turned in Iraq's favor in April of that year.[28]

The international response to the use of chemical weapons against civilians was more immediate than previous reactions to chemical weapons use, but ultimately even these efforts failed to exact a substantial political price from Iraq. Condemnations and calls for sanctions issued from the European Parliament, Western European Union, and France at the United Nations, but no concrete actions were taken. The U.S. Congress voted for sanctions, but they were never enacted into law due to pressure from the Reagan administration.[29] The British government similarly argued that sanctions would not be beneficial.[30] A widely shared conclusion of a Senate report sums up the situation:[31] "Since 1984 Iraq has used chemical weapons on a large scale without paying any price in political or economic relations with other countries. Global acquiescence in previous Iraqi use of chemical weapons has undoubtedly been a factor in Iraq's belief it could use gas on the Kurds with no international consequences."[32]

Unconventional Justifications

Encountering little international action to enforce the CW taboo, and given the publicized evidence of its use of chemical weapons, Iraq by the end of the war no longer felt compelled to deny it had used chemical weapons, a stance it otherwise had maintained throughout the conflict. In July 1988, the Iraqi foreign minister acknowledged that Iraq had used chemical weapons. But even here, Tariq Aziz claimed (falsely) that "Iran started its use. We were victims many times since the early beginning of the conflict."[33] In October Aziz obliquely justified the use of chemical weapons against Iranian forces by stating that "on several occasions, Iran attacked Iraq using hundreds of thousands of human waves whose objective was to either kill or get killed. In the face of this savage and barbaric assault, Iraq had no choice but to use its right to defend itself and protect its territorial integrity and its homeland."[34]

At first, the Iraqis also vehemently denied that they had used chemical weapons against the Kurds in August 1988.[35] Even internal Iraqi documents regarding the campaign against the Kurds did not refer to chemical weapons directly.[36] Eventually, however, an admission of the use of chemicals against the Kurds could be pieced together. A statement denying chemical attacks against the Kurds by Iraq's defense minister suggested that their use was not ruled out for humanitarian reasons but because the depth of the area of operations was not propitious. He did say that Iraq's policy was based on opposing the local or external usage of these weapons and affirmed that the general rule was not to use these weapons. After stressing that Iraq did not deviate from this rule, 'Adnan Khayrallah did nonetheless add that "If an enemy comes to your house to strike you on the head will you throw flowers at him or hit him with what he deserves?"[37] The implications of such ambiguities were confirmed in a little-noted statement by the Iraqi vice-president in November 1988, in which he admitted Iraqi use of chemical weapons in Halabja.[38]

A particular use of chemical weapons does not necessarily signal the simple death of the chemical weapons taboo, any more than the occurrence of a homicide indicates that there is not a generally robust societal norm proscribing murder (see Chapters 3 and 5). In fact, as Kratochwil and Ruggie have argued:

> Precisely because state behavior within regimes is interpreted by other states, the rationales and justifications for behavior which are proffered, together with pleas for understanding or admissions of guilt, as well as the responsiveness to such reasoning on the part of other states, all are absolutely critical component parts of any explanation involving the efficacy of norms. Indeed, such communicative dynamics may tell us far more about how robust a regime is than overt behavior alone.[39]

For our purposes, then, the question is to what extent the use of chemical weapons by Iraq reflected a conventionalizing of these weapons—and thus a severe erosion of the taboo—and to what extent it was treated as an exceptional practice.

Significantly, Iraq did not fundamentally question the humanitarian definition of the chemical weapons discourse. Like Italy in 1935–1936, Iraq made no explicit argument that chemical weapons were as legitimate as any other weapon or that they were humane. Indeed, the Iraqis contributed to the moral discourse by portraying chemical agents as a weapon of last resort that they would otherwise eschew for humanitarian reasons. The Iraqi foreign minister went so far as to claim that Iraq had reaffirmed that it "respects and abides by all the provisions of international law and international agreements accepted by the international community, including the Geneva Protocol of 1925 for the prohibition of the use in war of asphyxiating, poisonous or other gases and of bacteriological methods of warfare."[40]

One need not believe these above claims to notice that something significant had not occurred. Throughout all of the warnings, accusations, denials, admissions, and justifications, no attempt was made to conventionalize chemical weapons and re-open what has become the moral core of the chemical weapons taboo. Unlike the discourse that accompanied and followed the use of chemical weapons in World War I, the Iraqis never explicitly justified their use of such agents as a more humane type of warfare. Indeed, Iraq's leaders seem to have used chemical weapons on the understanding that it was a desperate and exceptional initiation of a terror weapon of last resort.

Moreover, the Iraqis sought to augment the significance of the weapon by emphasizing its special, nonstandardized status, as occurred in the sometimes larger-than-life warnings to the Iranians about the power of their secret weapon. They did so by portraying chemicals as a deterrent weapon on the order of nuclear weapons—a "weapon of mass destruction." Finally, any use of chemical weapons—even that restricted to soldiers—continued to attract political attention, consonant with past practices. The treatment of chemical weapons represented anything but a normalization process of the weapon as just one more standard component of the world's arsenal. Even in use its special status was reaffirmed.

The Poor Man's Bomb

Without question, the use of chemical weapons by Iraq and the tepid response of the international community dealt a potentially severe blow to the robustness of the norm, particularly among non-Western nations. Indeed, the failure to take strong measures to enforce the taboo during the Iran-Iraq War was to haunt the international community just a few years later during the Gulf War of 1990–1991. These events, however, could be seen as less than a universal assault on the norm to the degree they represented a continuation of the practice of bifurcating the international community into civilized and uncivilized areas, with the use of chemical weapons in the latter less impermissible in practice than in the former, though still formally taboo. As was the case after the Italo-Ethiopian war, the status of the norm would depend upon how this violation was understood and how these interpretations informed the subsequent course of events, whether in efforts to reinvigorate the norm or in the increasing allure of chemical weapons as a weapon of the weak.

The most significant contemporary development in the chemical weapons discourse has been the active employment of a discourse of the "poor man's bomb" and the inclusion of chemical weapons in a category of "weapons of mass destruction." The designation of chemical weapons as the "poor man's bomb" recalls the demarcation of the rules of statecraft and warfare between the core society of states and the non-industrialized world discussed in previous chapters. Notably, the condescending overtones of this disciplining discourse did not issue solely from the developed world. In his July 1988 statement defending CW, Aziz ventured to argue that "there are different views on this matter from different angles. You are living on a civilized continent. You are living on a peaceful continent."[41] Chemical weapons were indeed a symbol of unacceptable violence—at least among "civilized" countries.

Aziz expanded upon this view a year later. In response to a comment that the parallel between nuclear and chemical weapons (as implied in characterizing the latter as the "poor man's bomb") was a specious one, insofar as the former are deterrent and the latter have never prevented war, Aziz responded:

> The strategic conditions prevailing in Europe cannot be applied to our region. The Eastern and western countries have achieved a balance and war has become virtually impossible. The two sides have therefore shown their readiness to take disarmament measures. The situation in my region bears no resemblance to that. The causes of insecurity have not yet been eliminated. Neither Israel nor Iran has shown sufficient desire to live peacefully with its neighbours. It is therefore unrealistic to ask the Near East states to abandon a particular type of weapon until there is a real prospect of peace. But I do not say that we are opposed to the Paris conferences's objectives. We agree with them. We just hope that parallel disarmament efforts will be developed in both spheres—nuclear and chemical weapons.[42]

The emergent redefinition of chemical weapons as the "poor man's bomb" during the Iran-Iraq War was expressed in a Senate hearing on chemical warfare that occurred after the first confirmation of Iraq's use of chemical weapons against Iran. The chairman of the hearing asked: "The expression "a poor man's nuclear bomb" is sometimes used with regard, to make an analogy, to chemical weapons. Is that an accurate kind of generalization? I mean, are chemical weapons really a poor man's nuclear bomb? Is it that much easier, is it that much more able to be facilitated than nuclear?"[43]

In response, it was affirmed that chemical and biological weapons "are truly weapons of mass destruction, and they serve a deterrent function equivalent to that of nuclear weapons."[44] Senator Percy replied: "We all know that any proliferation of nuclear weapons threatens humanity. Now we are learning that for other, less costly, easier-to-make weapons, far less sophistication is required, although they may pose a threat approaching the horror of nuclear war and nuclear arms. That is why some are calling chemical and biological weapons the poor man's atomic bomb."[45]

The efforts of the non-industrialized world—the Arab countries in particular—to establish gas as a deterrent weapon on the order of nuclear weapons is ironic given the condescending connotations of the "poor man's bomb." This phrase recalls the disciplinary success of the poison taboo and its echoes of disdain for an equalizing weapon of the weak. Low-cost and efficient weapons of destruction are derided as an insufficient entry fee into the club of "civilized" warfare manned by industrial/technological powers. Indeed, J. P. Robinson has argued that the support in the developed world for renewed efforts towards international legal proscriptions against CW were generated by an understanding that chemical and biological weapons offered the potential to poor, weak countries of cheap, powerful force multipliers.[46] In that sense, the CWC and poison taboo have come to serve parallel purposes.

To point out this parallel is not to accede, of course, to the claim that the chemical weapons taboo is simply explained as another exercise of domination against a weapon of the weak. As previous chapters demonstrate, the process of getting to the point where chemical weapons have been defined in such terms has involved far more in the way of genealogical intrigue. There is nothing inevitable about chemical weapons being categorized in this fashion. Indeed, from the Hague through the interwar period chemical weapons occupied a place as potential weapons *of the strong*.

Importantly, the disciplinary implications of the "poor man's bomb" designation have been turned on their head by the situation of this definition within the discourse of "weapons of mass destruction," a category that has been widely accepted in the West. The designation of chemical weapons as a means of destruction on a par with nuclear weapons was given its earliest expression by the United Nations Commission for Conventional Armaments, which in 1948 adopted the following definition of "weapons of mass destruction": "Atomic explosive weapons, radioactive material weapons, lethal chemical and biological weapons, and any weapons developed in the future which have characteristics comparable in destructive effect to those of the atomic bomb or other weapons mentioned above."[47]

Efforts to further inscribe the chemical weapons discourse with this discursive identity gained particular momentum after the Iran-Iraq War, notably at the Paris Conference of January 1989, which had been proposed by the United States to reinvigorate the norm prohibiting CW in the aftermath of the Iran-Iraq War.[48] At this conference, representatives of Arab and other countries drew attention to the danger of nuclear armament, requesting the establishment of a link between nuclear disarmament and chemical disarmament. Some countries, such as Egypt and Algeria, went further, declaring that there could be no question of applying to chemical weapons so discriminatory a rationale as that of the Non-Proliferation Treaty on nuclear weapons. Romania and Syria both underlined the importance of eliminating all weapons of mass destruction, and insisted that a process of prohibiting chemical weapons must be part of a process of prohibiting that entire category, in particular nuclear weapons.[49] As Egypt's foreign minister stated at the conference:

> It would not be logical for the international community to permit to some countries in the most sensitive regions of the world the nuclear option without the least international control, while the same international community demands the total prohibition of chemical weapons. We consider that the progress in the field of the prohibition of chemical weapons is linked to the realization of a parallel prohibition on the level of nuclear weapons.[50]

Especially since the Iran-Iraq War, the special status of chemical weapons has largely been subsumed to this larger category of weapons of mass destruction. For the industrialized world, this category has served as the touchstone for efforts to curb the proliferation of advanced weapons systems in the third world. The Arab world, however, has appropriated the "weapons of mass destruction" discourse in a manner that has made explicit the double standard in the anti-proliferation designs of the industrialized world: whereas the third world is prevented from acquiring "deterrents" such as nuclear or chemical weapons, the Western powers are permitted to retain their weapons of mass destruction—conventional and otherwise—as legitimate tools of statecraft.[51] Israel's undeclared nuclear arsenal is the foremost immediate concern in this strategy of linkage, and it was on these grounds that the Paris Conference polarized opposition between a North anxious about proliferation and a South intent on redressing the selectivity and imbalance in the international proliferation regime.[52] The dichotomy between civilized and uncivilized is a tenuous one indeed if the possession of "weapons of mass destruction" is the key qualification for inclusion or exclusion.

The interpretive reversal in this appropriation of the mass destruction discourse recalls the kinds of operations examined in the genealogical studies of Nietzsche and Foucault. As Foucault wrote: "The successes of history belong to those who are capable of seizing these rules, to replace those who had used them, to disguise themselves so as to pervert them, invert their meaning, and redirect them against those who had initially imposed them."[53]

The Gulf War

A central puzzle to emerge from the Gulf War of 1991, as from World War II, is why chemical weapons were not used. Not only did the political and military leaders of the coalition forces expect that Iraq might employ chemical weapons as a weapon of last resort, but they also suspected that the war would be "chemical probably from the very first hour."[54] After briefly outlining the contending explanations for the non-use of chemical weapons by Iraq, I address the issues that more directly engage the genealogical problematic of the chemical weapons taboo.

The Non-Use of Chemical Weapons

There have been several reports regarding the release of chemical agents during the Gulf War, as well as evidence of traces of chemical materials in the field of operations.[55] Despite these reports, and although suspicions existed regarding chemical agents as a possible source of illnesses of Gulf War veterans (the so-called Gulf War syndrome),[56] U.S. and British officials initially maintained that chemical agents were not intentionally introduced into the combat theater and that Iraq did not employ chemical weapons during the war.[57] The two major explanations offered for the failure of Iraq to use its chemical arsenal are technical or logistical constraints and deterrence.

Some analysts believed that chemical weapons "never got distributed down to the battlefield" from storage sites north of the Euphrates River.[58] Explanations of this sort attributed to logistical miscalculations the failure of Iraq to introduce battlefield weapons. According to this view, Iraqi officers thought that they would have time to deploy the chemical munitions once the ground attack started but were never able to deliver it. In the words of a senior U.S. officer: "I think we caught them with their pants down and they couldn't get it done in time. I think the leadership assumed that their distribution system was better than it was, and that when the attack started they thought they would have a period of days, perhaps even weeks, to infiltrate this stuff down."[59]

Vice-Admiral Stanley Arthur, commander of U.S. naval forces in Desert Storm, was convinced that an abrupt shift of the wind from a southerly direction at the beginning of the ground war was the deciding factor in Iraq's restraint: "I'm pretty sure the poor folks who are sitting in the field looking at the prospect of this stuff blowing right back on them simply decided against them."[60] General Norman Schwarzkopf has speculated that Iraq's hesitancy was related either to the massive destruction of delivery systems, Baghdad's fear of nuclear retaliation, or Iraq's inability to replenish its stocks after chemical-production facilities were bombed at the start of the war.[61] In any case, some U.S. intelligence analysts contended that they never had solid evidence that Iraqi president Saddam Hussein had given his field commanders at the corps or division level permission to use chemicals, though some authors have claimed otherwise.[62]

It was not until June 1996 that the Pentagon publicly acknowledged evidence (provided to the United States by the UN in 1991) that chemical agents were present in the theater of operations during the Gulf War. Shortly after the war American combat engineers blew up an Iraqi munitions bunker near the southern Iraqi village of Kamisiyah, and UN inspections in October 1991 revealed that the bunker had contained chemical weapons including sarin and mustard.[63] These findings belie the argument that logistical problems prevented the forward deployment of battlefield chemical weapons, though the paucity of other incidents suggests that such deployments might well have been very limited. In any case, these revelations do not refute the U.S. claim that Iraq did not intentionally use chemical weapons during the Gulf War.

We must also account for why CW was not waged by other means. It has been claimed that Iraq did not have the technical capacity to deliver chemicals in the form of missile warheads, and that Iraq did not have enough missiles to make a chemical attack effective.[64] The former Iraqi head of military intelligence, however, has maintained that Iraq did have operational Scud missiles armed with chemical warheads.[65] The United Nations Special Commission (UNSCOM), which has the mandate of carrying out the provisions of UN Security Council Resolution 687, has revealed that Iraq declared it had weaponized chemical weapons in the form of aerial bombs and missile warheads.[66] Political restraints—rather than merely logistical ones—were therefore clearly decisive in preventing the use of chemical weapons by Iraq. What was the nature of these political constraints?

The Mass Destruction Threshold

As a prelude to the Iraqi invasion of Kuwait that began the Gulf War, Saddam Hussein announced in April 1990 that Iraq had advanced chemical weapons and provocatively declared: "By God, we will burn half of Israel, if it tries to harm or attack Iraq, or any part of Iraq. We do not need a nuclear bomb. We possess the binary chemical. Whoever threatens us with nuclear weapons, we will destroy him with chemical weapons."[67]

This statement can be interpreted as part of the effort to extend the taboo against using chemical weapons into a deterrent for war in general by explicitly linking chemical weapons to nuclear weapons and thereby defining chemical weapons as deterrent weapons.[68] Such statements could have been interpreted simply as threats to use chemicals, but the primary intent seems to have been to forestall the use of any weapons of mass destruction in a possible conflict with the U.S.-led coalition forces. Thus in August 1990 Aziz remarked in a little-noted statement that Iraq would not use chemical weapons unless the United States used nuclear weapons first.[69]

Chemical weapons were established as a threshold by both sides in the Gulf War, a weapon whose use would change the character of the war. For the coalition, the use of chemical weapons by Iraq would invite the possibility of unrestrained retaliation. According to a U.S. officer, chemicals would not have changed the outcome of the war but would have had a substantial impact on the peace, because Iraq would have broken the global taboo against chemical weapons and provoked a massive response by the United States.[70] In this respect, the chemical weapons taboo functioned in the same way it had during World War II, as a threshold of acute political importance that set the boundaries of conduct even in war.

Public exchanges in the initial days of the crisis and during the period preceding the attack by coalition forces illustrate these developments. In August 1990, Iraq's envoy to Greece warned that "we possess very destructive chemical weapons and we will use them if attacked."[71] President Bush declared that "the use of chemical weapons . . . would be intolerable and would be dealt with very, very severely."[72] The British, warning against the "madness" of using chemical weapons, indicated that such use would be met with a strong response.[73] Continuing the line of ambiguous threat, U.S. Secretary of State Cheney warned Iraq that "the U.S. military has a wide range of capabilities that could be brought to bear against Iraq should Saddam Hussein be foolish enough to try to use chemical weapons on American forces."[74]

As the outbreak of war came closer, Iraqi National Assembly Speaker Sa'di Mahdi Salih announced in December 1990 that "the Iraqi Army will use all types of its weapons to defend itself," adding that while Iraq does not possess nuclear weapons, chemical weapons are also effective.[75] The next day U.S. Secretary of Defense Cheney announced that "were Saddam Hussein foolish enough to use weapons of mass destruction, the U.S. response would be absolutely overwhelming and it would be devastating."[76]

This understanding was reiterated as an attack on Iraq grew more likely. At a meeting in Geneva on January 9, U.S. Secretary of State James Baker delivered to Aziz a letter for Saddam Hussein from President Bush, in which Bush indicated that Iraqi use of chemical weapons would result in the coalition adopting as a war aim the elimination of the regime in Baghdad. On February 8, 1991, senior administration officials let it be known that the United States would target Saddam Hussein and his ruling circle if Iraq violated the Geneva Protocol by introducing chemical agents.[77] On February 20, a senior Bush administration official involved in the final preparations for a ground war said that major use of chemical weapons would cross a "red line beyond which all previous bets are off. It's a red line that would compel the coalition to change its own objectives—adopting, for instance, a march on Baghdad to find Saddam and eliminate his regime."[78]

According to the Saudi commander of the joint forces, Hussein knew full well that should he use chemical warfare, "it would cause the total destruction of Iraq."[79] Allied forces went so far as to attempt to discourage front-line artillery crews from obeying possible orders to fire chemical shells, notifying them in leaflets that they would be pursued individually after the war as war criminals.[80]

The coalition never explicitly threatened to use chemical or nuclear weapons in response to a possible chemical attack, and a chemical response in particular seemed to be ruled out. As early as August 1990, General Michael Dugan, U.S. Air Force chief of staff, stated that "we would avoid in every possible circumstance even talking about deploying or using chemical weapons. We've made a national policy of getting rid of [them]."[81] Also in August, Israeli leader Yitzhak Shamir was moved to make clear that he did not support the remark of one of his ministers that Israel could produce chemicals as an answer to Iraqi threats.[82] Cheney's August 1990 statement included the comment that "I cannot conceive of a situation in which the United States would want to use chemical weapons."[83] As French prime minister Michel Rocard stated, any use of CW to crush Iraqi rebels would be "unbearable for the international community."[84]

Administration officials reported that the idea of using nuclear or chemical weapons had "never been on the table" in discussions involving top policy makers, though some junior military officers had advocated threatening or even using tactical nuclear weapons to save soldiers' lives.[85] Nuclear and chemical arms were not incorporated into U.S. planning for a possible military engagement.[86] A senior Arab official confirmed that the coalition allies had prepared specific plans for retaliation if Iraq waged chemical war, maintaining that "We'll use the unimaginable, short of nuclear weapons."[87]

Still, the warnings of the coalition members were intended to cultivate ambiguity as to whether the threat of massive retaliation might include "weapons of mass destruction." According to Secretary of Defense Richard Cheney, Deputy National Security Advisor Robert Gates, and Chairman of the Joint Chiefs of Staff General Colin Powell, the coalition's threat was left deliberately vague so that Saddam Hussein might believe the coalition would respond to a chemical attack with nuclear weapons. This was so even though the issue of using nuclear weapons was never even discussed, and the U.S. officials did not believe nuclear weapons ever would have been used. Cheney indicated that the threat was meant "to convey the message to Saddam Hussein that he was much better off if he never, never crossed over that line of actually using chemical weapons against us."[88]

The dominant view of the U.S. administration, as articulated by CIA Director William Webster, was that the use of conventional weapons was understandable to other nations in the region, but "when you get Western use of chemical weapons or other non-conventional weapons, I think you invite a new dimension that may carry heavy costs . . . in future relationships," and the United States couldn't proceed in ways others would find appalling.[89]

Whatever the exact nature of a response to the use of chemical weapons might have been, the threshold drawn by the issue of CW could not have been more plain. General Wafic al Sammarai claimed that he told Saddam Hussein very clearly that should he use chemical weapons the coalition would use their nuclear weapons. In light of this threshold, Foreign Minister Aziz states simply that the Iraqi leadership did not think it wise to use "such kind of weapons in such kind of a war, with such an enemy."[90]

The Iraqi strategy of linking chemical to nuclear weapons could be said to have failed in the sense that it worked only to prevent the use of chemical weapons and did not serve as a more general deterrent to war itself. To the extent that an objective of the Iraqis was to prevent the use of nuclear weapons by coalition forces, however, the linkage between chemical and nuclear weapons was successful. Nuclear weapons were as subject to a taboo against use as chemical weapons, and the weapons-of-mass destruction discourse during the conflict reinforced these restraints. The coalition could no more use its most powerful weapons than the Iraqis could employ their "weapons of mass destruction." Indeed, had the coalition used nuclear weapons, Iraq likely would have responded with its own weapons of mass destruction. According to a UNSCOM report, Iraq has stated "that authority to launch biological and chemical warheads was pre-delegated in the event that Baghdad was hit by nuclear weapons during the Gulf War."[91]

Nuclear and chemical weapons, however, were not the only inhabitants of the mass destruction category during the conflict. The designation of unacceptable weapons as those that have "mass destruction" capabilities is a remarkable development because it invites the question of why other enormously destructive "conventional" weapons are not included in this category. Indeed, the current Western version of what counts as a "weapon of mass destruction" is not universally accepted. The Soviets, for their part, had defined high-precision conventional munitions as weapons of mass destruction in the military literature of the 1980s.[92] Precisely this kind of contestation of the category emerged during the Gulf War.

Iraq's envoy to the United Nations, Abdul Amir Anbari, hinted Iraq would be justified in using chemical weapons by drawing a parallel between CW and allied bombing raids. He observed that "we consider use of mass destructive weapons against Iraq would justify Iraq to use, unfortunately, mass destructive weapons." Answering a question by the British ambassador whether Iraq would respect the international treaty prohibiting the use of chemical weapons, Anbari responded that his government had made a commitment not to use chemical weapons unless weapons of mass destruction were used against Iraq. He added that, in his opinion, if the massive bombing from high altitude continued, these bombs could then be considered weapons of mass destruction.[93] Hussein underlined this threat of equivalence while responding to a question of whether Iraq would use chemical weapons: "We will use weapons that match those used against us by our enemy . . . weapons that are equivalent to those used against us."[94]

In the end, the disjuncture between the category of weapons of mass destruction and the capabilities of modern "conventional" weapons has remained at the margins of the discourse on acceptable weapons. So too, however, has the reverse operation of questioning the unacceptability of nuclear and chemical weapons as uncontested members of the club. This is not to say that the view has never been expressed privately that to die by chemical weapons is neither more nor less horrible than to die by bullet or flame.[95] Only rarely, however, has that view been expressed in public discourse. A singular example during this period had the intent of condemning all weapons rather than legitimizing chemical weapons. As an editorial in a Jordanian newspaper stated, "Killing a man is condemned, irrespective of the means used. In this regard, an old rifle, hand-to-hand fighting, nuclear bombs, and mustard gas are all equal."[96]

The crucial point for the purposes of this book is that the inclusion of chemical weapons in the mass destruction discourse represents the unparalleled possibility of an extension of the category of proscribed weapons, rather than the historical pattern of constant erosion. Thus, even though the common wisdom that emerged from the Gulf War was the assessment that chemical weapons had failed to live up to the deterrent status of the "poor man's bomb," the overall thrust of the weapons discourse has been to try to expand the definition of unacceptable weapons rather than to restrict it.[97]

A Standard Anomaly?

The linking of chemical to nuclear weapons in an effort to delegitimize them as weapons of mass destruction is thus a novel development not only in the chemical weapons discourse but also from the historical perspective of the reception of weapons innovations. There are, however, parallels between the role of chemical weapons in the Iran-Iraq War and the Italo-Ethiopian War, and between World War II and the Iran-Iraq and Gulf Wars. Assessments of the utility of chemical weapons and the robustness of international norms that were made in the aftermath of the Iran-Iraq War bear a striking resemblance to the kinds of interpretations voiced after the Italo-Ethiopian conflict. As Charles Floweree points out: "Although the failure of Iraq's chemical weapons to play any role in the Persian Gulf War has undoubtedly dimmed the luster of these weapons as "the poor man's atomic bomb," against an enemy less well equipped defensively and less powerfully armed than the coalition forces, chemical weapons can play a significant role, as was demonstrated in the Iran-Iraq War."[98]

Do such assessments herald a new cycle of efforts to standardize chemical weapons, at least for use against "uncivilized" nations? The position of Iran is particularly illustrative, if ultimately ambiguous, in this regard. In January 1989, the Iranian foreign minister stated that Iran does not have such weapons and "does not need them because we do not want to use them." Velayati also said that "these are horrible weapons which nobody can imagine being used on modern battlefields. The main reason why we are opposing their use is that they kill civilians, soldiers, children and old people indiscriminately."[99]

Despite such statements, Iran's official disavowals of their possession of chemical weapons have become increasingly suspect, for these were not the only lessons that Iran learned in its war with Iraq. In the aftermath of the war with Iraq, Rafsanjani told the Revolutionary Guards:

> With regard to chemical, bacteriological, and radiological weapons training, it was made very clear during the war that these weapons are very decisive. It was also made clear that the moral teachings of the world are not very effective when war reaches a serious stage and the world does not respect its own resolutions and closes its eyes to the violations and all the aggressions which are committed in the battlefield. . . . We should fully

equip ourselves both in the offensive and defensive use of chemical, bacteriological, and radiological weapons.[100]

Although Iran has signed the Chemical Weapons Convention banning the development, production, stockpiling, transfer, and use of chemical weapons, it has not ratified the agreement, and there are indications that Iran is pursuing a chemical weapons capability.[101] They do not, however, regard chemical weapons as simply another usable weapon to be added to their arsenal. Rafsanjani again: "Chemical and biological weapons are the poor man's atomic bombs and can easily be produced. We should at least consider them for our defense. . . . Although the use of such weapons is inhuman, the war taught us that international laws are only drops of ink on paper."[102] Another senior Iranian official adds: "We reserve the right for ourselves to get technological know-how necessary to confront the chemical agents our enemies might use against us."[103]

The characterization of chemical weapons as the poor man's equivalent to nuclear weapons represents a definitional struggle to transcend on the cheap the demarcation between the industrialized and nonindustrialized worlds. Although there are parallels between the use of chemical weapons by Italy in 1935–1936 and Iraq in the 1980s, a crucial difference is that the allure of CW has changed. Whereas chemical weapons were previously seen as effective weapons that would actually be used, their "effectiveness" now derives as much or more from the political value of manipulating the threat that they might be used—a threat that is politically significant only because the accumulated practice of non-use has resulted in the assumption that such weapons should never be used. This assumption is the source of the unusual status accorded to chemical weapons. It is also the source of the central tension that has characterized the negotiations over a global ban on the possession and production of chemical weapons, and it accounts for the resistance of certain nations to signing the Chemical Weapons Convention.

The Chemical Weapons Convention

Spurred by the end of the Cold War between the U.S. and Soviet Union and by concerns over CW generated by the Iran-Iraq War and Gulf War, agreement was finally reached in September 1992 on a Chemical Weapons Convention, after years of negotiation.[104] The document was opened for signature in January 1993, and by January 1997, it had been signed by 160 nations, 66 of which had deposited their instruments of ratification.

The CWC entered into force April 29, 1997—180 days after the date of the deposit of the sixty-fifth instrument of ratification.

The convention is a significant extension of the prohibition against the use of chemical weapons embodied in the Geneva Protocol. The CWC's provisions—including its reaffirmation of the protocol's ban on use—are not subject to the kind of reservations that rendered the protocol a no-first-use pledge by some forty states.[105] The convention further extends the prohibition on use to the production, transfer, and possession of chemical weapons, and even prohibits signatories from assisting others in engaging in such proscribed activities. As contained in Article I:

1. Each State Party to this Convention undertakes never under any circumstances:

a) To develop, produce, otherwise acquire, stockpile or retain chemical weapons, or transfer, directly or indirectly, chemical weapons to anyone;

b) To use chemical weapons;

c) To engage in military preparations to use chemical weapons;

d) To assist, encourage or induce, in any way, anyone to engage in any activity prohibited to a State Party under this Convention.

These measures of the CWC are to be backed up by intrusive verification procedures, as well as by the provision of defensive assistance to parties facing chemical attacks or the threat thereof. Moreover, Article XII provides for "measures to redress a situation and to ensure compliance, including sanctions." Such means include referring situations of noncompliance to the United Nations Security Council for remedial action.

These stipulations not only redress lacunae in the Geneva Protocol that many have felt were critical for a truly effective prohibition, but they are also indicative of a more robust taboo insofar as they include far-reaching disciplinary measures to invite and even compel compliance. As one observer has noted, "By criminalizing all of the activities associated with procuring chemical weapons, the CWC provides an indisputable, concrete basis for action by the international community."[106] Provisions for the regularized punishment of the violation of prohibitionary social norms is both a primary means of accomplishing their instantiation and a signal of their strength through the encouragement of self-discipline. As Foucault writes: "Disciplinary punishment is, in the main, isomorphic with obligation itself; it is not so much the vengeance of an outraged law as its repetition, its reduplicated insistence."[107] The criminalization of stipulated activities thus also has the productive effect of defining criminals—"outlaw" or pariah states who do not conform to the legal regime.[108]

Beyond simple punishment, then, the surveillance functions to be taken up by the Organization for the Prohibition of Chemical Weapons (OPCW) will seek to create conforming international subjects by a variety of techniques that provide an international analogue to those outlined in Foucault's analysis of the operations of institutions of disciplinary power. According to Foucault, such power

> refers individual actions to a whole that is at once a field of comparison, a space of differentiation and the principle of a rule to be followed. It differentiates individuals from one another, in terms of the following overall rule: that the rule be made to function as a minimal threshold, as an average to be respected or as an optimum towards which one must move. It measures in quantitative terms and hierarchizes in terms of value the abilities, the level, the 'nature' of individuals. It introduces, through this 'value-giving' measure, the constraint of a conformity that must be achieved. Lastly, it traces the limit that will define difference in relation to all other differences, the external frontier of the abnormal. . . . The perpetual penalty that traverses all points and supervises every instant in the disciplinary institutions compares, differentiates, hierarchizes, homogenizes, excludes. In short, it *normalizes*.[109]

Acceptance of the bureaucratic routines of the OPCW will have significant effects. The rendering of practices to abide by the chemical weapons taboo as routine technical issues through the operation of the OPCW will signify that the reign of the chemical weapons taboo has become less overt but more telling than achieved through more visible events. It represents a potential movement of the issue of chemical weapons away from the political and towards the legal and technical as it becomes routine.

An important contemporary adjunct to the disciplinary measures of the international community to police the chemical weapons taboo is the enforced disarmament of Iraq's weapons of mass destruction in the aftermath of the Gulf War. The UN Security Council Resolution 687, adopted in April 1991, mandates the destruction of Iraq's nuclear, chemical, biological, and ballistic missile weapons capabilities. To ensure compliance, Resolution 687 demands that Iraq submit declarations of the locations, amounts, and types of proscribed materials, submit to inspections carried out by a Special Commission (UNSCOM), and agree to establish a regime of future ongoing monitoring.[110] Sanctions enacted by the Security Council against Iraq (Resolution 661 of 1990) will be lifted only upon satisfactory compliance with these demands.

These measures seek to impose on Iraq a principle of "compulsory visibility" through the technique of inspection under international supervision, and they provide a disciplinary companion to the verification regime of the CWC through the designation and punishment of an international criminal.[111] A persistent feature of this delegitimizing process has been the castigation of chemical weapons as the weapon of the weak and of the possessors of such weapons as unworthy international citizens. In ratification hearings of the CWC in the U.S. Senate, it was stated that "chemical weapons, to be blunt, are a poor man's weapon, not a rich man's," and that "a rich nation like the United States should seek to maintain and strengthen the barriers against the proliferation of cheap weapons of mass destruction."[112]

Refining and Defining Lethal War

An additional feature of the CWC is its inclusion of nonlethal agents in its prohibition of chemical weapons. The wording of the Geneva Protocol gave rise to ambiguities as to whether nonlethal substances such as riot-control agents were included in the prohibited category of "asphyxiating or deleterious gases." Even though the United States did not ratify the protocol until 1975, successive U.S. leaders had signalled their adherence to the prohibition on the first-use of lethal chemical weapons.[113] Still, although most nations since the League of Nations Disarmament Conference in the 1930s indicated that they regarded even nonlethal agents as prohibited by the Geneva Protocol, the United States did not. It was on the basis of these ambiguities that U.S. officials argued during the Vietnam War that its use of riot-control agents and defoliants did not constitute chemical warfare as prohibited by the protocol. Article I(5) of the CWC attempts to close this loophole by unambiguously stating that "each State Party undertakes not to use riot control agents as a method of warfare."

The definition of chemical weapons according to the CWC is contained in Article II(1), and includes the following, together or separately:

a) Toxic chemicals and their precursors, except where intended for purposes not prohibited under this Convention, as long as the types and quantities are consistent with such purposes;
b) Munitions and devices, specifically designed to cause death or other harm through the toxic properties of those toxic chemicals specified in subparagraph (a), which would be released as a result of the employment of such munitions and devices;

c) Any equipment specifically designed for use directly in connection with the employment of munitions and devices specified in subparagraph (b).

Toxic chemicals in turn are defined in Article II (2) as meaning "any chemical which through its chemical action on life processes can cause death, temporary incapacitation or permanent harm to humans or animals." Interestingly, because of the way toxic chemicals are defined for the purposes of the convention, herbicides are by definition excluded.[114] The preamble to the CWC does, however, expressly recognize "the prohibition, embodied in the pertinent agreements and relevant principles of international law, of the use of herbicides as a method of warfare."

Walter Krutzsch and Ralf Trapp have noted that this way of defining a weapon departs from the practice of most other international weapons agreements, in which "a weapon is usually considered to be the entirety of its components, and characterized by more or less objective criteria." In the case of chemical weapons under the CWC, however, "each of the components of a chemical weapons system in itself already has to be regarded as the prohibited weapon."[115] This had to be done in order to take account of binary chemical weapons, which contain separated chemical compounds that become lethal chemical weapons only after the weapon is fired.

Significantly, the principle behind the CWC's definition of chemical weapons is not based on the objective characteristics of the materials but on the intent behind the use of chemicals.[116] The reasoning here is to recognize that virtually any chemical could be defined as "toxic" in sufficient dosages and to accommodate peaceful applications of dual-use chemicals. A significant lesson drawn from the actual experience of chemical warfare is that the fog of war does not easily permit of fine distinctions between lethal and nonlethal chemical agents. Supposedly nonlethal agents such as tear gases can be lethal in sufficient dosages. Conversely, agents such as mustard gas typically cause blisters on their victims rather than death; therefore, defining prohibited substances as lethal chemicals could exclude mustard. What matters is the concentration of the agents involved. To take into account these features:

What remained, in the end, was a definition based on the intent to abuse the toxic properties of a chemical, or the intent to use a chemical system made up of comparatively non-toxic chemicals to produce a toxic chemical, for chemical weapons purposes. . . . That approach leads initially to covering all toxic chemicals, and all precursor chemicals for them, and then excluding from the definition those which are used for purposes not prohibited.[117]

In other words, to secure an absolute prohibition on the possession of chemical weapons, the relevant materials had to be defined in terms of how they are intended to be used. The logic of defining chemical agents that are prohibited from possession parallels the logic of the usual restraints on the use of other weapons (that is, do not ban weapons technologies themselves but only certain uses). This intriguing development demonstrates the significant accomplishment embodied in a ban on the possession of chemical weapons. A ban on tanks, for example, would not incur the same difficulties—one would not have to ban only tanks "intended for use in war," as that is the sole reason tanks exist. Chemical weapons, by contrast, are the ultimate "dual-use" technology, and they present difficulties for prohibiting possession far beyond that of many other weapons technologies.

The prohibitions on the use of nonlethal agents in warfare by the CWC represent a significant institutional refinement of the definition of the category of chemical weapons. However, controversies over the use of nonlethal agents have not been entirely eliminated. Although the convention prohibits the use of riot-control agents as a method of warfare, Article II stipulates that the prohibition of chemical weapons does not extend to the use of toxic chemicals "intended for purposes not prohibited under this Convention." Articles II(9)(c) and II(9)(d) define such purposes and include "military purposes not connected with the use of chemical weapons and not dependent on the use of the toxic properties of chemicals as a method of warfare" and "law enforcement purposes including domestic riot control."

This formulation leaves a grey area concerning what constitutes "law enforcement" and "a method of warfare." The policy of the United States on nonlethal agents had been guided by Executive Order No. 11850 of April 1975 forbidding "the first use of riot control agents in war except in defensive military modes to save lives," which had been interpreted to include operations such as evacuations and control of rioting prisoners. In June 1994, President Clinton transmitted to the U.S. Senate his administration's review of the impact of the CWC on Executive Order No. 11850, indicating that the United States interprets the CWC prohibition on riot-control agents (RCAs) as a method of warfare to mean the following:

> The CWC applies only to the use of RCAs in international or internal armed conflict. Other peacetime uses of RCAs, such as normal peacekeeping operations, humanitarian and disaster relief missions, counter-terrorist and hostage rescue operations, and non-combatant rescue operations conducted outside such conflicts are unaffected by the Convention.

The CWC does not apply to all uses of RCAs in time of armed conflict. Use of RCAs solely against noncombatants for law enforcement, riot control, or other noncombat purposes would not be considered as a 'method of warfare' and therefore would not be prohibited. Accordingly, the CWC does not prohibit the use of RCAs in riot control situations in areas under direct US military control, including against rioting prisoners of war, and to protect convoys from civil disturbances, terrorists, and paramilitary organization in rear areas outside the zone of immediate combat.

The CWC does prohibit the use of RCAs solely against combatants. In addition, according to the current international understanding, the CWC's prohibition on the use of RCAs as a 'method of warfare' also precludes the use of RCAs even for humanitarian purposes in situations where combatants and noncombatants are intermingled, such as the rescue of downed air crews, passengers, and escaping prisoners and situations where civilians are being used to mask or screen attacks. However, were the international understanding of this issue to change, the United States would not consider itself bound by this position.[118]

The issue of the status of nonlethal agents is revealing for several reasons. On one level, permitting the use of riot-control agents for domestic purposes while proscribing nonlethal methods in warfare establishes the chemical weapons taboo as embodied in the CWC as a distinctively *international* norm in the literal sense: the same activity permitted in the domestic context (the use of irritant agents) is prohibited in the international context. Significantly, with the enactment of domestic penal legislation as required by Article VII of the CWC, activities prohibited by the CWC are to be regarded as violations of domestic law.

Furthermore, the extension of the chemical weapons taboo to nonlethal chemicals in warfare raises questions about the purpose of the use of force and the objectives of warfare. As we have seen, this issue has been involved in the question of banishing CW since the debates at the Hague Conferences at the turn of the century: does banning nonlethal methods of warfare constitute an advance towards the elimination of the violence of warfare, or does it actually prevent warfare from being conducted on a more humane basis?

The CWC will be at the core of this debate in the face of ongoing technological investigations of alternative means of warfare. Simultaneous with the conclusion of the CWC, there has been a surge of interest in nonlethal means of warfare. Among the projects under consideration in the U.S. and Russian militaries as possible nonlethal technologies are electronic, audio, laser, and other means. Various chemical-related methods also have been under investigation, including chemical immobilizers, neural inhibitors, and anti-material compounds, but such means run head-on into the CWC's prohibition on nonlethal chemicals.[119] This conflict has not gone unnoticed. An article in a Moscow newspaper has argued that international agreements "are a serious obstacle to the development and application of chemical and biological means of nonlethal action." On the same issue, a Russian general has contended that the CWC does not prohibit the use of "nonlethal chemical weapons." Although he apparently had in mind antimaterial methods such as agents for destroying internal-combustion engines, he did claim that "the text of the convention does not give a clear answer as to whether the use of immobilizers as chemical weapons is prohibited."[120] Thus, while the CWC's prohibition of nonlethal means of warfare at first glance would seem to eliminate the ambiguities surrounding the taboo as incurred by the Geneva Protocol, it might nevertheless occupy the center of controversy, given the searches underway by military establishments for new missions in a changing world.

These developments have significant implications. On the one hand, the exclusion of nonlethal chemicals from war reproduces the division of the political world into distinct domestic and international realms. On this level, the institutionalized definition of chemical weapons indicates an abjuring of one avenue for the domestication of the violence of international space. War is to occupy a distinct space, characterized by parameters of violence unique to the international.

On the other hand, it is entirely possible that this space of violence might be drawn increasingly narrowly. Military establishments investigating nonlethal technologies are interested in such means for operations "short of war." As such, the employment of nonlethal chemicals is not necessarily foreclosed from what would presently count as international operations—warfare—if those events themselves come to be redescribed in terms other than war such as humanitarian interventions or the policing of international crimes such as terrorism.

A Discriminatory Universal Regime?

The CWC is the most comprehensive and intrusive arms control agreement ever achieved. Several countries have been unwilling to sign the document, however—most notably a contingent of Arab states including Egypt, Syria, Libya, Jordan, Chad, Iraq, and the Sudan.[121] By transforming the chemical weapons taboo from a norm against use into a prohibition on possession, the convention is perceived to perpetuate a discriminatory disarmament regime by denying the non-nuclear nations a war-preventing weapon on par with nuclear weapons, while Israel in particular remains outside the Treaty on the Non-Proliferation of Nuclear Weapons. The effort to extend the taboo against chemical weapons has brought to the surface the disparity between the delegitimizing implications of the category of "weapons of mass destruction" and the continued legitimacy of the possession of nuclear weapons for some nations as a tool of politics, if not war. This disparity is the source of the resistance to the discipline of the discriminatory mass destruction proliferation regime, and it is the axis upon which rests truly universal acceptance of the extension of the chemical weapons taboo to even the possession of such weapons.

Taken to its extreme, the definitional linkage of chemical to nuclear weapons through the discursive usurpation of the "weapons of mass destruction" category could have deleterious implications for the robustness of the chemical weapons taboo. The non-nuclear nations could aim to subvert the anti-proliferation designs of the West by emphasizing the unwillingness of the nuclear nations to give up their mass destruction weapon of choice and might thereby justify the possession of their own mass destructive arsenal. Moreover, the disciplinary discourse of "civilization" could conceivably be turned on its head to justify the use of chemical weapons. If it is accepted by all that the non-industrialized nations are not yet "civilized," why would the "civilized" world find so disturbing the contained use of chemical weapons within and among such "barbaric" nations? Finally, the linking of chemical weapons with nuclear weapons could be taken as an erosion of the nuclear weapons taboo, insofar as violations of the former have been more prevalent than the latter.

In contrast, however, the discursive operation of situating chemical weapons in the category of mass destruction has the effect of reinforcing the illegitimacy of CW. As mentioned previously, acceptance of the legitimacy of the "weapons of mass destruction" discourse invites the question of why other enormously destructive "conventional" weapons are not included in this category. Rather than being implicated in a reopening of questions about the relative humanity of chemicals vis-à-vis other weapons, this discursive move portends the possibility of a further rupture in the value-neutral weapons discourse.

Moreover, inclusion of chemical weapons in this category constitutes an utterly unique development in the history of the legitimacy of weapons technologies. Quite unlike the usual pattern of receding moral restraints on weapons, the "weapons of mass destruction" discourse is in one respect an unparalleled extension of the category of illegitimate weapons. Rather than banishing the moral rejection of chemical weapons into the quaint dustbin of protests against new weapons technologies, the invention of nuclear weapons has perpetuated and reinforced the chemical weapons taboo via the discourse of mass destruction. The inclusion of chemical weapons in the category of weapons of mass destruction is in this way indicative of a further closure of the once-controversial humanitarian aspect of the chemical weapons discourse. The invention of nuclear weapons has to this point not made gas seem less horrible and more humane.

Finally, while the linkage to nuclear weapons could serve to justify the possession of chemical weapons as a deterrent, the linkage to nuclear weapons has not legitimized the actual use of chemical weapons. This development plays on the central paradox of the deterrent function of nuclear weapons—their political and symbolic value as deterrents depends on their status as being too horrible to use. Whereas the possession of nuclear weapons has maintained legitimacy for some members of the international system, their use in warfare has not. Nuclear weapons derive a degree of legitimacy not from belief in their ability to win wars but belief in their ability to prevent wars. If anything, the taboo against using nuclear weapons is in all likelihood stronger than the taboo against using chemical weapons.[122] Thus, while the coupling with nuclear weapons is not unambiguously a positive development for the robustness of the chemical weapons stigma, on balance the effect has been to further remove chemical weapons from the arsenal of standard and acceptable means of warfare. The use of chemical weapons has become no less controversial a political event by virtue of the invention of nuclear weapons.

Still, the universality of this delegitimizing operation with respect to chemical weapons and perhaps biological weapons as well ultimately seems contingent upon a corresponding decrease in the allure of possessing nuclear weapons. This remains a primary axis of contestation concerning the universal acceptability of a prohibitionary norm against chemical warfare.

Significantly, then, the identities of the nations who have expressed the desire to eliminate war by the threat of destruction has shifted from those who opposed a ban on chemical weapons (the United States at the Hague) to those who support it, if only in the context of a prohibitionary regime based on the category of weapons of mass destruction (most notably some Arab nations). This reversal of opposition has occurred because chemical weapons over time have been redefined from a weapon of the strong to a weapon of the weak.

The ground upon which the chemical weapons taboo is being contested has shifted from the military advantages of the *use* of chemical weapons as a technology of war to their *possession* as an instrument in the mass destruction toolbox of war-preventing diplomacy. My argument is that this shift is indicative of the consolidation of the taboo. It is no longer deemed legitimate to argue, and few even think, that the use of chemical weapons is acceptable, much less humane.

On Technology and Morality

Every technology of significance to us implies a set of political commitments . . . what appear to be merely instrumental choices are better seen as choices about the form of society we continually build, choices about the kind of people we want to be.
—Langdon Winner

The use of chemical weapons stands out in the minds of most as an especially egregious infliction of humanity's technology upon itself. The study of the origins, development, and functions of the chemical weapons taboo reveals the value of a genealogical analysis of meanings which searches out the relations of dominance and resistance, the processes of identity construction, and the contingencies involved in the operation of a moral discourse. While exhibiting all these things, the chemical weapons taboo also testifies to the genuine moral rejection of a means of modern warfare—a protest that arose at a particular historical juncture when people questioned the untrammelled application of technological warfare among the advanced technological states of the "civilized" world.

The chemical weapons taboo arose from, and was implicated in, larger historical developments concerning international politics and the conduct of modern industrial warfare, and in this respect the taboo differs sharply from the usual protests against novel weapons encountered in the history of warfare. The first institutionalized ban on CW was a product of the golden era of efforts to limit warfare through international law. The emergence and rise of societal questioning of the institution of war during this period coincided with the self-conscious identification of leading nations as members of an international society of civilized states whose conduct with one another could be regularized in ways that would distinguish them from mere savages in an international state of nature.

This heyday of efforts to restrict international war was no doubt in part a result of the increasing destructiveness of modern industrial means of conducting warfare. But the efforts to contain the horrors of warfare were not simply determined by considerations of technology. From the order of Christendom to the Western society of civilized states, and, more recently, to the industrially advanced liberal democracies of modern capitalism, a normative dimension of these orders has been to put the conduct of relations among the members of the club on a different footing from the relations with less privileged areas of the world, however defined.

Such pretensions of civilization were dealt a shattering blow with the savagery of World War I. The unquestioned faith in technology as a unilinear force for the progress of humankind was ruptured. Chemical weapons, which had been temporarily singled out during the Hague's grand deliberations on international arbitration and the law of war, became an effective scapegoat for the disillusionment with the promise of technology that followed World War I. Throughout continued efforts to reinscribe the prohibition buttressed by a genuine moral opposition to CW by important political figures, chemical weapons have been implicated in the gradual delegitimation of major war among the primary technological powers by serving as a most potent symbolic threshold of the limits of acceptable conduct.

In this respect, the protests against the introduction of the category of chemical weapons have differed from the opposition to past weapons. The larger international normative contexts concerning the value of technology and legitimacy of violence, within which particular weapons protests have been situated, has transformed. A comparison with the experience of the reception of firearms illustrates the difference. The introduction of firearms occasioned a variety of arguments against their use, from arguments of efficiency to moral protests against this new contrivance that surely issued from the devil himself. But despite such protests the allure of guns and cannon proved too seductive, and, as J. R. Hale has documented, these new forms of destruction came to be extolled and admired as thrilling, impressive contraptions expressive of the exuberance of a new age of invention and discovery. Roaring cannon were said to be a "pleasure to behold."[1] Guns provided ammunition for those arguing on moderns' side of the ancients versus the moderns controversy that was just beginning around the fifteenth century. Technological wonders such as firearms fueled the contention that wisdom was to be found not in the observations of ancient sages but through modern scientific knowledge and finding out for oneself by doing—that is, by technology.

The significance of the symbolic effect of the chemical weapons discourse lay in large part in the fact that the protests against this weapon occurred during the first serious questioning of the Enlightenment faith in progress. The protests against chemical weapons took place during a rupture in the "dare to know" tradition of the Enlightenment and all the intimations of progress it had previously implied. A primary expression of disillusionment with that promise of progress was the first serious societal questioning of the nature, value, and inevitability of warfare. The introduction of firearms took place in an age almost innocent of pacifism, where "war was thought to be necessary to the state and good for the individual."[2] Although the end of the nineteenth century witnessed a gradual challenge to the notion that war was healthy, natural, necessary, and unavoidable, it was the shock of World War I that dealt a more decisive blow to an unthinking faith in the progress of "civilized" Western society. Commitment to the technological society of modernity has remained dominant, but chemical weapons occupied a space of contestation that presented a challenge to the naturalizing discourse of war and technological progress.

Chemical weapons appeared at a germinal moment that witnessed an emerging awareness that a civilization based upon progress in technology might be turned upon itself. This category of weapons was impregnated with institutionalized symbolic value. Chemical weapons portended that humankind might already had reached the moment of ultimate self-mastery implied by technology—the very capability to decide the fate of the species itself. Chemical weapons themselves never actually lived up to such omnicidal capabilities, certainly no more so than other means such as high explosives, but as a presage of such a capability they served as a forerunner to nuclear weapons. Gas has served as a litmus test and symbol of unease in the twentieth century that humankind might actually not be able to extricate itself from the nihilistic spiral of seductive destruction wrought by technology. If the most "civilized" peoples in the world could not resist such possibly suicidal temptations among themselves there would be little hope for humankind.

In these crucial respects, the reception of protests against chemical weapons departed significantly from its historical precursors. But how was this new type of weapon distinguished from its contemporaries? Several new weapons participated in the catastrophic violence of modern warfare that was World War I. The submarine, airplane, and flamethrower all had their time (however brief), inviting excoriation as barbaric means of warfare. The protests against the new chemical weapons might well have gone the way of these and other protests through history were it not for a conjunction of rather fortuitous circumstances. In the interwar period, the propaganda efforts of the chemical lobby in the United States effectively mobilized and politicized an impending scenario of future catastrophe wrought by gas warfare. This massive campaign backfired and created enough public momentum to lead to efforts to (re-)banish gas warfare through international law.

Even so, the institutional opprobrium of CW during the interwar years might very well have failed to catch hold without the political space created by the Hague Declaration. The military powers that accepted the interwar agreements to prohibit chemical weapons did so largely because their framers believed they were merely reconfirming an already existing norm. This norm was embodied in the Hague Declaration, whose violation during World War I had left little confidence in such treaties, and Article 171 of the Versailles Treaty, an essentially anti-German provision that was itself a reinscription of the Hague ban. In genealogical fashion, the invocation of this legacy as the rationale for a renewed ban on CW obscured a less than glorious ancestry but operated nonetheless as moral support for the rejection of CW.

As seen in Chapter 2, the Hague Declaration itself was made possible because it banned a weapon that had yet to be developed as a standard tool of warfare. This development is crucial in understanding the success of the chemical weapons taboo: the Hague Declaration represented a prohibition in international law which anticipated a weapons innovation that had not yet occurred. It thus represented an exercise in anticipatory and mutual self-denial rather than after-the-fact recrimination for having suffered the surprise of being the first victim of a new weapon at the hands of an enemy. The incipient protest against CW was not simply the usual castigation of an enemy's advantage—it was in fact a mutual litmus test of how humankind would deal with the novel moral situation of technological modernity.

If the Hague ban was made possible for these reasons, these reasons also explain why the ban was not seen as a terribly significant achievement. Similar assessments accompanied the Washington and Geneva prohibitions, though by then the international community generally believed that the ban on using chemical weapons was unlikely to prevent gas warfare or even preparations for it. Noting the putative weakness of the Geneva Protocol, L. F. Haber has argued that it, "to this day, attracts attention and is given attributes which exceed its real significance. It is a declaration of intent and as such may have moral influence, but as there are no provisions for verification, or for enforcement of the ban, or penalties for infringement, it is without teeth."[3]

If it is true that the nations of the world could not place much confidence in these articles of international law to prevent the use of chemical weapons in future war, it is not at all the case that these efforts were therefore "a waste of time."[4] Chapter 5 discussed the institutionalized moral discourse embodied in the protocol which established gas as a weapon of particular political and symbolic importance. Years of thinking about chemical weapons as only weapons of retaliation eventually had the effect of retarding their acceptance by military establishments and ultimately worked towards preventing their use. Throughout World War II, abstinence from the use of chemical weapons was shaky and almost always in doubt. In the end, however, the moral and legal restraints against CW in conjunction with other factors critically tipped the balance in favor of non-use by establishing a politicized barrier that required unusual justification for resort to chemical weapons.

In other words, the chemical weapons taboo operated as a norm in international society. In the absence of the ready excuse provided by the international prohibition, it is not hard to imagine that chemical weapons eventually would have become a standard component of the world's military arsenals, and the use of chemical weapons would have proceeded as an unquestioned, unpoliticized, and uncontroversial practice of warfare. Humankind has not had the opportunity to get used to chemical weapons, and this anachronistic strangeness for soldiers and civilians alike has kept vivid the special moral repulsion and fear usually reserved for the initial encounter with a novel technology of warfare. Strangeness breeds fear, and as Nietzsche noted, "Being moral means being highly accessible to fear."[5] Chemical weapons remain novel beyond their time, representing an obstinate refusal of humankind to succumb to the temptations of technology.

Defining Features

How were chemical weapons constituted and successfully distinguished as a category apart from other weapons? In Chapter 2 I explained how the absolute ban against asphyxiating shells enacted at the Hague stood in sharp contrast to the usual type of limitations sought on weapons. Whether gas shells were lethal or merely irritants, and whether they were employed against defenseless civilians or against protected soldiers, the first use of this entire category of weapons was to be proscribed. This absolute definition of a category of odious weaponry was carried through at the Washington and Geneva Conferences, and the same understanding ultimately informed the significant expansion enacted in the Chemical Weapons Convention of 1993. This latter agreement categorically prohibits not only the use of all forms of chemical warfare, but the possession and production of such weapons as well.

It was seen that with the Hague Declaration, gas weapons were first singled out as a potential and special threat to civilian populations. Since then, this association has proven critical in the successes and failures in prohibiting CW. In the absence of this legitimizing discourse, the need to proscribe chemical weapons has faltered, as occurred with the resistance to the Geneva Protocol by the U.S. Senate. This development suggests the value of emphasizing the threat to innocent civilians for future efforts to attain bans on other weapons such as land mines.

The designation of the civilian threat as the defining political feature of chemical weapons is of particular theoretical interest from a constructivist standpoint. The political salience of this association was far from inevitable and indeed was arbitrary in the sense that other weapons before and since have presented at least as much of a threat to noncombatants. Indeed, the lesson drawn from the experience of World War I was not that gas could effectively be restricted to the battlefield, as it had been during that conflict. Rather, the lack of exposure of civilian populations to CW actually made the interwar fear of chemical weapons more galvanizing than it might have been had civilians been exposed to gas bombing as a regular feature of war—in which case the world would likely, if resignedly, have accepted gas as an unavoidable and unremarkable—though horrible—feature of modern technological warfare. In short, it was not so much the facts themselves (the possibility of effective restraint from using chemical weapons versus civilian populations) as the political inscription of a particular interpretation of chemical weapons (their use meant unparalleled catastrophe) that proved crucial in the development of the chemical weapons taboo during this period.

For similar reasons, the effectiveness of portraying humanity as defenseless before the threat of CW makes the persistence of the taboo especially remarkable. Of all the notable means of destruction of modern warfare such as the machine gun and high-explosive shell, defenses are most likely to be effective against chemical weapons.[6] Thus, less so than the cases of poison or nuclear weapons, nothing is so compelling in the nature of the weapon that singles it out as a suicidal technology to be avoided at all costs.[7] The chemical weapons taboo is a social and political construction.

An understanding of the features of the chemical weapons taboo reveals that the explanation for this norm resists the parsimonious expectations posited by rationalist approaches in the social sciences, such as regime theory in the scholarly field of international relations.[8] Such approaches maintain that states act according to their rational self-interest. The problem of applying such an approach to CW is that there is nothing inherently more or less rational about avoiding chemical warfare as there is in avoiding a variety of other violent practices. Truth be told, one could quite plausibly argue in hindsight that the chemical weapons taboo appears quite rational indeed and makes an awful lot of sense— but if so, it is the plethora of other less-restricted practices of warfare that are irrational and thus in need of explanation. Rationalist explanations are simply indeterminate, and in order to account for what is politically defined as rational self-interest, one must turn to constructivist approaches such as the genealogical analysis offered in this book.

The Political Construction of Technology

Not only does the chemical weapons taboo resist adequate explanation by rationalist approaches to international regimes, it also defies the conventional realist dictum that effective bans are only realized for useless weapons. The discussion of the chemical and poison taboos in earlier chapters reveals that the realist truism is not an empirical statement of fact but serves a legitimation function for the conduct of violence and its acceptable forms. The relentless march of ever more destructive weapons innovations is less inevitable than is often assumed.

Besides engaging theories of international regimes and the predominant realist wisdom regarding weapons restraints, the distinctive feature of the chemical and poison taboos is relevant to another body of scholarly work that has thus far largely remained outside the purview of international relations scholarship—the social construction of technology.[9] A prominent concern for the large tradition of literature on the issues raised by modern technology is the debate over technological determinism and the moral and political status of technology. To oversimplify matters greatly: for some thinkers in this tradition, technology is a morally neutral phenomenon; technology is neither inherently good nor bad, but its moral value depends upon how it is used. For others, technology is a social construction that embodies moral and political values.[10]

The genealogies of the poison and chemical weapons taboos call into question the determinism implied by the belief that "no effective weapons are banned." In demonstrating the political implications of these prohibitions, this book has also denuded the veil of value-neutrality from the discourse on weapons technologies. A genealogical understanding of these bans reveals that the determinism of the value-neutral technology discourse operates as an emasculating device that sanitizes the political and moral implications of how weapons technologies operate to legitimate power in the international system. Albeit the use of ever more powerful technologies of warfare often is accepted as an inevitable and therefore natural occurrence, the cases interrogated in this study demonstrate that this is not simply nor necessarily the case. The way that these technologies have been politically constituted is underscored by an understanding of the roles of poison and CW as weapons of the weak.

Weapons of the Weak

Although there is a close connection between the prohibition against the use of poison and the chemical weapons taboo, the origins and functions of these prohibitionary norms are not simply identical; they reveal fascinating departures and interpretive graftings. Chemical weapons were considered a weapon of the strong at the dawn of the twentieth century, and efforts to ban them were seen as a pledge of mutual self-denial of the powerful. By the close of the century, the predominant understanding of chemical weapons had metamorphosed them into a weapon of the weak, like poison. A central purpose of the taboo has thus been transformed from a privilege of civilized self-restraint to a coercive means of other-denial.

The poison ban served the political function of institutionalizing acceptable warfare in a certain way; this function has largely been forgotten over time with the dominance of the unquestioned moral authority of the prohibition. Indeed, the delegitimation process has been so spectacular a success that despite the taboo against poison, the realist thesis that "only useless weapons are banned" has maintained its place as a piece of unchallengeable wisdom about the inevitability of war and human affairs.

The genealogy of the poison taboo reveals that it is a particular definition of military power that has been legitimated in the international system. Contrary to the implications of the realist thesis about restraints on weapons, the absolute technological ability to kill—by any and all means—does not designate who will count as a powerful actor in international politics. Rather, the ability to apply a particular and politically legitimated means of force influences the hierarchical ordering of the system. Terrorists who threaten to poison the water supplies of whole cities are not deemed legitimate actors in the international system, and neither are nations who would commit such an unimaginably heinous act. Still, the threat posed by more technologically and economically demanding means of destruction such as massive conventional capabilities and nuclear weapons is much more readily assumed to be an inevitable and natural feature of the contest of international war and diplomacy.

Given the virtually limitless possibilities for violation, the taboos against poison and chemical weapons are remarkably robust. The terror-ist use of nerve gas in subways by members of a cult in Japan in 1995 is the kind of exception that proves the rule, as witnessed by the novel level of moral outrage and utter shock at an event that killed relatively few people in terms of the unfortunate standards set by other horren-dous acts of violence against civilians. States and terrorists alike have largely eschewed—and rarely even countenanced—methods such as the poisoning of water supplies of cities as a means of violence.[11]

Defining the Boundaries of Violence

The successful castigation of the disciplinary discourse of "weapons of the weak" has circumscribed the legitimacy of poison and contempo-rary chemical weapons, and the definition of the category of chemical weapons plays a role in the ordering of the space of international politics by states. As the contemporary embodiment of the taboo, the Chemical Weapons Convention reproduces the international and domestic bound-aries in its definition of prohibited chemical weapons. The use of certain chemical means—riot-control agents—is actually prohibited in interna-tional conflict while permitted in domestic policing functions. This ap-parent anomaly is brought about by the reproduction of distinct bound-aries between the international and the domestic, the realms of lethal violence between state communities, and controlled violence within communities.

The tension between the prohibition of nonlethal chemical weapons and the contemporary interest in nonlethal technologies of war may strain the definition of the chemical weapons taboo embodied in the CWC. Whether it does so depends upon the extent to which trans-do-mestic exercises of force by the most powerful state actors is understood as methods in the same conceptual framework as "warfare," or, con-versely, as something more resembling the policing functions of "law enforcement" permitted by the CWC. To the extent that the latter sce-nario prevails, it will indicate a deepening of international society.

Whether in the "war on drugs," peacekeeping missions, or human-itarian interventions such as that of Somalia in the 1990s, major states are likely to be increasingly involved in transnational policing functions as opposed to outright warfare. For such activities, the trappings of con-ventional state-to-state war are less appropriate, and the preferred methods of contemporary policing—such as nonlethal means—are more apposite. To the extent that nonlethal weapons thus become the weapon of the strong in the future, the self-denial of nonlethal chemical weapons as embodied in the CWC can only be maintained by the redefinition of such exercises of coercion as something other than international war—that is, by the domestication of international space into a transnational criminal space.

Mass Destruction

The notion of a weapon of the weak tells us much about the function of processes of legitimation and delegitimation in international politics, and its importance has been resurrected with the equivalence drawn between chemical and nuclear weapons in the discourse of weapons of mass destruction. The allure of chemical weapons for some nations is not simply that they are technologically advanced weapons of military value in certain tactical and strategic situations. Rather, the opposition to the CWC for some nations represents an effort to acquire on the cheap the kind of diplomatic, symbolic and political currency enjoyed by the possession—not use—of nuclear weapons.

The current resistance to the CWC therefore differs from the opposition to earlier efforts to ban CW. At the Hague, the United States did not want to deny itself a potentially useful weapon to employ against future enemies. Some twenty-five years later, the Geneva Protocol was rejected by the U.S. Senate in an atmosphere that regarded the use of chemical weapons in future wars as all but unavoidable. By the 1990s, assessments of the role of chemical weapons have changed, and the primary objectives sought by the majority of the countries opposed to a ban on CW have shifted. With one relatively inexpensive shot, otherwise poor nations hope to gain admission into the zone of advanced technological and industrial powers among whose members large-scale general warfare has lost legitimacy to the point of becoming obsolescent. Failing that, certain nations, led by a group of Arab countries, aspire to extend the scope and efficacy of the nuclear non-proliferation regime, especially as regards Israel.

The transformation of the allure of chemical weapons, to the point where they are now being harnessed in an effort to eliminate other weapons of mass destruction, is a moral novelty of real importance. The inclusion of chemical weapons in a broader category of weapons of mass destruction portends an especially remarkable development from the perspective of the history of weapons protests, which all too often has been a tale of the gradual erosion of moral protests and the reluctant acquiescence to the use of ever-novel technologies of destruction.

Is this delegitimation simply because chemical weapons lack military utility? The previous chapters demonstrate that this argument cannot be sustained empirically in accounting for the chemical weapons taboo. Still, the use of this discursive strategy has played an important role in legitimizing the taboo. Support for the CWC within the United States has been justified by a particular variant of this strategy of minimalizing the need for chemical weapons. According to the U.S. Department of Defense:

> The ability to retaliate with chemical weapons is no longer an essential element in countering the possibility of possession of chemical weapons by other states. . . .
>
> Fundamentally, the Defense Department supports giving up the right to retaliate with chemical weapons because we have an effective range of alternative retaliatory capabilities. . . .
>
> We have reached the judgment that we do not need to retain chemical weapons to deliver an effective response to the use of chemical weapons against us.[12]

This development is of no small analytical importance. The analysis of this book shows that this effort to legitimize the CW taboo reflects a process of rationalizing the marginal place that chemical arms have come to occupy for political reasons more than the objective characteristics of the technology. The debate over the utility of chemical weapons has never been decisively settled. In the absence of a taboo against chemical weapons, no one would have ever have bothered to search for alternatives in the first place. It is impossible to tell a "non-norms" story about the desuetude of chemical warfare.

Moral Norms

The genealogies of the chemical and poison taboos provide valuable insights into the operation of prohibitionary norms in international politics. The chemical weapons taboo has come to exhibit some of the features that characterize the operation of the prohibition on poison. As with the poison ban, the chemical weapons taboo has increasingly served as its own rationale, in need of no further humanitarian justification. This has not always been the case. The moral obloquy against gas has coalesced around the existence of articles of international law prohibiting these weapons, whose persistence has made it increasingly unacceptable to reopen what was once the controversial debate over the humanitarian effects of CW.

This is one way by which the legal norm institutionalized in successive international forums has reinforced the broader moral odium with which chemical weapons are generally regarded. The existence of international treaty law has tended to serve as the taboo's own justification and to confer a degree of legitimacy to the position that chemical weapons are odious, thereby foreclosing (though not eliminating) the questioning of the designation of these weapons as inherently immoral. Once international treaty law was in place, the usual arguments that "all weapons are cruel and are a regrettable but inevitable features of international life" were not enough to undo the prohibitive success of international agreement. Even if all weapons are cruel, that is no reason to reject a prohibition that affirms the principle for one particular weapon. The burden of proof to undo the taboo has henceforth been to make the positive case that chemical weapons were a desirable invention.

Conversely, the rejection of chemical weapons has been articulated more successfully in the absence of considerations regarding the humanity of other weapons technologies. The moral castigation of chemical weapons actually subverts itself by a comparison with other weapons by implying that being riddled by bullets, ripped apart by bayonets, burned alive, or mutilated by explosives must be something less than a dreadful experience.

In addition, the genealogical tracing of the taboo reveals that a generational tradition of the non-use of chemical weapons—regardless of the reasons—has become a crucial constituent of the moral discourse regarding CW and thus of the international norm proscribing the use of chemical weapons. This point can be illuminated by an episode from the period of the Iran-Iraq war. During U.S. Senate hearings over Iraq's use of chemical weapons in the early 1980s, it was remarked in one exchange that gas weapons surely were reprehensible since even Hitler did not use them against Allied armies or cities. No one present knew why Germany refrained from waging CW in World War II, but the salient fact remained: "We do know it did not happen."[13] Thus, the legacy of resistance in incorporating chemical weapons as standard agents of war in turn instantiates the moral discourse, and chemical weapons are understood to be particularly immoral.

This anecdote has implications for assessing the robustness of the taboo. A common suggestion for measuring the robustness of such a prohibitionary norm is to ascertain whether particular cases of chemical weapons non-use were the direct result of a belief that their use was illegal and immoral.[14] The genealogical approach of this book highlights the fact that events and circumstances of a less intentional character nevertheless can prove no less important in the development of a norm. Over time, the process of forgetting the origins and functions of such prohibitions—to the point of never even questioning their authority, such as with the ban on poison—indicates the strength of the norm. In the case of chemical weapons, the question of the humanitarian status of these weapons has gone from being a hotly contested issue to being a more or less taken-for-granted assumption that they are peculiarly odious. The moral rejection of gas coalesced around the legal proscription, and it is the increasingly unquestioned status of chemical weapons as particularly heinous which in turn has buttressed the authority of the prohibition in international law. Moreover, the institutionalization of the taboo in international law has sustained the continued treatment of the use of chemical weapons as a violation of an international norm, a development very different from the treatment of past weapons such as firearms. The genealogical focus on the discursive closure of contested features of prohibitionary norms is a valuable tool in the assessment of norms in international politics.

These observations on the meaning and functions of the chemical weapons taboo dispel the lawlike inevitability ascribed to war by the realist belief that war is inevitable and attempts to circumscribe it are doomed to failure. The undifferentiated quality to the contest of power in international politics imparted by such realist truisms is unwarranted. Moreover, the thesis that technology is morally neutral is less benign or inevitable than this dominant contemporary discourse implies, as revealed by the fact that some technological means of destruction are legitimized whereas others are not. If struggle seems inevitable in international politics, the form that those struggles take is neither inevitable nor monolithic but is constructed in politics.

Against the political and technological determinism ascribed to conflict by realist accounts of political life, this book supports the position that war is a variable social institution politically constituted and bounded in all but the most absolute of extermination campaigns. The tools used to conduct violence are themselves political artifacts, the products of moral and political commitments and not merely the outcome of an autonomous technological determinism to which we are all captive. If the argument of this book is successful, the "irrational" attitude toward chemical weapons ceases to appear as the central anomaly in need of explanation. "For the mere fact that certain abuses have been remedied," Alexis de Tocqueville observed, "draws attention to the others and they now appear more galling."[15] Why indeed endure as if inevitable the sufferings wrought not by nature but by human artifice?

Notes

Chapter 1. Weapons, Morality, and War

1. This book focuses on the history of chemical weapons and how they have been defined, and it deals with related weapons categories such as biological weapons, poison, and weapons of mass destruction insofar as they relate to the categorization and prohibition of chemical weapons.
2. L. C. Green, "Lawful and Unlawful Weapons and Activities," in *Essays on the Modern Law of War*, ed. Green (New York: Transnational Publishers, 1985), p. 173; W. H. Oldendorf, "On the Acceptability of a Device as a Weapon," *Bulletin of the Atomic Scientists* 18:1 (January 1962), 35–37.
3. John Tompkins, *The Weapons of World War III: The Long Road Back from the Bomb* (Garden City, N.Y.: Doubleday, 1966), p. 138.
4. Alfred T. Mahan, U.S. delegate to the Hague Peace Conferences, in *The Proceedings of the Hague Peace Conferences*, ed. James Brown Scott (New York: Oxford University Press, 1920), p. 366.
5. Nicholas Fotion and G. Elfstrom, *Military Ethics: Guidelines for Peace and War* (London: Routledge & Kegan Paul, 1986), p. 159.
6. Julius Stone, *Legal Controls of International Conflict* (New York: Rinehart, 1959), p. 551.
7. For the importance of the taboo for theories of international relations, see Richard Price, "A Genealogy of the Chemical Weapons Taboo," *International Organization* 49:1 (Winter 1995), 73–103.
8. Gas was, of course, used by the Nazis in their extermination camps and by the Japanese against the Chinese, as will be made clear in Chapter 5.
9. Stockholm International Peace Research Institute (hereafter SIPRI), *The Problem of Chemical and Biological Warfare*, vol. 4: *CB Disarmament Negotiations, 1920–1970* (Stockholm: Almqvist & Wiksell, 1971), p. 21.
10. See Frederic J. Brown, *Chemical Warfare: A Study in Restraints* (Princeton: Princeton University Press, 1968); Kenneth Adelman, "Chemical Weapons: Restoring

the Taboo," *Orbis* 30:3 (Fall 1986), 444; Susan Wright, "The Military and the New Biology," *Bulletin of the Atomic Scientists* 41:5 (May 1985), 10; John Ellis van Courtland Moon, "Chemical Warfare: A Forgotten Lesson," *Bulletin of the Atomic Scientists* 45:6 (August 1989), 40–43; and Moon, "Chemical Weapons and Deterrence: The World War Two Experience," *International Security* 8:4 (Spring 1984), 3–35.

11. The implications of these anomalies for rational choice and constructivist theories of social science are pursued in Richard Price and Nina Tannenwald, "Norms and Deterrence: The Nuclear and Chemical Weapons Taboos," in *The Culture of National Security: Norms and Identities in World Politics*, ed. Peter Katzenstein (New York: Columbia University Press, 1996), pp. 114–152.

12. The United States did not employ lethal CW in Vietnam but did use riot-control agents (CS) and defoliants, maintaining that use of these agents did not constitute chemical warfare. Allegations of Soviet use of CW in Afghanistan, while rampant in the atmosphere of the Cold War, have never been substantiated.

13. Not all assessments of the potential value of CW in Japan were as enthusiastic as Waitt's, but even more cautious evaluations concluded that CW would be effective, especially in combination with other weapons. See John Ellis van Courtland Moon, "Project Sphinx: The Question of the Use of Gas in the Planned Invasion of Japan," *Journal of Strategic Studies* 12 (1989), 313.

14. Jeffrey Legro makes a thoughtful case for the restraints of military culture during World War II in *Cooperation under Fire: Anglo-German Restraint during World War II* (Ithaca: Cornell University Press, 1995).

15. See, for example, Fotion and Elfstrom, *Military Ethics*, p. 168.

16. John Haldane, "Ethics and Biological Warfare," *Arms Control* 8:1 (May 1987), 31. Though made regarding biological weapons, the comments are still relevant.

17. Martin van Creveld, *Technology and War* (New York: Free Press, 1989), p. 72.

18. See Michael Mandelbaum, *The Nuclear Revolution* (Cambridge: Cambridge University Press, 1981), pp. 38–39.

19. J. R. Partington, *A History of Greek Fire and Gunpowder* (Cambridge: W. Heffer & Sons, 1960).

20. Michel Foucault, "Nietzsche, Genealogy, History," in *The Foucault Reader*, ed. Paul Rabinow (New York: Pantheon Books, 1984), p. 78.

21. Friedrich Nietzsche, *On the Genealogy of Morals*, trans. Walter Kaufmann and R. J. Hollingdale (New York: Vintage Books, 1989), pp. 77–78.

22. Foucault, "Nietzsche, Genealogy, History," p. 80.

23. See Alexander Nehamas, *Nietzsche: Life as Literature* (Cambridge: Harvard University Press, 1985), pp. 98–113.

24. On discourses and power, see Foucault, *The History of Sexuality*, vol. 1: *An Introduction* (New York: Vintage Books, 1990); *Power/Knowledge: Selected Interviews and Other Writings, 1972–1977*, ed. Colin Gordon (New York: Pantheon Books, 1980); *Discipline and Punish* (New York: Vintage Books, 1979); and *Politics, Philosophy, Culture* (New York: Routledge, 1990).

25. David Couzens Hoy, "Introduction," in *Foucault: A Critical Reader*, ed. Hoy (Oxford: Basil Blackwell, 1989), p. 15.

26. Conflicts over interpretive truths—that is, the exercise of power—are located at different sites from the power relations usually examined in international relations scholarship. While a Nietzschean genealogy shares with realism a focus on relations of power in human affairs, its focus on multiple sites of power challenges the state-centrism of realism. See James Der Derian, *On Diplomacy* (Oxford: Basil Blackwell, 1987), p. 83. Moreover, a genealogy does not presume that the results of power interactions that forge norms necessarily reflect the inten-

tions of actors. See James Keeley, "Toward a Foucauldian Analysis of International Regimes," *International Organization* 44:1 (Winter 1990), 96. The genealogical method that frames this book makes no assumption that the dominion of a moral interpretation simply reflects the balance of military capabilities. Indeed, Nietzsche came to quite the opposite conclusion in his genealogies of dominant moral interpretations: for Nietzsche, the weak often prevail over the powerful through the appropriation of an interpretive structure of the world.

27. This approach is suggested in the research program outlined by Keeley, "Toward a Foucauldian Analysis," 83–105.

28. In the end, an interpretive understanding of the meanings of norms will often provide a good part of the explanation for their existence and efficacy. See Charles Cross, "Explanation and the Theory of Questions," *Erkenntnis* 34 (March 1991), 237–260; Richard Price, "Interpretation and Disciplinary Orthodoxy in International Relations," *Review of International Studies* 20 (April 1994), 201–204; and Charles Taylor, *Sources of the Self* (Cambridge: Harvard University Press, 1989).

29. Friedrich Kratochwil and John Gerard Ruggie, "International Organization: A State of the Art on the Art of the State," *International Organization* 40:4 (Autumn 1986), 753–775.

Chapter 2. The Origins of the Chemical Weapons Taboo

1. The history of such methods can be found in Rudolf Hanslian, ed., *Der Chemische Krieg*, vol. 1 (Berlin: E. S. Mittler & Son, 1937), pp. 1–8; Louis Lewin, *Die Gifte in der Weltgeschichte* (Berlin: Julius Springer, 1920); Wyndham Miles, "The Idea of Chemical Warfare in Modern Times," *Journal of the History of Ideas* 31:2 (January/March, 1970), 297–304; SIPRI, *The Problem of Chemical and Biological Warfare*, vol. 1: *The Rise of CB Weapons* (Stockholm: Almqvist & Wiksell, 1971), pp. 125–127; and Alden Waitt, *Gas Warfare* (New York: Duell, Sloan & Pearce, 1942), pp. 6–12.

2. As stated in the SIPRI study, precursors of chemical weapons had been used before 1914, but "it was not until World War I that that confluence of chemical science and military technology had occurred which could make their use at all significant." See SIPRI, *Rise of CB Weapons*, pp. 125–126.

3. The Russian Circular is reprinted in James Brown Scott, ed., *The Reports to the Hague Conferences of 1899 and 1907* (Oxford: Clarendon Press, 1917).

4. The Conventions, Declarations, and other relevant documents of the Hague Conferences are reprinted in James Brown Scott, ed., *The Hague Peace Conferences of 1899 and 1907*, vol. 2: *Documents* (Baltimore: Johns Hopkins Press, 1909).

5. A. M. Prentiss, *Chemicals in War* (New York: McGraw-Hill, 1937), p. 686.

6. Calvin DeArmond Davis, *The United States and the First Hague Peace Conference* (Ithaca: Cornell University Press, 1962), p. 175.

7. Article 6 of the Convention (VIII) Relative to the Laying of Automatic Submarine Contact Mines. See Scott, *Reports to the Hague Conferences*, p. 650.

8. Note in particular the meticulous account of the historical development of this notion in James Turner Johnson, *Just War Tradition and the Restraint of War* (Princeton: Princeton University Press, 1981), and Michael Walzer's application of just-war doctrine in *Just and Unjust Wars* (New York: Basic Books, 1977).

9. T. J. Lawrence, *The Principles of International Law* (Boston: D.C. Heath, 1923), p. 518.

10. The only other weapon perhaps treated comparably is the expanding "dum-

dum" bullet, which was prohibited by virtue of a declaration also reached at the Conference of 1899.

11. Mandelbaum, *Nuclear Revolution*, chap. 2.
12. Lawrence, *Principles of International Law*, pp. 55–56.
13. The Manual of the Laws of War on Land produced by the Institute of International Law in 1880 also bans poison, simply stating in Article 8(a) that poison in any form is forbidden. See James Lorimer, *The Institutes of the Law of Nations* (Edinburgh: Blackwood & Sons, 1883), app. 3.
14. Ibid., app. 2.
15. William I. Hull, *The Two Hague Conferences* (Boston: Ginn, 1908), pp. 232–233.
16. Georg Schwarzenberger, *The Legality of Nuclear Weapons* (London: Stevens & Sons, 1958), p. 27.
17. The Lieber Code can be found reprinted in many sources, including Lorimer, *Law of Nations*, app. 1.
18. See Hugo Grotius, *The Law of War and Peace* (*De Jure Belli ac Pacis Libri Tres*), trans. Francis Kelsey (New York: Bobbs-Merrill, 1925), bk. 3, chaps. 15, 16; and A. A. Roberts, *Poison in Warfare* (London: William Heinemann, 1915), pp. 52–57.
19. *The Odyssey of Homer*, trans. Richmond Lattimore (New York: Harper Colophon, 1975), bk. 1, l. 260 (p. 34).
20. *The Laws of Manu*, trans. G. Bühler (Oxford: Clarendon Press, 1886), p. 230.
21. Silinius quotation from Grotius, *Law of War and Peace*, bk. 3, chap. 16.
22. Alberico Gentili, *De Iure Belli Libri Tres* (1612), trans. John C. Rolfe (Oxford: Clarendon Press, 1933), bk. 2, chap. 6.
23. Louis Lewin, *Die Gifte in der Weltgeschichte* (Berlin: Julius Springer, 1920), p. 524.
24. Bynkershoek, *Quaestiones Juris Publici Libri Duo* (1737), bk. 1, chap. 1, p. 3; cited in Schwarzenberger, *Legality of Nuclear Weapons*, p. 31.
25. Gentili, *De Iure Belli Libri Tres*, bk. 2, chap. 6.
26. See Lewin, *Die Gifte in der Weltgeschichte*.
27. See J. R. Hale, *War and Society in Renaissance Europe, 1450–1620* (New York: St. Martin's Press, 1985), p. 83. Da Vinci did, however, remark that the use of poisoned arrows "should not be used except against traitors, for it comes from them." *The Notebooks of Leonardo da Vinci*, arranged by Edward McCurdy, vol. 1 (New York: George Braziller, 1958), p. 810.
28. Robert Ward, *Enquiry of the Law of Nations in Europe* (London, 1795), 1:252, cited in Lewin, *Die Gifte in der Weltgeschichte*, p. 524.
29. Grotius, *Law of War and Peace*, bk. 3, chap. 4 (1).
30. Schwarzenberger, *Legality of Nuclear Weapons*, pp. 30–31.
31. Lewin, *Die Gifte in der Weltgeschichte*, pp. 561–563.
32. Schwarzenberger, *Legality of Nuclear Weapons*, p. 27.
33. Gentili, *De Iure Belli Libri Tres*, p. 158.
34. Margaret Hallissy, *Venomous Woman* (Westport, Conn.: Greenwood Press, 1987), pp. 5–6.
35. Gentili, *De Iure Belli Libre Tres*, pp. 155, 160.
36. Schwarzenberger, *Legality of Nuclear Weapons*, 34.
37. Grotius, *Law of War and Peace*, bk. 3, chap. 4 (15) (emphasis added).
38. See Emer de Vattel, *Le Droit des gens* (Leiden: Aux depens de la compagnie, 1758), vol. 2, bk. 3, chap. 8, para. 155.
39. Ann Van Wynen Thomas and A. J. Thomas, *Development of International Legal Limitations on the Use of Chemical and Biological Weapons*, vol. 2 (Prepared for the U.S. Arms Control and Disarmament Agency, 1968), p. 254.
40. Robert O'Connell, *Of Arms and Men: A History of War, Weapons, and Aggression* (Oxford University Press, 1989), p. 113.

41. Ibid., p. 117.
42. Hale, *War and Society in Renaissance Europe*, p. 31; see also pp. 16, 29–30, 58.
43. Ibid., p. 37.
44. See Niccolò Machiavelli, *The Prince*, trans. Harvey Mansfield (Chicago: University of Chicago Press, 1985), bk. 12.
45. Hale, *War and Society*, pp. 42–45.
46. Roberts, *Poison in Warfare*, p. 55. The passage continues, "but its usage in warfare was countenanced to a marked degree." This seems correct in the comparative sense that poison was more prevalent as a weapon of assassination than a weapon on the battlefield, but the argument here is that poisoning rulers was in effect an act of warfare given the political circumstances of the times in which war was "the sport of kings." Further, Lewin's lengthy documentation of the use of poison in warfare dispels the notion that such means were absent from the warfare of the period. See *Die Gifte in der Weltgeschichte*, bk. 12.
47. William McNeill has argued that this concern contained the scale of violence until the French Revolution. See *The Pursuit of Power: Technology, Armed Force, and Society since A.D. 1000* (Chicago: University of Chicago Press, 1982), p. 161.
48. Martin van Creveld, *The Transformation of War* (New York: Free Press, 1991), p. 82.
49. In that sense, the taboo against biological weapons is more simply explained and politically less intriguing than that of chemical weapons. Chemical agents in shells or missiles, for example, do not suffer from such a liability.
50. On the sovereign state's elimination of non-state forms of violence see Janice Thomson, *Mercenaries, Pirates, and Sovereigns* (Princeton: Princeton University Press, 1994).
51. One could argue that civilians did not benefit from the poison taboo if one thinks that humankind during this period could have countenanced an outright ban on war itself and thus have spared centuries of unfortunate civilian populations hence.
52. J. Servan cited in Foucault, *Discipline and Punish*, pp. 102–103.
53. See Gerrit W. Gong, *The Standard of 'Civilization' in International Society* (Oxford: Clarendon Press, 1984).
54. Elaine Scarry, *The Body in Pain* (Oxford University Press, 1985).
55. Robert O'Connell observes astutely that there is a tendency throughout history and across cultures to prefer weapons that are loud, confrontational, big, and visually impressive (*Of Arms and Men*, pp. 254, 266, 306).
56. See Lewin, *Die Gifte in der Weltgeschichte*, p. 524.
57. See the meticulously researched account of Michael Adas, *Machines as the Measure of Men* (Ithaca: Cornell University Press, 1989).
58. Lawrence, *Principles of International Law*, p. 541.
59. See Friedrich Nietzsche, *The Use and Abuse of History*, trans. Adrian Collins (New York: Macmillan, 1957), and passages in *Human, All-Too-Human*, trans. Marion Faber (Lincoln: University of Nebraska Press, 1986), and *Genealogy of Morals*.
60. A conclusion also reached by Schwarzenberger, *Legality of Nuclear Weapons*, p. 36.
61. Lawrence, *Principles of International Law*, p. 533.
62. M. W. Royse, *Aerial Bombardment and the International Regulation of Warfare* (New York: H. Vinal, 1928), pp. 131–132.
63. W. T. Mallison, "The Laws of War and the Juridical Control of Weapons of Mass Destruction in General and Limited Wars," *George Washington Law Review* 36:2 (December 1967), 318.
64. William V. O'Brien, "Biological/Chemical Warfare and the International Law of War," *Georgetown Law Journal* 51:1 (Fall 1962), 7.

65. Roberts, *Poison in Warfare*, p. 56.
66. Foucault, *Discipline and Punish* p. 49; see also pp. 105, 111 for proposed punishments for poisoners by legal reformers.
67. Scott, *Proceedings of the Hague Peace Conferences*, pp. 365–366.
68. Ibid., pp. 365–366 (emphasis added).
69. F. Stansbury Haydon, "A Proposed Gas Shell, 1862," *Journal of the American Military History Foundation* 2:1 (Spring 1938), 52–54.
70. Thomas and Thomas, *International Legal Limitations*, p. 56. See also Joseph Burns Kelly, "Gas Warfare in International Law," *Military Law Review*, Department of the Army pamphlet no. 27-100-9, (July 1960), p. 44; and O'Brien, "Biological/Chemical Warfare," p. 22.
71. This debate is reprinted in Scott, *Proceedings of the Hague Peace Conferences*, pp. 365–367.
72. Ibid.
73. Britain supported the ban, but on the condition that support for it be unanimous; hence the negative vote in 1899. See Memorandum from Sir J. Fisher to Marquess of Salisbury, July 20, 1899 in Roberts, *Poison in Warfare*, p. 142.
74. Report of the U.S. Commission, in Scott, *Hague Peace Conferences*, vol. 2: *Documents*, p. 33.
75. Andrew D. White, *The First Hague Conference* (Boston: World Peace Foundation, 1912), pp. 82–83.
76. The idea of noncombatant immunity of course has a long history in just-war doctrine, and just-war theory provided the normative context in which the Hague deliberations were embedded.
77. See Miles, "Idea of Chemical Warfare," p. 298; Amos Fries and Clarence West, *Chemical Warfare* (New York: McGraw Hill, 1921), pp. 1–4; and Clarence J. West, "The History of Poison Gases," *Science* 49:1270 (1919), 412–417.
78. On the rise of the society of states see Hedley Bull, *The Anarchical Society* (New York: Columbia University Press, 1977); Bull and Adam Watson, eds., *The Expansion of International Society* (Oxford: Clarendon Press, 1984); Adam Watson, *The Evolution of International Society* (New York: Routledge, 1992); and Gong, *Standard of 'Civilization'*.
79. On the evolution of ideas discrediting war, see John Mueller, *Retreat from Doomsday: The Obsolescence of Major War* (New York: Basic Books, 1989).
80. See van Creveld, *Technology and War*, p. 71.
81. See O'Connell, *Of Arms and Men*.
82. Quoted in Heinz Leipmann, *Poison in the Air*, trans. Eden Paul and Cedar Paul (Philadelphia: J. B. Lippincott, 1937), p. 33.
83. Lewin, *Die Gifte in der Weltgeschichte*, pp. 571–572.
84. We must recall, of course, that the United States in its role as chief opponent to the ban sought to legitimize any use.
85. Adas, *Machines as the Measure of Men*.
86. Scott, *Hague Peace Conferences*, vol. 2: *Documents*, p. 37.
87. Britain voted against the declaration in 1899 but was to accede by 1907.
88. Hull, *Two Hague Conferences*, p. 78.
89. Although the United States supported a humanitarian formula to ban dum-dum bullets, it rejected the declaration because its delegates found the language unsatisfactory. See "Report of Captain Crozier to American Delegation," in Scott, *Instructions to the American Delegates to the Hague Peace Conferences and Their Official Reports* (New York: Oxford University Press, 1916), pp. 29–35.
90. In Scott, *Hague Peace Conferences*, vol.2: *Documents*, pp. 7–8.
91. Ibid., p. 20.

92. Davis, *United States and the First Hague Peace Conference*, p. 41.
93. Alfred Mahan, "The Peace Conference and the Moral Aspect of War," *North American Review* 169:4 (October 1899), 445.
94. Among the numerous authors who make such an argument are Francis Fukuyama, *The End of History and the Last Man* (New York: Free Press, 1992); Mueller, *Retreat from Doomsday*; and Richard Rosecrance, *The Rise of the Trading State* (New York: Basic Books, 1986). Martin van Creveld, in *Transformation of War*, makes a comparable argument that conventional war is being replaced by low-intensity conflict.
95. Just-war doctrine can be seen—somewhat paradoxically—as compatible with realism. Since realism holds that the existence of war is an unavoidable feature of international political life, there is some merit to efforts to render warfare somewhat more endurable and less horrible than it otherwise could be in all its worst extremes. However, accepting the doctrine of military necessity (which lies at the core of much of just-war doctrine) at some point makes just-war theory virtually indistinguishable from realism. As Mallison has noted, the just-war principle of "humanity" verges on tautology, since it only prohibits the use of force which is not permitted under the principle of "military necessity." See Mallison, "Laws of War," 313; Jean Bethke Elshtain, "Critical Reflections on Realism, Just Wars, and Feminism in a Nuclear Age," in *Nuclear Weapons and the Future of Humanity*, ed. Avner Cohen and Steven Lee (Totowa, N.J.: Rowman and Allanheld, 1986), pp. 255–272; Robert Holmes, *On War and Morality* (Princeton: Princeton University Press, 1989); and David Luban, "Just War and Human Rights," and "The Romance of the Nation-State," in *International Ethics*, ed. Charles Beitz et al. (Princeton: Princeton University Press, 1985).
96. Seth Low, "The International Conference of Peace," *North American Review* 169:5 (November 1899), 631.
97. Scott, *Hague Peace Conferences*, vol. 1: *Conferences*, p. 109.
98. Scott, *Hague Peace Conferences*, vol. 2: *Documents*, p. 524.
99. Indeed, the commitment to the abolition of warfare voiced by U.S. delegates at the Hague can be portrayed as a rhetorical one at best, given statements such as the following in a later article by U.S. delegate Mahan: "Peace, indeed, is not adequate to all progress; there are resistances that can be overcome only by explosion. . . . Power, force, is a faculty of national life; one of the talents committed to nations by God." Mahan, "The Peace Conference and the Moral Aspect of War," 444.
100. Hull, *Two Hague Conferences*, p. 84 (emphasis added).
101. See David Campbell, *Politics without Principle* (Boulder, Colo.: Lynne Rienner, 1993); and Chris af Jochnick and Roger Normand, "The Legitimation of Violence: A Critical History of the Laws of War," *Harvard International Law Journal* 35:1 (Winter 1994), 49–95.

Chapter 3. World War I

1. A. M. Prentiss, *Chemicals in War* (New York: McGraw-Hill, 1937), p. 689.
2. James Morgan Read, *Atrocity Propaganda: 1914–1919* (New Haven: Yale University Press, 1941), p. 198.
3. Thomas and Thomas, *Legal Limits on the Use of Chemical and Biological Weapons*, p. 141.

4. SIPRI, *The Problem of Chemical and Biological Warfare*, vol. 3: *CBW and the Law of War* (Stockholm: Almqvist & Wiksell, 1973), p. 103.

5. See also Paul Fauchille, *Traité de Droit International Public*, vol. 2 (Paris: Rousseau, 1921), pp. 118–123; William E. Hall, *A Treatise on International Law*, ed. A. Pearce Higgins (Oxford: Clarendon Press, 1924), p. 637; and Alberic Rolin, *Le Droit moderne de la guerre*, vol. 1 (Bruxelles: Albert DeWit, 1920), pp. 325–326.

6. See L. F. Haber, *The Poisonous Cloud* (Oxford: Clarendon Press, 1986), pp. 15–16.

7. Ibid., p. 21.

8. Ibid., p. 224.

9. See Max Bauer, "Denkschrift betreffend den Gaskampf und Gasschutz," in *Chemische Kriegführung — Chemische Absrüstung: Dokumente und Kommentare*, ed. Hans Günter Brauch and Rolf-Dieter Müller (Berlin: Berlin Verlag, 1985), p. 69.

10. Hermann Geyer, "Der Gaskrieg," in *Der Grosse Krieg: 1914–1918*, ed. Max Schwarte, vol. 4 (Leipzig: Johann Ambrolius Barth, 1922), p. 489; "'New Terrible Force' Hit Oppau, Haber Says," *New York Times*, September 25, 1921, sec. 2, p. 9. This charge may not have been incorrect, but as with all the postwar accounts examined in this chapter, we must keep in mind that the authors of such writings were sensitive to the issue of which side violated the Hague Declaration, which could have influenced their postwar recollections.

11. SIPRI, *Rise of CB Weapons*, pp. 27–28; and Haber, *Poisonous Cloud*, pp. 24–25.

12. Geyer, "Der Gaskrieg," pp. 491–500. Geyer's account must be treated with caution insofar as this volume was preoccupied with refuting the Allied charges of German breaches of international law during World War I. Geyer also argues that Ni-Schrapnel was not a prohibited gas shell, as it contained no lethal agents and did not cause "unnecessary suffering" (p. 496). Other authors have made the claim that these shells were designed on the understanding that any new agent had to observe the letter—if not the spirit—of the Hague Declaration. See Charles Heller, *Chemical Warfare in World War I: The American Experience, 1917–1919* (Fort Leavenworth, Kan.: Combat Studies Institute, 1984), p. 6.

13. SIPRI, *Rise of CB Weapons*, p. 133.

14. Otto Hahn, *Mein Leben* (Munich: F. Bruckmann KG, 1968), p. 117, quoted from Brauch and Müller, *Chemische Kriegführung*, pp. 82–83.

15. Haber, *Poisonous Cloud*, p. 28.

16. Ibid., p. 42.

17. Bauer, "Denkschrift betreffend den Gaskampf und Gasschutz," in Brauch and Müller, *Chemische Kriegführung*, p. 70.

18. Haber claims that there is an inconsistency between the attitude ascribed to the leadership and the actual policy. He thus draws the unsupported conclusion that there must have been an attempt by Fritz Haber (his father) to cover up (*Poisonous Cloud*, p. 28). A less conspirational conclusion might be that consideration of the norm turned on whether certain kinds of gas were permissible and some not. That is, there does not appear to be a belief that all use of any kinds of gas were proscribed, but that certain kinds were allowable under the Hague norm—Haber's analysis fails to differentiate consistently among different kinds of gas weapons.

19. Geyer, "Der Gaskrieg," p. 500. Hanslian contended that Germany's use of chlorine gas from cylinders was not a violation of the Hague insofar as it was not as toxic as materials already introduced by the French (*Der Chemische Krieg*, p. 16).

20. Berthold von Deimling, *Aus der alten in die neue Zeit* (Berlin, 1930), p. 210, cited in Brauch and Müller, *Chemische Kriegführung*, p. 84.

21. Hanslian, *Der Chemische Krieg*, pp. 8–9.

22. Geyer, "Der Gaskrieg," pp. 491, 503–504. While this charge is for the most part accepted in the literature, the French position is not an unreasonable one, as will be seen in the pages that follow.
23. A rich collection of such statements is to be found in James Garner, *International Law and the World War* (London: Longmans, Green, 1920), pp. 278–282. These claims that the prosecution of war in this fashion was the most humane—insofar as it shortened the duration of war—bear a striking resemblance to the language employed by the United States at the Hague Conferences.
24. J. H. Morgan, trans., *The War Book of the German General Staff* (New York: McBride, Nast, 1915), p. 85.
25. Ibid., p. 69.
26. Ibid., pp. 70, 87.
27. Ibid., p. 86.
28. In addition to Geyer, "Der Gaskrieg," see also Hanslian, *Der Chemische Krieg,* and Haber, *Poisonous Cloud,* p. 291.
29. See the material in War Office file WO/32/5177 at the Public Record Office (PRO) in Kew near London.
30. See *Times* (London), April 13, 1915, p. 8; April 14, p. 8; and April 19, p. 8; see also SIPRI, *Rise of CB Weapons,* pp. 29–30.
31. In the London *Times* of April 21, 1915, p. 8, Sir John French erroneously accused the Germans of having already employed asphyxiating gases at Ypres.
32. Emphasis added. See *Times* (London), April 24, 1915, p. 7, and the initial British response to such arguments in *Times* (London), April 26, 1915, p. 10.
33. *Times* (London), April 29, 1915, p. 6. See also Garner, *International Law,* pp. 274–276.
34. The quotation is attributed to the German press in *Times* (London), May 6, 1915, p. 9. This challenge to the moral desirability of the norm was especially the case with an article that appeared in the Kölnische Zeitung, which is discussed below.
35. Haber, *Poisonous Cloud,* p. 23.
36. Ministry of Munitions, *History of the Ministry of Munitions,* vol. 11: *The Supply of Munitions, Part II: "Chemical Warfare Supplies"* (London: HMSO, 1921), p. 1.
37. C. H. Foulkes, *Gas! The Story of the Special Brigade* (London: William Blackwood & Sons, 1934), p. 23.
38. Ibid.
39. Haber, *Poisonous Cloud,* p. 22.
40. PRO file WO/188/357.
41. The possible use of nonlethal gases was considered for the Dardanelles campaign, but even these were curtailed by Churchill because "it would not be expedient to introduce into the War, elements which might justify the enemy in having recourse to inhuman reprisals." Winston Churchill, *The World Crisis,* vol. 2: *1915* (London: Scribner, 1923), p. 75. Given his later interest in the use of gas (which approached enthusiasm), the moral tone of much of Churchill's recollections are to be treated with great circumspection at best. In a note to the Dardanelles Committee (October 20, 1915), Churchill observed that the winds in the region "would afford a perfect opportunity for the employment of gas by us. . . . I trust that the unreasonable prejudice against the use of gas upon the Turks will now cease." PRO file CAB/42/4.
42. Ministry of Munitions, *History,* p. 2.
43. Ibid., p. 4.
44. General French's dispatch to the War Office of April 23, 1915, reads: "Urge that

immediate steps be taken to supply similar means of most effective kind for use by our troops. Also essential that our troops be immediately provided with means of counter-acting effect of enemy gases which should be suitable for use when on the move." See Foulkes, *Gas!*, p. 19.

45. PRO file WO/32/5177, telegram from Lord Kitchener to Sir John French, April 24, 1915.

46. According to the director of gas services, the decision to retaliate had been made by May 18, 1915. See Henry Thuillier, *Gas in the Next War* (London: Geoffrey Bles, 1939), p. 22.

47. Until December 1915, research, design, and supply rested with Jackson; actual use (cylinders and grenades) lay with Foulkes's special brigade of Royal Engineers. Jackson's section became the Trench Warfare Department in June 1915. "This department was responsible for the supply of service mortars and grenades, and for research, design and supply duties in regard to novel weapons for trench warfare and all special stores, i.e., chemical substances, gas cylinders and special projectiles, including chemical bombs and grenades. In general the functions of the Ministry at its formation excluded responsibility for design; but this duty was expressly reserved to the Trench Warfare Department by the Army Council on the ground that it was impracticable to sever design from supply in the case of experimental stores. . . . One result of this arrangement was that the chemical warfare authority was more closely concerned with the provision for the chemical weapons used by the Special Brigade of Engineers than with other chemical projectiles, *viz.*, artillery shell. The authority for designing artillery shell was the Director of Artillery." In December 1915, the Trench Warfare Supply Department was constituted a separate unit within the Ministry, being responsible, among other things, for the production of chemicals and containers for chemicals, but not for the chemical shell. Ministry of Munitions, *History*, pp. 13–15.

48. Letter from Asquith of April 27, 1915. PRO file CAB 37/127.

49. Ref. No. OA 2/23C from Sir John French, GHQ, British Army in the Field, to the Secretary, War Office, on June 16, 1915. PRO file WO 32/5170.

50. Ministry of Munitions, *History*, p. 5.

51. Ibid.; Foulkes, *Gas!*, p. 305.

52. Charles Howard Foulkes, "Chemical Warfare Now and in 1915," *REJ* 76 (March–December 1962), 177, cited in Donald Richter, *Chemical Soldiers: British Gas Warfare in World War I* (Lawrence: University Press of Kansas, 1992), p. 23.

53. See the documentation in Ministry of Munitions, *History*, pp. 8–9.

54. On the one hand, one might argue that any British use of gas, even in retaliation, constituted a breach of the Hague Declaration since the declaration's prohibition made no distinction between first use and retaliation. On the other hand, retaliatory use of CW might not have constituted a legal violation of the declaration since, like any treaty of international law, the declaration could be regarded as having ceased to remain in force once its terms had been violated by a principal party. More sustainable is the legal interpretation offered to the War Office, that the German use of gas was not a violation of the Hague because Servia [sic] was not a party to the Declaration and thus the agreement was not legally binding for any of the belligerents during the war. See the legal notes by Edmonds in PRO file WO/158/122. This argument seems legally correct insofar as the language of the declaration specifically states that it "shall cease to be binding from the time when, in a war between the contracting powers, one of the belligerents shall be joined by a non-contracting Power." In short, a precise legal

interpretation would lead to the rather surprising conclusion that the Hague Declaration was in fact not violated during World War One.

55. Charles Howard Foulkes, "Fire, Smoke, and Gas," *Journal for the Society for Army Historical Research* 19 (1940), 148, cited in Richter, *Chemical Soldiers*, p. 16.

56. War Committee Papers, October 1916. PRO file CAB 42/22.

57. PRO file CAB 23/1. Minutes of Cabinet, January 21, 1917.

58. SIPRI, *Rise of CB Weapons*, p. 127.

59. See, for example, the matter-of-fact "eyewitness" report of the new German weapon at Ypres in *Times* (London), April 30, 1915.

60. See *Times* (London), April 21–28, 1915. This line is also generally followed in the French press; see *Le Temps*, April 26, 1915, p. 1.

61. See *Times* (London), April 26, 1915, p. 9. The outcry raised when gas was first used by the Germans at Ypres "was not directed primarily against the brutality of the weapon as a weapon, but against its employment, without warning, on unprotected troops in defiance of the spirit of the Hague Conventions" Lecture on Chemical Warfare to Staff College, February 26, 1926, in PRO file WO/188/48.

62. Read, *Atrocity Propaganda*, pp. 195–196.

63. The important fact that the Allies did not officially condemn the gas attack at Ypres as a violation of the Hague Declaration is surprisingly underemphasized in the literature; exceptions include Kelly, "Gas Warfare," 36; and O'Brien, "Biological/Chemical Warfare," 23. Geyer, "Der Gaskrieg," 496, points out that the Allied press did not even mention the use of Ni-Schrapnel. Julius Stone, *Legal Controls of International Conflict* (New York: Rinehart, 1959), p. 554, argues that the Allies denounced the attack at Ypres as a violation of Articles 23(a) and (e) of the Hague Regulations, and did so because a cloud attack was not forbidden by the declaration. The basis for this argument is unclear.

64. Although the British press at first ridiculed the German's resort to the technicalities of the Hague ban, an inconspicuous sentence on page 10 of *Times* (London), April 29, 1915, admits that the word "sole" is required to give the correct meaning of the clause.

65. PRO file WO/188/48.

66. *Times* (London), April 26, 1915, p. 10. The importance of the lack of official protests is put in sharper relief when it is recognized that the German poisoning of wells in South-West Africa was officially protested, insofar as it constituted a violation of the Hague injunction against the use of poison. See, for example, *Times* (London), May 6, 1915, p. 9.

67. An article concerning the report of Dr. Haldane upon the use of asphyxiating gases makes first mention of the "diabolical contrivance" which fills the German name with "a new horror." *Times* (London), April 29, 1915, p. 9. See also *Times* (London), May 1, 1915, p. 7; May 6, p. 10; May 7, p. 9; May 8, p. 5. It is interesting to compare Sir John French's first matter-of-fact descriptions of gas warfare in April 1915 with his later, much more embellished dispatches (such as London *Times*, July 12, 1915, p. 9).

68. Frederic Brown, *Chemical Warfare: A Study in Restraints* (Princeton: Princeton University Press, 1968), pp. 14–15.

69. Churchill's writing after the war argued that British developments "could not depart from the accepted Laws of War." Memo, Churchill to Lord Dundonald, January 1, 1915, in Churchill, *World Crisis*, vol. 2: *1915*, p. 75.

70. See, e.g., Haber, *Poisonous Cloud*, pp. 24, 53.

71. See Hanslian, *Der Chemische Krieg*; and SIPRI, *Rise of CB Weapons*, pp. 127–131.

West, "History of Poison Gases," refers to French use of irritant-filled cartridges for cartridge-throwing rifles.

72. Haber, *Poisonous Cloud*, p. 24.
73. E. Vinet, "La Guerre des gaz et les travaux des services chimiques francais," *Chemie et Industrie* 2:1 (January 1919), 1377.
74. R. Cornubert, "La Guerre des gaz," *Revue Generale des Science Pures et Appliques* 31 (1920), 45–56.
75. Hanslian, *Der Chemische Krieg*, p. 20; and SIPRI, *Rise of CB Weapons*, p. 45.
76. Foulkes, *Gas!*, p. 305.
77. Vinet, "La Guerre des gaz," 1403.
78. SIPRI, *Rise of CB Weapons*, p. 33.
79. *Le Temps*, April 28, 1915, p. 1; May 1, 1915, p. 1. Aerial bombardments by the Germans attracted at least as much attention in the French press as gas—see, e.g., *Le Temps*, May 7, 1915, p. 1.
80. Fries and West, *Chemical Warfare*, p. ix.
81. See Brown, *Chemical Warfare*, p. 19.
82. Fries and West, *Chemical Warfare*, p. 72.
83. U.S. War Department, *Annual Report, 1917*, vol. 1 (Washington, D.C.: Government Printing Office, 1918), p. 42. Heller, *Chemical Warfare*, p. 35, has attributed this lack of attention to gas to, first, a restricted propaganda, which gave the impression that gas was not used much or not effective, and that it was in any case disreputable; and, second, Wilson's neutrality, which hampered preparations.
84. See Fries and West, *Chemical Warfare*, p. 135; Heller, *Chemical Warfare*, pp. 44–45; and Haber, *Poisonous Cloud*, pp. 167–169.
85. Heller, *Chemical Warfare*, p. 87.
86. Ibid., p. 90.
87. Brown, *Chemical Warfare*, p. 24.
88. Ibid., p. 18.
89. *New York Times*, September 21, 1917, p. 6. Brown, in *Chemical Warfare*, adds that "the lack of public concern is indicated by the placement of the announcement on p. 6. This was consistent with the general attitude about gas" (p. 25).
90. John Pershing, *My Experiences in the World War I* (New York: Frederick A. Stokes, 1931), p. 165.
91. Fries and West, *Chemical Warfare*, pp. 6–7.
92. General Fries explained that the reaction to gas was due to the "newness of the weapon. Moreover, its first great use was coupled with the breaking of a solemn pledge not to use it." "Science Versus Butchery," speech by Fries on January 16, 1922, in PRO file WO 188/125.
93. Joachim Krause and Charles K. Mallory, *Chemical Weapons in Soviet Military Doctrine* (Boulder, Colo.: Westview Press, 1992), p. 26.
94. Thomas and Thomas, *Legal Limits*, p. 141.
95. *History of the Ministry of Munitions*, pp. 10–11; Haber, *Poisonous Cloud*, pp. 224–225.
96. Foulkes, *Gas!*, p. 296.
97. Ibid., p. 246.
98. Ibid., p. 240.
99. Bombers had been contracted for by the British in 1918, but only 3 delivered by end of war; see Brown, *Chemical Warfare*, p. 43.
100. Brown, *Chemical Warfare*, p. 45, citing J. Harbord, *The American Army in France, 1917–1919* (Boston: Little, Brown, 1936), p. 223.

101. S. J. Auld, *Gas and Flame in Modern Warfare* (New York: George Doran, 1918), pp. 22–23.

102. George Quester, *Deterrence before Hiroshima* (New Brunswick, N.J.: Transaction Books, 1986), pp. 44–45. His sources for this contention are not convincing, however.

103. Brown, *Chemical Warfare*, p. 46.

104. Despite this evidence, Haber argues that a more likely reason is that they did not want to waste then-scarce mustard gas by dispersing it thinly in the rear of the German army, an interpretation that is given no support; see Haber, *Poisonous Cloud*, p. 205.

105. Ibid.

106. Fries and West, *Chemical Warfare*, p. 399.

107. SIPRI, *Rise of CB Weapons*, p. 233. The highest casualties (675) were sustained by the people of Armentières who refused to leave the area in July 1917—86 died in the attacks. See Andy Thomas, *Effects of Chemical Warfare: A Selective Review and Bibliography of British State Papers* (Philadelphia: Taylor and Francis, 1985), pp. 20–23, for an account of civilian casualties.

108. Brown, *Chemical Warfare*, p. 44.

109. Haber, *Poisonous Cloud*, pp. 249–250.

110. *Times* (London), February 11, 1918, p. 5; February 27, 1918, p. 5. The only other such appeal was President Wilson's unsuccessful proposal in May 1915 (after the sinking of the Lusitania) that Germany end the use of gas and attacks on merchant ships in exchange for a British lifting of the blockade of neutral ports. In both cases, the motivating concern seems to have been the increasing threat posed to civilians by the war.

111. Haber concurs that "the belligerents avoided deliberate gas attacks on civilians. The French planned all their gas-cloud operations so that populous sectors behind the German lines were not involved; the Special Brigade took no such precautions. The Germans claimed that they had urged civilians to leave exposed areas, but that the French had opposed voluntary, let alone forced, evacuations." That did not stop the Germans, Haber continues, "from discharging cylinders or firing gas shells even when they knew that non-combatants were still living or working in an area." Haber writes of "careless indifference shown to civilians in the first two to two-and-a-half years of CW," an assessment that seems overstated, given that he cites only three such incidents for the duration of the war. See Haber, *Poisonous Cloud*, p. 248.

112. See Quester, *Deterrence before Hiroshima*.

113. Read, *Atrocity Propaganda*, pp. 193–194.

114. This response is to be expected of the initial human encounter with such a novel experience. In this respect, the reaction to gas was not that different from the historical reactions to other novel technologies, though the rest of the book shows how reactions to CW differed in very important ways on other grounds.

115. Erich Maria Remarque, *All Quiet on the Western Front* (New York: Fawcett Crest, 1982), p. 282.

116. Haber, *Poisonous Cloud*, p. 41. He adds that gas defense had to be seen to work, to demonstrate that the threat posed by the new weapon could be contained (p. 78).

117. Read, *Atrocity Propaganda*, pp. 195–196.

118. Reprinted in *Times* (London), June 28, 1915, p. 10. Not only is this quote suggestive of the fear that sustained anti-gas sentiments, but it also indicates the German understanding concerning the permissibility of irritant gases versus the illegality of lethal ones.

119. Garner, *International Law*, p. 288.
120. See Foulkes, *Gas!*, and Richter, *Chemical Soldiers*.
121. B. H. Liddell Hart, *The Remaking of Modern Armies* (London: John Murray, 1927), pp. 80–87.
122. Haber, *Poisonous Cloud*, p. 230.
123. SIPRI, *Rise of CB Weapons*, p. 141.
124. Brown, *Chemical Warfare*, p. 16.
125. Allegations were made of a few incidences of biological warfare during World War I. See SIPRI, *Rise of CB Weapons*, pp. 216–217.
126. Legal aspects, notes by Edmonds in PRO file WO158/122.
127. I do not claim that the use of CW against civilian populations could not have caused enormous casualties, but only emphasize that CW are at the least no less susceptible to defensive measures than other weapons such as high explosives.

Chapter 4. The Interwar Period

1. See especially Brown, *Chemical Warfare*, chaps. 2, 3; Haber, *Poisonous Cloud*; Thomas and Thomas, *Legal Limits on the Use of Chemical and Biological Weapons*; and SIPRI, *CBW and the Law of War* and *Rise of CB Weapons*.
2. SIPRI, *Rise of CB Weapons*, p. 234.
3. In 1920 the International Committee of the Red Cross proposed to General Assembly of the League of Nations a variety of arms-limitation measures, including an absolute prohibition on asphyxiating gas; six months later the International Conference of the Red Cross urged supplementing the Hague Declaration to make the ban on gas warfare more explicit and extensive.
4. SIPRI, *CB Disarmament Negotiations*, p. 44 (emphasis added).
5. In 1922, the Temporary Mixed Commission appointed a subcommittee of scientists from around the world to study the development of CW. The reports were inconclusive; Senator Paterna of Rome University saw no ground to believe that new substances of greater military value than any yet known could be discovered and manufactured on a large scale, and that "we must neither hope nor fear that progress of chemistry will lead to any greater success in the discovery of gases than in discovering explosives." Although some people emphasized that gas was a new and terrible weapon and the threat to unprepared populations must be recognized, others argued that "chemical warfare on protected troops has not introduced any such horrors as generally believed," and that it was difficult to foresee future forms. The Commission's report incorporated these opinions, and concluded that "all nations should realize to the full the terrible nature of the danger which threatens them" (ibid., pp. 48–56).
6. Address given by William Hale of Dow Chemical Company to Flint Rotary Club, December 16, 1921, during the Nye Committee hearings. See Senate, *Munitions Industry: Hearings before the Special Committee Investigating the Munitions Industry*, 73d Cong. pt. 11: December 6, 7, and 10; pt. 12: December 11 and 12, 1934 (Washington: Government Printing Office, 1935), pp. 2564–2568. To cite a few examples, an internal cable from du Pont of December 3, 1920, reads: "Urge attention of League be drawn to danger of resumption of German organic chemical and dye monopoly. . . . Disarmament is a farce while Germany retains organic chemical monopolies" (pp. 2398–2399). A March 25, 1921, internal letter from the publicity manager of du Pont reads: "It is, of course, a fact

and is quite apparent that American dye manufacturers want to protect and develop their industry as a business proposition . . . I think with the present unsettled condition of world affairs, and with Germany's attitude toward the peace treaty arguments based on the question of disarmament are very much stronger than any others" (p. 2569).

7. See *New York Times*, March 13, 1921, p. 1; also April 20, 1919, sec. 7, p. 1; May 25, 1919, p. 1; April 21, 1921, p. 11; June 5, 1921, p. 16.

8. *New York Times*, November 11, 1920, p. 1; March 20, 1921, p. 20; June 15, 1921, p. 3; July 19, 1921, p. 10; July 21, 1921, p. 14; and September 25, 1921, sec. 2, p. 9.

9. The headline article from the *New York Times* was picked up as "A Rain of Death" in the London *Times*, March 14, 1921, p. 11. See also claims by the president of the Society of Chemical Industry, *Times* (London), September 1, 1921, p. 9.

10. *Times* (London), March 28, 1919, p. 14; July 20, 1920, pp. 13–14; July 29, 1920, pp. 13–14; August 7, 1920, p. 7; August 13, 1920, p. 14; December 8, 1920, p. 16; September 8, 1921, p. 12; September 9, 1921, p. 9.

11. See, e.g., the headline story "War Work Shocks British Chemists," reported in *New York Times*, November 11, 1920, p. 1; the accident at a gas plant in France which injured six thousand villagers (*New York Times*, January 20, 1922, p. 3); and French protests against Haber (*New York Times*, January 26, 1920, p. 12).

12. An oft-cited example is the depiction of a few "Lewisite" bombs eradicating London in Will Irwin's *Next War* published in 1921.

13. A most important example of the acceptance of CW as inevitable is the report of the Committee on Chemical Warfare Organization (the Holland Committee) in Britain, which was commissioned to assess the future of chemical warfare. On the similarity to new weapons in the past, see *New York Times*, December 8, 1921, p. 18.

14. A well-known defense of the humanity of chemical warfare was J. B. S. Haldane, *Callinicus: A Defence of Chemical Warfare* (London: Kegan Paul, Trench, Trubner, 1925). See also *Times* (London), September 1, 1921, p. 9; *New York Times*, December 8, 1921, p. 19; December 9, 1921, p. 2.

15. *Times* (London), September 8, 1921, p. 12.

16. For example, while General Fries of the Chemical Warfare Service championed the military value of CW, the chief of staff of the army, General Pershing, thought gas weapons were cruel and "abhorrent to civilization."

17. Occasional statements testify to the general temper of the time regarding CW which some sought to counter: "Contrary to popular belief, gas is regarded by responsible American Army officials as one of the most humane weapons of war" (*New York Times*, November 26, 1919, p. 6).

18. See Brown, *Chemical Warfare*, pp. 49–96.

19. Legro, *Cooperation under Fire*, p. 154.

20. SIPRI, *Rise of CB Weapons*, p. 247.

21. *Times* (London), April 3, 1923, p. 7.

22. SIPRI, *Rise of CB Weapons*, pp. 247–248. Dr. Finn Sparre of du Pont admitted in the Nye Committee hearings that the opinions made linking the chemical industry to war and disarmament were exaggerated; see Senate, *Munitions Industry*, pp. 2403–2404, 2411, 2470–2471.

23. Brown, *Chemical Warfare*, p. 180.

24. Haber, *Poisonous Cloud*, p. 307.

25. David Campbell, *Writing Security* (Minneapolis: University of Minnesota Press, 1992).

26. Mary Douglas, *Rise and Blame: Essays in Cultural Theory* (New York: Routledge, 1992); *Risk Acceptability according to the Social Sciences* (New York: Russell Sage Foundation, 1985); and Douglas and Aaron Wildavsky, *Risk and Culture: An Essay on the Selection of Technological and Environmental Dangers* (Berkeley: University of California Press, 1982).
27. Haber, *Poisonous Cloud*, p. 288.
28. As Brown has argued, "the danger to which the American public was most responsive was that exemplified by German use of gas in World War I" (*Chemical Warfare*, p. 58).
29. On the background of the conference, see Robert Kaufman, *Arms Control during the Pre-Nuclear Era* (New York: Columbia University Press, 1990); and Harold Sprout and Margaret Sprout, *Toward a New Order of Sea Power: American Naval Policy and the World Scene, 1918–1922* (Princeton: Princeton University Press, 1940).
30. State Department, *Conference on the Limitation of Armament* (Washington, D.C.: Government Printing Office, 1922), p. 4.
31. State Department, *Foreign Relations of the United States 1921*, vol. 1 (Washington, D.C.: Government Printing Office, 1936), p. 70.
32. State Department, *Conference on the Limitation of Armament*, p. 436.
33. Ibid., p. 412.
34. Ibid.
35. As Hughes argued, whereas "any definite program regarding limitation of land armament was impracticable . . . a point might soon be reached where an announcement might be made, to show the public that the Conference had taken due note of this important matter" (ibid., p. 414).
36. Ibid., p. 440.
37. As summarized by Admiral de Bon of France; ibid., p. 512.
38. Ibid., p. 486.
39. Ibid., p. 490.
40. Ibid., p. 492.
41. Ibid., p. 488.
42. Ibid., p. 508 (emphasis added).
43. Ibid., p. 730.
44. Quoted in Brown, *Chemical Warfare*, p. 62.
45. State Department, *Conference on the Limitation of Armament*, p. 730.
46. In Britain, War Office documents indicate that no line could be drawn between gases having a permanent disabling effect and those having a temporary effect, for the effect depends upon the concentration of gas. See PRO file WO/188/388.
47. State Department, *Conference on the Limitation of Armaments*, p. 376.
48. Ibid.
49. Ibid.
50. Partington, *History of Greek Fire and Gunpowder*, pp. 27–28.
51. *New York Times*, October 11, 1926, p. 23. There were voices of opposition, however, such as the letters of British soldiers who could not agree with CWS spokesmen that gas was humane (*New York Times*, November 30, 1919, sec. 3, p. 1).
52. J. E. Mills, "Chemical Warfare: Its Limitations and Possibilities," PRO file WO 188/125 dated September 25, 1925.
53. "Chemical Warfare versus Cold Steel and High Explosive," PRO file WO 188/125.
54. Haldane, *Callinicus*, p. 22.
55. Statement by Brad Roberts in Senate Committee on Foreign Relations, *Chemical*

Warfare: Arms Control and Nonproliferation: Joint Hearing before the Committee on Foreign Relations and the Subcommittee on Energy, Nuclear Proliferation and Government Processes, 98th Cong., 2d sess., June 28, 1984, pp. 60–61. See also Manfred R. Hamm, "Deterrence, Chemical Warfare, and Arms Control," *Orbis* 29:1 (Spring 1985), 120.

56. Roberts, in Senate Committee on Foreign Relations, *Chemical Warfare.*
57. Moreover, the common explanation leaves out altogether the crucial role of the institutionalization of the CW taboo accomplished at the Hague before World War I.
58. *The Portable Nietzsche,* ed. Walter Kaufmann (Viking Penguin, 1982), p. 74.
59. "Science versus Butchery," speech by Fries on January 16, 1922, in PRO file WO/188/125.
60. *Portable Nietzsche,* p. 243.
61. George Raudzens, "War-Winning Weapons: The Measurement of Technological Determinism in Military History," *Journal of Military History* 54:4 (October 1990), 403–433.
62. Partington, *A History of Greek Fire and Gunpowder,* p. 129.
63. Ibid. (my translation).
64. Quoted in Haber, *Poisonous Cloud,* p. 293. See also the assessments of gas as an extremely useful auxiliary weapon in PRO files WO/188/143 and WO/188/48.
65. Indeed, the subject of aircraft, which was discussed after the issue of gas, was eventually also handled using this approach.
66. State Department, *Conference on the Limitation of Armament,* p. 732.
67. Brown, *Chemical Warfare,* pp. 64, 68.
68. State Department, *Conference on the Limitation of Armament,* p. 732. The committee did, however, admit in its report that such arguments existed.
69. Ibid., p. 732.
70. Ibid.
71. Ibid.
72. Charles E. Hughes, "Possible Gains," in *Proceedings of the American Society of International Law* (Washington, D.C., 1927), 1–2. It has been suggested that Hughes—who had near complete control over foreign policy matters in the Harding administration—sought this ban so earnestly in part to atone for the disappointment of the U.S. failure with the League of Nations and to provide some redemption in a war-weary atmosphere that looked with hope towards disarmament and peace. See Brown, *Chemical Warfare,* pp. 45–46.
73. Hughes, "Possible Gains," 7.
74. Brown, *Chemical Warfare,* p. 67. Article 171 of the Treaty of Versailles declares that "the use of asphyxiating, poisonous and other gases and all analogous liquids, materials or devices being prohibited, their manufacture and importation are strictly forbidden in Germany." The same article also prohibits manufacture and importation of armored cars and tanks.
75. Despite skepticism regarding the importance of the prohibition, not all of the delegates regarded the provision as an utterly empty declaration.
76. "Chemical Warfare Policy," November 1924, PRO file WO 188/144.
77. Reprinted in State Department, *Conference on the Limitation of Armament,* pp. 1604–1611.
78. Similar prohibitions were contained in Article 135 of the Treaty of Saint-Germain; Article 82 of the Treaty of Neuilly; and Article 119 of the Treaty of Trianon. Although the United States never ratified the Treaty of Versailles, it did conclude the 1921 Treaty of Berlin, which contained a similar provision.
79. However, this narrow focus was not at all the case with the Washington Treaty

itself, in which the five powers prohibited themselves from using gas weapons. The motive behind Article 171 seems not to have been an attempt to emasculate German industry, but rather the fear that Germany might develop a new gas weapon to attack the Allies. Wilson objected to the first proposals on the grounds that the intrusions into the commercial chemical industry did not come within the purview of the military terms. State Department, *Foreign Relations of the United States: The Paris Peace Conference, 1919*, vol. 5 (Washington, D.C.: Government Printing Office, 1946), pp. 310–311.

80. State Department, *Conference on the Limitation of Armament*, p. 732.
81. *New York Times*, January 8, 1922, p. 17.
82. See Brown, *Chemical Warfare*, p. 68. Haber "is not so confident" about such assessments given the lack of compelling evidence either way (*Poisonous Cloud*, pp. 297–298).
83. Thomas H. Buckley, "The Washington Naval Treaties," in *The Politics of Arms Control Treaty Ratification*, ed. Michael Krepon and Dan Caldwell (New York: St. Martin's Press, 1991), pp. 73, 103.
84. *Congressional Record*, 67th Cong., 2d sess., 1922, 62, pt. 5, p. 4727.
85. Ibid., p. 4728.
86. Ibid., p. 4730.
87. Balfour, quoted in State Department, *Conference on the Limitation of Armament*, p. 750.
88. Ibid., p. 594.
89. League of Nations, *Proceedings of the Conference for the Supervision of the International Trade in Arms and Ammunition and in Implements of War* (Geneva, 1925), p. 308.
90. Ibid., pp. 535–536.
91. Ibid., p. 307.
92. Ibid., p. 307, 309.
93. Ibid., pp. 309–310, 308–315. According to Burton, "a clear basis for agreement is already in existence," given the Washington Treaty and the Convention for the Limitation of Armaments of Central American States of 1923 which contains an article prohibiting the use of asphyxiating gases. A gas prohibition was also contained in Article (c) of the Fifth Agreement of the Fifth International Conference of American States of May 3, 1923.
94. The Norwegian delegate stated he would abstain, because it is impossible to prevent the use of the most horrible methods of war; the problem is the abolition of war, not regulation: "Why have the legal systems of the various countries never considered the possibility of regulating murder? No attempt has ever been made to find out whether the use of certain weapons would be permissible in getting rid of an enemy; no decision has ever been taken that it is admissible, for example, to resort to the pistol, but that it is unlawful to use poison" (ibid., pp. 312–313).
95. Ibid., p. 597.
96. Ibid., p. 739.
97. Ibid., p. 530.
98. Haber, *Poisonous Cloud*, p. 296.
99. *Congressional Record*, 69th Cong., 1st sess., 1927, 68, pt. 1:144.
100. Ibid., p. 145.
101. Ibid., pp. 151–152.
102. Ibid., p. 153.
103. Ibid., p. 363.

104. General deterrence refers to the prevention of war on the whole, as opposed to specific deterrence which seeks the prevention only of a particular means of war.

105. Although the idea of acquiring gas weapons to prevent their use in kind developed in the 1920s, explicit formulations of the logic of general deterrence based upon chemical capabilities in this period are relatively rare. A significant exception is the statement of the CWS in its first annual report that the knowledge of U.S. research, development and training in CW "will go a long way toward deterring them [potential foes] from forcing hostilities" (report printed in Brown, *Chemical Warfare*, pp. 86–87).

106. As noted by Frances V. Harbour, *Chemical Arms Control: The U.S. and the Geneva Protocol of 1925*, Case Studies in Ethics and International Affairs, no. 4 (New York: Carnegie Council on Ethics and International Affairs, 1990).

107. Besides Borah, who had responsibility to shepherd the treaty through the Senate, Senator Heflin argued that poison gas is horrible and submitted a letter from a dissenting member of the Legion which invokes the argument that gas will threaten women and children in the next war (*Congressional Record*, 68, pt. 1:367–368).

108. Ibid., pp. 146–147.

109. The General Order is reprinted in *New York Times*, July 13, 1922, p. 32.

110. See Brown, *Chemical Warfare*, for a more extensive treatment of U.S. military policy in this period.

111. PRO files WO/188/48, WO/188/388, and WO/188/389.

112. A central failure in this regard was the absence of an influential Senator on the Geneva delegation, a practice which Hughes had carefully taken at Washington following the debacle of the Versailles Treaty in the U.S. Senate. See William C. Widenor, "The League of Nations Component of the Versailles Treaty," pp. 17–64; Thomas H. Buckley, "The Washington Naval Treaties," pp. 65–124; and Rodney McElroy, "The Geneva Protocol of 1925," pp. 125–166; all in Krepon and Caldwell, *Politics of Arms Control Treaty Ratification*.

113. McElroy, "Geneva Protocol of 1925," pp. 125–166.

114. Britain withheld ratification until the German Reichstag approved the protocol in 1929 with "honest intentions" and "relief," according to the chief of German CW during World War II. As he wrote, "general feeling in all German government and military circles as well as public opinion in Germany definitely rejected the use of chemical warfare agents. If for no other reasons, than because of the moral ground that had been so heavily stressed by the League of Nations." See Lt. Gen. Herman Ochsner, *History of German Chemical Warfare in World War II, Part I: The Military Aspect* (Aberdeen Proving Ground, Md.: Historical Office of the Chief of the Chemical Corps, MS. P-004a, 1949), pp. 12–13. The Soviets embraced the goals of the protocol, as they had only grudgingly accepted the necessity of preparedness. The Soviet commissar for war remarked in the 1920s that "the use of poison gas in the last war requires us to keep even this means of warfare in reserve for the defense of our nation against the enemy." See Krause and Mallory, *Chemical Weapons in Soviet Military Doctrine*, p. 36.

115. Accessions and reservations are documented in App. 5 of SIPRI, *CB Disarmament Negotiations*.

116. See SIPRI, *CB Disarmament Negotiations*.

117. SIPRI, *CB Weapons and the Law of War*, pp. 92–93 (emphasis added).

118. See Brown, *Chemical Warfare*, pp. 177–178.

119. "Military Men Say Poison Vapors Are No More Inhumane than Shrapnel or Shell," *New York Times,* July 27, 1919, sec. 7, p. 5; September 21, 1920, p. 2.
120. See the statements of Colonel Brigham and General Fries of the CWS in *New York Times,* September 10, 1926, p. 6; November 26, 1926, p. 12.
121. *New York Times,* December 11, 1926, p. 3.
122. *New York Times,* August 5, 1925, p. 21; October 1, 1925, p. 26.
123. See, e.g., *New York Times,* July 31, 1919, p. 8; February 25, 1920, p. 11; September 13, 1922, p. 31; January 26, 1925, p. 14; March 10, 1925, p. 4; March 15, 1925, sec. 8, p. 12.
124. *New York Times,* February 15, 1925, p. 22.
125. For example, *New York Times,* June 19, 1925, p. 20, and August 25, 1926, p. 23.
126. A *New York Times* editorial (February 16, 1927, p. 22) concluded that stories of cities being reduced to tombs by gas were "sheer romancing" and that high explosives were far more destructive as the last war had shown. This opinion echoed military claims that tales of the obliteration of whole cities were ridiculous views meant to terrorize people like stories of the "bogey man" (*New York Times,* February 2, 1925, p. 3).
127. Lawrence Douglas, "The Submarine and the Washington Conference of 1921," *Naval War College Review* 26:5 (1974), 96.
128. Reprinted in Senate Subcommittee on Disarmament, *Disarmament and Security: A Collection of Documents 1919–1955,* 84th Cong., 2d sess. (Washington: Government Printing Office, 1956), p. 701.
129. Nehamas, *Nietzsche,* pp. 104, 107–108.
130. Ibid., p. 110.

Chapter 5. Colonizing Chemical Warfare

1. I often refer to the "non-use" of chemical weapons in World War II, but there were a few isolated instances of the use of gas as a method of warfare in Europe. These occasions were either accidental or undertaken by local commanders without the knowledge of higher authorities. See SIPRI, *Rise of CB Weapons,* chap. 2. In addition, the Japanese employed both chemical and biological weapons in its war against China, and gas was used by the Nazis as a method of extermination in their concentration camps. On the latter see *Nazi Mass Murder: A Documentary History of the Use of Poison Gas,* ed. Eugen Kogon, Hermann Langbein, and Adalbert Rücherl (New Haven and London: Yale University Press, 1993). The phrase "non-use of CW" refers to the surprising fact that chemical weapons were nevertheless not employed as a military weapon on the major battlefields between the Allied and Axis powers nor used against civilians in raids on their cities.
2. See especially Brown, *Chemical Warfare;* SIPRI, *Rise of CB Weapons;* Legro, *Cooperation under Fire;* and Moon, "Chemical Weapons and Deterrence."
3. For an overview of alleged uses of chemical weapons in the inter-war period, see SIPRI, *Rise of CB Weapons,* pp. 125–230; and J. P. Perry Robinson, "Origins of the Chemical Weapons Convention," in *Shadows and Substance: The Chemical Weapons Convention,* ed. Benoit Morel and Kyle Olson (Boulder, Colo.: Westview Press, 1993), pp. 37–54.
4. Dorothy Kneeland Clark, "Effectiveness of Toxic Chemicals in the Italo-Ethiopian War," Staff Paper ORO-SP-87 (Bethesda: Operations Research Office, Johns Hopkins University, 1959), p. 11.

5. *New York Times,* March 22, 1936, p. 25.
6. See A. J. Barker, *The Civilizing Mission* (New York: Dial Press, 1968); Angelo Del Boca, *The Ethiopian War, 1935–1941* (Chicago: University of Chicago Press, 1969); Dorothy Kneeland Clark, "Effectiveness of Toxic Chemicals"; Stanley Fair, "Mussolini's Chemical War," *Army* 35 (January 1985), 44–53; SIPRI, *Rise of CB Weapons,* pp. 142–146; and George Steer, *Caesar in Abyssinia* (Boston: Little, Brown, 1937).
7. See the reports in *Times* (London), December 31, 1935, pp. 11, 12; March 23, 1936, p. 12; and July 1, 1936, p. 16.
8. An newspaper editorial several months before the war described a new Italian military invention that involved sprinkling corrosive fluid on the ground. According to the article, this method was relatively humane compared to the use of agents which blinded or destroyed lungs, and showed commendable self-restraint on the part of the Italian high command (*New York Times,* July 9, 1935, p. 20). Even as late as April 4, 1936, Ethiopian officials noted with alarm and surprise that official evidence of the use of chemical weapons had not yet reached Britain (*New York Times,* April 4, 1936, pp. 1, 7).
9. One of the few instances of public protest against the Italian's use of chemical weapons was a cable sent to the League of Nations by an American committee of religious and welfare organizations. See *New York Times,* April 9, 1936, p. 14.
10. A complete account of the League's consideration of these matters is given in SIPRI, *CB Disarmament Negotiations,* chap. 6.
11. Ibid., p. 176.
12. *New York Times,* April 9, 1936, pp. 1, 17; and April 11, p. 8.
13. Though informed Italian circles emphasized that their refusal to confirm or deny the allegations should not be interpreted as a tacit admission of guilt. *New York Times,* April 10, 1936, p. 16.
14. SIPRI, *CB Disarmament Negotiations,* p. 180.
15. Ibid., p. 178.
16. Dorothy Kneeland Clark, "Effectiveness of Toxic Chemicals in the Italo-Ethiopian War," p. 9.
17. *New York Times,* March 26, 1936, p. 16.
18. This absence of protest until lethal gas was used may suggest that the use of tear gas was not regarded by the Ethiopians as a violation of the norm, though it is unclear whether such use was treated as taboo by the Italians, Ethiopians, or the international community.
19. The full significance of this dimension of the incident has gone virtually unremarked; one exception was the Archbishop of Canterbury, as reported in *New York Times,* March 31, 1936, p. 12.
20. Kratochwil and Ruggie, "International Organization: A State of the Art on the Art of the State."
21. Daniel Waley has documented two Italian apologists in Britain who defended the use of gas, one of whom was heckled when doing so in a public speech; see *British Public Opinion and the Abyssinian War* (London: Maurice Temple Smith, 1975), pp. 128–130.
22. On this point, see Friedrich Kratochwil, "Regimes, Interpretation and the 'Science' of Politics: A Reappraisal," *Millennium* 17:2 (Summer 1988), 263–84, and Kratochwil and Ruggie, "International Organization: A State of the Art on the Art of the State."
23. See, for example, Charles Taylor, "Interpretation and the Sciences of Man," in *Interpretive Social Science: A Second Look,* ed. Paul Rabinow and William Sullivan

(Berkeley: University of California Press, 1987), pp. 33–81, and Alexander Wendt, "Anarchy is What States Make of It: The Social Construction of Power Politics," *International Organization* 46:2 (Spring 1992), 391–425. I use the term "interpretive" to highlight the differences between "how" questions of understanding meaning and "why" questions of explaining causal outcomes, while the term "constructivist" calls attention to the ontological assumptions and causal models as distinguished from positivist approaches.

24. SIPRI, *CBW and the Law of War*, p. 107.
25. *New York Times*, April 21, 1936, p. 18; *Times* (London), April 20, 1936. One of the effects of such assessments of the Abyssinian crisis on CW policy was to induce the British government to authorize a program of chemical warfare preparation. See Paul Harris, "British Preparations for Offensive Chemical Warfare 1935–1939," *Journal of the Royal United Services Institute for Defence Studies* 125:2 (June 1980), 57.
26. Legro, *Cooperation under Fire*, p. 182. Economic sanctions were adopted by the League as a general response to the Italian aggression, and they included an embargo on CW materials. Also, the League Council adopted a resolution that emphasized the importance attached to observance of the protocol.
27. See *New York Times*, January 12, 1936, sec. 2: p. 1; March 10, 1936, p. 18; and April 26, 1936, sec. 4, p. 5.
28. Rolf-Dieter Müller, "World Power Status through the Use of Poison Gas? German Preparations for Chemical Warfare 1919–1945," in *The German Military in the Age of Total War*, ed. Wilhelm Deist (Warwickshire, U.K.: Berg Publishers, 1985), p. 183.
29. Ibid., p. 189.
30. Brown, *Chemical Warfare*, p. 145. Brown goes on to state that "the major impact of the Italo-Ethiopian campaign was to reconfirm the attitude of those who already viewed gas as an inhumane horror weapon and to resuscitate cries for prohibition of all chemical warfare," noting that the State Department considered issuing a new plea for ratification of the Geneva Protocol in April 1937.
31. J. Kendall, cited in SIPRI, *Rise of CB Weapons*, p. 334. One author has argued that the Italian's use of CW was an act of desperation to disrupt an Ethiopian incursion into Eritrea, but this interpretation is not supported by the commanding Italian General's memoirs. See G. Steer, *Caesar in Abyssinia*, and P. Badoglio, *The War in Abyssinia* (New York: G. P. Putnam's Sons, 1937).
32. Robert Harris and Jeremy Paxman, *A Higher Form of Killing* (New York: Hill and Wang, 1982), p. 50.
33. George Quester, *Deterrence before Hiroshima*, p. 78. Thus, while reports of Japan's use of CW against the Chinese were ignored, even the suggestion that CW was being contemplated in Spain drew preemptory attention from Britain. The use of tear gas by government forces was reported and the insurgents claimed that they too had gas but "refuse to break the international law which forbids its use" (*Times* [London], August 19, 1936, p. 10). In response, Britain sent its diplomats to investigate these allegations and convey the grave consequences that might follow from the use of gas even in reprisal (*Times* [London], September 8, 1936, p. 12).
34. Harris and Paxman recount that in August 1919, Foulkes in India had urged the War Office to use CW versus the Afghans and tribesmen on NW frontier, meeting stiff opposition from much of the cabinet. Foulkes argued that "on the question of morality . . . gas has been openly accepted as a recognized weapon for the future, and there is no longer any question of stealing an unfair advantage

by taking an unsuspecting enemy unawares. Apart from this, it has been pointed out that tribesmen are not bound by the Hague Convention and they do not conform to its most elementary rules." It has been claimed by the chemical advisor to the British Army in India that it was decided as policy to use gas. Gas was rumored to have been used, though firm confirmation is lacking (*Higher Form of Killing*, pp. 43–44).

35. See Rudibert Kunz and Rolf-Dieter Müller, *Giftgas Gegen Abd el Krim: Deutschland, Spanien, und der Gaskrieg in Spanisch-Marokko, 1922–1927* (Freiberg: Rombach, 1990), and Müller, "World Power Status," p. 183. It has also been claimed that the Soviets waged CW against groups in Central Asia during its civil war until as late as 1930; see V. Pozdnjakow, "The Chemical Arm," in *The Red Army*, ed. Basil Liddell Hart (New York: Harcourt, Brace & Company, 1956), pp. 384–394. On these incidents, see SIPRI, *Rise of CB Weapons*.

36. The Vietnam case is of course controversial insofar as the United States used herbicides and tear gases, means many considered proscribed methods of chemical warfare. The United States maintained that such means were outside the prohibitions on chemical warfare. See SIPRI, *Rise of CB Weapons*.

37. See Legro, *Cooperation under Fire*, p. 156.

38. Mueller, *Retreat from Doomsday*.

39. Francis Fukuyama, *The End of History and the Last Man* (New York: Free Press, 1992).

40. Richard Rosecrance, *The Rise of the Trading State* (New York: Basic Books, 1986); James Goldgeier and Michael McFaul, "A Tale of Two Worlds: Core and Periphery in the Post–Cold War Era," *International Organization* 46:2 (Spring 1992), 467–491.

41. Michael Doyle, "Kant, Liberal Legacies, and Foreign Affairs," pts. 1 and 2, *Philosophy and Public Affairs* 12 (Summer/Fall, 1983), 205–235, 323–353.

42. Racism may have played a part in the increased willingness to use gas against "uncivilized" peoples, as John Ellis has argued of the early uses of the machine gun; see *The Social History of the Machine Gun* (Baltimore: Johns Hopkins University Press, 1975). One Ethiopian official charged that the savage use of CW would result in the hatred of whites by all of Africa (*New York Times*, October 22, 1935, p. 22). Race mattered, but the level of technological capability—rather than race *per se*—was more important as a gauge of "civilization." It was with such a category in mind that even Ethiopian officials themselves could refer to their own people as "ignorant" and "savage" (*New York Times*, October 14, 1935, p. 11). See Adas, *Machines as the Measure of Men*, for a more general statement of this argument concerning the use of technology—rather than race, morality, or religion—as the primary standard of "civilization."

43. Donald Puchala and Raymond Hopkins, "International Regimes: Lessons from Inductive Analysis," in *International Regimes*, ed. Stephen Krasner (Ithaca: Cornell University Press, 1983), p. 70.

44. *Giornale d'Italia*, as reported in *New York Times*, July 4, 1935, p. 1.

45. Moon, "Chemical Weapons and Deterrence," p. 32.

46. SIPRI, *Rise of CB Weapons*, p. 321.

47. Brown, *Chemical Warfare*, p. 296.

48. SIPRI, *The Rise of CB Weapons*, p. 334.

49. Ibid., p. 322.

50. Brown, *Chemical Warfare*, p. 293.

51. Ibid., p. 295.

52. Legro, *Cooperation under Fire*, pp. 157, 176, 206, 222–223.

53. Harris and Paxman claim that "at no point was the fact that chemical weapons were banned under international law a major consideration in the decision not to go ahead and use them," but even they are unable to sustain the blanket claim, since, as they continue, an exception was the "personal antipathy of Roosevelt—ironically one of the few countries free from legal obligation not to use gas was led by one of the few world leaders with a moral aversion to this weapon" (*Higher Form of Killing*, p. 136).

54. An exception to this tendency is Legro, who notes the elasticity of arguments from deterrence based on calculations of "national interest" and relative advantage or disadvantage. As it is not always obvious what is in the national interest, and as some advantage or disadvantage for any policy can always be found, the crucial questions are how "interests" and "advantages" are interpreted, why certain asymmetries and not others are highlighted, and "who decides, and what assumptions do they make?" (*Cooperation under Fire*, pp. 166–167).

55. Incendiary weapons were regarded as illegal prior to the war, though not by all countries. See SIPRI, *CBW and the Law of War*, p. 40. The British regarded the use of white phosphorous as an anti-personnel weapon to be forbidden by the Geneva Protocol to which Britain was committed and by Hague Convention Article 23(e) prohibiting materials causing unnecessary suffering (PRO file PREM 3/89).

56. See Price and Tannenwald, "Norms and Deterrence."

57. In the United States, the General Board of the Navy policy of April 1922 remained in effect until the war. Based on the assumption that the United States would not initiate CW, it stated that "the United States be prepared to make full use of gas warfare in retaliation" (quoted in Brown, *Chemical Warfare*, p. 160). In line with the Washington Treaty and Geneva Protocol, Britain in the interwar period adopted a retaliation-only policy similar to the French. SIPRI, *Rise of CB Weapons*, chap. 4, gives a summary of national interwar policies and preparations. On the Soviet no-first use policy, see Krause and Mallory, *Chemical Weapons in Soviet Military Doctrine*.

58. As Moon shows, the adoption of a no-first-use stance was taken with some equivocations; see "Chemical Weapons and Deterrence," pp. 9–24.

59. PRO files WO/188/48 and WO/188/388.

60. *Times* (London), September 4, 1939, p. 4.

61. Brown, pp. 230–231.

62. *New York Times*, February 23, 1938. This policy was not merely declaratory, for military plans from the 1920s to the start of World War II confined chemical weapons to a retaliatory role. Prominently placed on the first page of the 1936 field service regulations was a special order by Voroshilov which stated that "the means of chemical attack, which are referred to in this manual, will only be used by the WPRA [Red Army] in the case where our enemies have used them against us first." Kraus and Mallory, *Chemical Weapons in Soviet Military Doctrine*, pp. 82–83.

63. Brown, *Chemical Warfare*, p. 248.

64. *New York Times*, January 30, 1944, p. E3.

65. Brown, *Chemical Warfare*, p. 249.

66. The British and French began to collaborate on joint CW policy in May 1939, and, according to a secret report by the head of the British delegation, the attitude of the two governments was broadly similar: "The French think that the chemical industries in Germany and Italy are so highly developed that the use of gas by these countries may be regarded as certain. Their delegation had not

considered the possibility that either Germany or Italy might refrain from using gas in the early stages to avoid retaliation in kind" (Harris and Paxman, *Higher Form of Killing*, p. 51). More important, the joint development of British–U.S. gas policy held that CW use could be initiated only in joint consultation or independently in case of retaliation; the requirement for consultation was extended to other commonwealth members of the alliance (PRO file PREM 3/89).

67. Steven Rose, ed., *CBW: Chemical and Biological Warfare* (Boston: Beacon Press, 1968), p. 14. In another incident, a German air-raid on the port at Bari in December of 1943 hit an American supply ship loaded with mustard bombs, causing over 600 gas casualties including 83 deaths. The allies attempted to cover-up this accident, but when it became apparent that it could not be kept secret, the combined chiefs of staff issued a statement which reiterated that "Allied policy is not (repeat not) to use gas unless or until the enemy does so first but that we are fully prepared to retaliate and do not deny the accident, which was a calculated risk" (PRO file WO/193/712). See Harris and Paxman, *Higher Form of Killing*, pp. 119–123, and D. Saunders, "The Bari Incident," *United States Naval Institute Proceedings* 93 (September 1967), 35–39.

68. Legro offers a cultural explanation of these and other incidents in *Cooperation under Fire*, pp. 199–200.

69. The Japanese also used biological weapons in Asia and had plans for employing them against the United States. See Sheldon Harris, *Factories of Death: Japan's Biological Warfare 1932–45 and the American Cover-Up* (New York: Routledge, 1994), and Peter Williams and David Wallace, *Unit 731: Japan's Secret Biological Warfare in World War II* (New York: Free Press, 1989).

70. General Ismay reported as late as June 28, 1944, in a letter to Churchill that there was not sufficient evidence to prove allegations of Japanese use of CW (PRO file PREM 3/89).

71. See Gerrit Gong, "China's Entry into International Society," in *The Expansion of International Society*, ed. Hedley Bull and Adam Watson (Oxford: Clarendon Press, 1984), pp. 171–183.

72. Müller, "German Preparations for Chemical Warfare," p. 191.

73. Dr. Hans Fischer, "German Doctrine and Viewpoint on Tactical and Strategical Advantages and Disadvantages of Chemical Warfare," in *German Chemical Warfare [in World War II], Part II: Civilian Aspects* (Aberdeen Proving Ground, Md.: Historical Office of the Chief of the Chemical Corps, MS. P-004, 1956), p. 2 (emphasis added).

74. Dr. Hans Fischer and Dr. Wirth, "What Were the Plans and Intentions of the German High Command in the Question of Using Chemical Warfare? What Were the Reasons for Refraining from the Use of Chemical Warfare?" in *German Chemical Warfare*, pp. 331, 333.

75. Ibid. See also Hermann Ochsner, "U.S. Army Chemical Warfare Project: Berich über Production von K-Stoffen, Raumexplosions und Raumbränden, P-004a," reprinted in Brauch and Müller, *Chemische Kriegführung*, pp. 253–254.

76. Müller suggests that Hitler agreed at beginning of the war to declare officially his intention to refrain from first use of gas in response to Western declarations because he wanted an arrangement with Britain which would free him in the west for his conquest in the east, and the use of gas—because it was regarded as particularly unacceptable—would not have encouraged the British to make such deals ("German Preparations for Chemical Warfare," p. 189).

77. Harris and Paxman, *Higher Form of Killing*, p. 109.

78. Brown, *Chemical Warfare*, p. 251.

79. Ibid., and Moon, "Chemical Weapons and Deterrence," pp. 29–30.

80. Brown, *Chemical Warfare*, pp. 258–260.
81. Quoted in Krause and Mallory, *Chemical Weapons in Soviet Military Doctrine*, p. 89.
82. "Washington Adopts Gas Ban," *New York Times*, January 8, 1922, p. 1.
83. J. R. Hale, "Gunpowder and the Renaissance: An Essay in the History of Ideas," in *From the Renaissance to the Counter-Reformation*, ed. Charles H. Carter (New York: Random House, 1965), pp. 117–120.
84. Ibid., pp. 127, 136.
85. Ibid., p. 131.
86. Ibid., p. 134.
87. Winston Churchill, *Their Finest Hour* (London, 1949). There were reports in 1940 that Italy was preparing to use gas in Ethiopia. The War Office squashed suggestions that a retaliatory threat be made to stop it, because it was feared that giving attention to cases of possible use without retaliating might signal to Germany that Britain feared gas war, providing incentives for German use. Even if the Italians used gas, it was decided that "publicity should not (repeat not) be given to the fact" (PRO file PREM 3/88/3).
88. Churchill, *The Grand Alliance* (London, 1950), cited in SIPRI, *Rise of CB Weapons*, p. 314.
89. *Times* (London), October 21, 1939, p. 6.
90. Olaf Groehler, *Der Lautlose Tod* (Berlin: Verlag der Nation, 1978), p. 123.
91. *Times* (London), July 26, 1941, p. 4.
92. *Times* (London), May 4, 1942, p. 3.
93. *New York Times*, May 11, 1942, p. 1.
94. *Times* (London), May 14, 1942, p. 3. On these incidents, see SIPRI, *Rise of CB Weapons*, pp. 153–155, and Mallory and Krause, *Chemical Weapons in Soviet Military Doctrine*, pp. 92–93.
95. *Times* (London), May 15, 1942, p. 3.
96. *Times* (London), June 6, 1942, p. 4.
97. *Times* (London), April 22, 1943, p. 4.
98. *Times* (London), April 24, 1943, p. 3.
99. *Times* (London), June 9, 1943, p. 4.
100. See Legro, *Cooperation under Fire*.
101. Ochsner, *German Chemical Warfare*, p. 23; Omar N. Bradley, *A Soldier's Story* (New York: Henry Holt, 1951), p. 279; and SIPRI, *Rise of CB Weapons*, pp. 297, 312. Harris and Paxman contend—too strongly—that the use of chemical weapons at Normandy could have turned around the outcome of the war, ultimately leading to a separate peace with Hitler (*Higher Form of Killing*, pp. 63–64). For British assessments see numerous documents in PRO file PREM 3/89.
102. SIPRI, *Rise of CB Weapons*, pp. 324–326.
103. Harris and Paxman, *Higher Form of Killing*, p. 135; Ochsner, *German Chemical Warfare*, p. 23.
104. Intelligence reports indicated that Hitler would consider using gas against England but would hesitate to employ it should it be made clear that such use would result in retaliation against German civilian populations. Intelligence report of April 1943, PRO file PREM 3/88/3.
105. Müller, "German Preparations for Chemical Warfare," p. 196. As Brown concisely wrote of Germany and England, "Each nation assumed that tactical employment of chemical weapons would escalate to strategic counter-city exchange. And fears of strategic retaliation precluded serious considerations of

tactical use. Similarly, it was assumed tacitly that there was no viable qualitative distinction between toxic and non-toxic agents" (*Chemical Warfare*, pp. 244–245). Moon also notes the assumption that initiation of CW anywhere would mean global gas warfare; see "Chemical Weapons and Deterrence," p. 25.

106. See Legro, *Cooperation under Fire*, pp. 163–166.

107. PRO file WO/193/732.

108. Ibid.

109. Memo of June 16, 1940, PRO file WO/193/732.

110. Although I think it likely that the British would have used chemical weapons in the event of a German invasion, claims that the British already had made such a decision in advance seem premature. Harris and Paxman state that a decision to unilaterally initiate had been made, but their support is not conclusive. They cite a Churchill memo of June 30, 1940, declaring that "in my view there would be no need to wait for the enemy to adopt such methods," but fail to note the significance of the final words of the memo: "The question of actual employment must be settled by the Cabinet." The claim is also based on the finding that in January 1941, during the 'Victor' anti-invasion exercise, the War Cabinet sanctioned the use of gas, but this authorization was only given in the context of an exercise. See PRO file "Chemical Warfare: Policy—Use in Home Defence 1940–1941," 28 April, 1941, WO 193/732. Harris and Paxman further cite a March 1942 official minute to the chiefs of staff which stated "It has been accepted that we should not initiate the use of gas unless it suited our book to do so during the invasion" (Harris and Paxman, *Higher Form of Killing*, pp. 111, 115). Based upon the same evidence, Legro also contends that a contingent decision to initiate CW in case of invasion was made but admits that whether such a decision would actually have been implemented is arguable (Legro, *Cooperation under Fire*, pp. 163–164, 177, 220).

111. "Chemical Warfare: Retaliation," Chiefs of Staff Committee memorandum, March 19, 1941, PRO file WO/193/732.

112. Ibid. (emphasis added).

113. Brown's comment that any such decision "would have been made in an atmosphere of desperation" is apt (*Chemical Warfare*, p. 228).

114. PRO file AIR 2/5117 dated June 16, 1940.

115. Churchill letter to Ismay, July 6, 1944, in PRO file PREM 3/89.

116. Memo in PRO file PREM 3/89.

117. Ibid.

118. Müller has argued that the German public feared allied gas attacks, and that this fear was important in forestalling the use of gas. He contends that Hitler and his inner circle were apprehensive of the ability of the populace to withstand the hardships of war and were wary of anything that might break morale; thus the Germans did not use gas against Britain after the fall of France, as it was feared that even a small-scale British retaliation could have a devastating effect ("World Power Status," pp. 192–195).

119. Ibid., p. 188.

120. The phrase is from a memo in PRO files PREM/3/89.

121. *New York Times*, January 30, 1944, p. E3.

122. *New York Daily News*, November 20, 1943; *Washington Times Herald*, February 1, 1944; see also "We Should Have Used Gas at Tarawa," *Washington Times Herald*, December 20, 1943; "We Should Gas Japan," *New York Daily News*, November 20, 1943; "Should We Gas the Japs?" *Popular Science Monthly*, August 1945; "Thoughts on the Use of Gas in Warfare," *Newsweek*, November 20, 1943. A

poll taken in June 1945 showed that 40 percent of respondents would favor the use of gas if U.S. casualties were reduced; see H. Cantril, ed., *Public Opinion 1935–1946* (Princeton: Princeton University Press, 1951), p. 249.

123. Brown, *Chemical Warfare*, p. 276.
124. Moon, "Chemical Weapons and Deterrence," p. 34.
125. Moon, "Project Sphinx," p. 313.
126. Quester, *Deterrence before Hiroshima*, p. 175.
127. O'Brien, *Civil Defence*, pp. 329–330.
128. Müller, "World Power Status," p. 198, citing A. Hillgruber, ed., *Staatsmänner und Diplomaten bei Hitler*, vol. 2 (Frankfurt a.M.: 1970), p. 403.
129. SIPRI, *The Problem of Chemical and Biological Warfare*, vol. 5: *The Prevention of CBW* (Stockholm: Almqvist & Wiksell, 1971), p. 26.
130. Brown, *Chemical Warfare*, pp. 291–292.
131. Ibid., pp. 150–151; Moon, "Chemical Weapons and Deterrence," pp. 7, 15.
132. E. Ehmann, "Organizational and Industrial Functions of the Army Ordnance Office in the Army High Command in the Field of Chemical Warfare Agents," in *German Chemical Warfare*, p. 494.
133. Fischer and Wirth, "What Were the Plans," p. 328.
134. See Legro, *Cooperation under Fire*, pp. 182–183.
135. Harris, "British Preparations," p. 61.
136. SIPRI, *Rise of CB Weapons*, pp. 328–330; Moon, "Chemical Weapons and Deterrence," pp. 9–30.
137. Fischer and Wirth, "What Were the Plans," pp. 329–331; Müller, "World Power Status," pp. 185, 188.
138. SIPRI, *Rise of CB Weapons*, p. 281.
139. Haber, *Poisonous Cloud*, p. 170.
140. Fischer and Wirth, "What Were the Plans," pp. 329–331; Müller, "World Power Status," p. 190.
141. Harris and Paxman, *Higher Form of Killing*, p. 59; SIPRI, *Rise of CB Weapons*, p. 325.
142. "Chemical Warfare," War Cabinet, Chiefs of Staff Committee memorandum, November 14, 1941, PRO file WO/193/711.
143. See, e.g., Ochsner, *German Chemical Warfare*.
144. While there has been no shortage of candidates for "war-winning" weapons throughout history, few have ever lived up to expectations. See O'Connell, *Of Arms and Men*; van Creveld, *Technology and War*; McNeill, *Pursuit of Power*; and George Raudzens, "War-Winning Weapons: The Measurement of Technological Determinism in Military History," *Journal of Military History*, 54:4 (October 1990), 403–433.
145. Hale, "Gunpowder and the Renaissance," pp. 114–115.
146. Brown, *Chemical Warfare*, pp. 151, 292.
147. Thus, whereas the lack of preparations was central to forestalling CW, those same preparations would have been far more advanced if Germany had any intention of initiating gas warfare. See Fischer and Wirth, "What Were the Plans," pp. 7–8.
148. SIPRI, *Rise of CB Weapons*, p. 334.
149. On the tendency of technology to subvert the means-ends relationship by supplying its own ends, see Tom Darby, "Reflections on Technology: An Excursus as Introduction," in *Sojourns in the New World*, ed. Darby (Ottawa: Carleton University Press, 1986), pp. 1–21.
150. Brown, *Chemical Warfare*, p. 293.

Chapter 6. A Weapon of the Weak

1. J. P. Perry Robinson, "Origins of the Chemical Weapons Convention," in *Shadows and Substance: The Chemical Weapons Convention*, ed. Benoit Morel and Kyle Olson (Boulder, Colo.: Westview Press, 1993), p. 48.
2. For an explanation of the role of the moral norm against CW in this outcome, see Robert McElroy, *Morality and American Foreign Policy* (Princeton: Princeton University Press, 1992), chap. 4. On the use of chemical agents in Vietnam, see SIPRI, *Rise of CB Weapons*, pp. 162–210.
3. Significantly, then, biological weapons were separated institutionally from chemical weapons, unlike their treatment under the Geneva Protocol. This development reflected a recognition in the early 1970s that a further prohibition on biological weapons would be more amenable to an international agreement than a ban on chemical weapons, since the former's unpredictability made them much less attractive as a military weapon than the latter. The chemical weapons taboo is in this way analytically more intriguing than the prohibition on biological weapons, albeit the two categories are often mentioned in the same breath.
4. See the discussions in Senate Committee on Foreign Relations, *Chemical Warfare: Arms Control and Nonproliferation: Joint Hearing before the Senate Committee on Foreign Relations and the Subcommittee on Energy, Nuclear Proliferation and Government Processes*, 98th Cong., 2d sess., June 28, 1984.
5. Anthony Cordesman and Abraham Wagner, *The Lessons of Modern War*, vol. 2 *The Iran–Iraq War* (Boulder, Colo.: Westview, 1990), pp. 512–513.
6. UN Document S/1995/284, pp. 11–12.
7. Cordesman and Wagner, *Lessons of Modern War*, p. 507.
8. Edward Spiers writes of the "fairly limited and exploratory manner" of Iraq's introduction of CW, and their "circumscribed" employment during the following several years; see "The Role of Chemical Weapons in the Military Doctrines of Third World Armies," in *Security Implications of a Global Chemical Weapons Ban*, ed. Joachim Krause, (Boulder, Colo.: Westview, 1991), pp. 52–53.
9. Quoted in Cordesman and Wagner, *Lessons of Modern War*, p. 514.
10. He added that the weapon is not nuclear, chemical, or internationally prohibited; see "Use of 'Secret Weapon' against Iran Threatened," Monte Carlo Radio, in Arabic, October 25, 1982, *Foreign Broadcast Information Service* (hereafter *FBIS*) MEA, October 26, 1982, p. E1.
11. "Baghdad Reiterates Use of 'New Weapon' on Iran," Baghdad, in Persian to Iran, November 5, 1982, *FBIS* MEA, November 9, 1982, p. E6.
12. Cordesman and Wagner, *Lessons of Modern War*, p. 514.
13. Philip A. G. Sabin, "Escalation in the Iran-Iraq War," in *The Iran-Iraq War*, ed. Efraim Karsh (New York: St. Martin's Press, 1989), p. 285.
14. Iraq denied the first Iranian claim of CW use in 1981. See "Claim of Chemical Weapons Use against Iran Denied," Baghdad, INA, in Arabic, *FBIS* MEA, July 21, 1981, p. E2.
15. *Newsweek*, August 2, 1982, p. 11.
16. "Commentary Warns Tehran against Using Chemicals," Baghdad, in Persian to Iran, July 24, 1981, *FBIS* MEA, July 29, 1981, p. E3. According to one author, Iraq in 1982 conceded tear gas use in response to Iranian allegations of Iraqi CW; C. Raja Mohan, "Chemical Weapons in the Gulf: A Dangerous Portent," *Strategic Analysis* 8:1 (April 1984), 70.
17. Spiers, "The Role of Chemical Weapons," p. 52; see also John Bulloch and Harvey Morris, *The Gulf War* (London: Methuen, 1989), pp. 261–262.

18. Cordesman and Wagner, *Lessons of Modern War*, p. 514.
19. Efraim Karsh, *The Iran-Iraq War: A Military Analysis*, Adelphi Papers, no. 220 (London: Institute for Strategic Studies, Spring 1987), p. 56.
20. Stephen Krasner, "Structural Causes and Regime Consequences: Regimes as Intervening Variables," in *International Regimes*, ed. Krasner (Ithaca: Cornell University Press, 1983), p. 9.
21. Senate Committee on Foreign Relations, *Chemical Weapons Use in Kurdistan: Iraq's Final Offensive* (Washington, D.C.: Government Printing Office, 1988), p. 30.
22. Julian Perry Robinson, "Chemical and Biological Warfare: Developments in 1984," in *SIPRI Yearbook 1985: World Armaments and Disarmament* (New York: Taylor and Francis, 1985), pp. 181–183; Cordesman and Wagner, *Lessons of Modern War*, p. 514.
23. J. P. Robinson, "Chemical and Biological Warfare: Developments in 1985," in *SIPRI Yearbook 1986: World Armaments and Disarmament* (Oxford: Oxford University Press, 1986), p. 160.
24. UN missions were sent in March 1984, April 1985, February–March 1986, April–May 1987, March–April 1988, July 1988 (two), and August 1988; each time, investigators found that Iraq had used chemical weapons.
25. Cordesman and Wagner, *Lessons of Modern War*, p. 516.
26. "While this pause in Iraq's use of gas may have been because of the hostile reaction in the West and the Third World, it may also have been because Iraq lacked the organization and dispensers to use gas safely. There are indications that unfavourable winds caused Iraqi deaths at Haji Omran in August 1983, at Majnoon in March 1984, and near Fish Lake in 1987. Iran also seems to have become more cautious after the U.S. formally condemned Iraqi use of chemical weapons in March 1985" (Cordesman and Wagner, *Lessons of Modern War*, p. 514). This does not mean, however, that in the light of Iraqi resumption of gas warfare in 1987 we should unreservedly conclude that supply, at least as much as scruple, had been a substantial constraint in Iraqi resort to these prohibited weapons; see S. J. Lundin, J. P. Robinson, and Ralf Trapp, "Chemical and Biological Warfare: Developments in 1987," in *SIPRI Yearbook 1988: World Armaments and Disarmament* (Oxford: Oxford University Press, 1988), p. 115. Such a reading back into history does not take into account the fact that Iraq's use of chemicals was so circumscribed that serious international efforts to prevent further use may very well have had the desired effect.
27. On April 10, 1987, residential sections of Khorramshahr were reportedly subjected to chemical bombardment, the first deliberate chemical attack of civilian areas in the war; see *SIPRI Yearbook 1988*, p. 114. On the attacks against the Kurds, see Human Rights Watch/Middle East, *Iraq's Crime of Genocide* (New Haven: Yale University Press, 1995).
28. See *Chemical Weapons Convention Bulletin*, no. 27 (March 1995), 26.
29. See S. J. Lundin, "Chemical and Biological Warfare: Developments in 1988," in *SIPRI Yearbook 1989: World Armaments and Disarmament* (Oxford: Oxford University Press, 1989), p. 101.
30. *Guardian* (London), September 30, 1988, p. 12.
31. Senate Committee on Foreign Relations, *United States Policy toward Iraq: Human Rights, Weapons Proliferation, and International Law: Hearing before the Committee on Foreign Relations*, 101st Cong., 2d sess. June 15, 1990. Claiborne Pell, chairman, stated that "the Reagan administration opposed my efforts to sanction Iraq for its use of chemical weapons against its Kurdish minority. As a result, Iraq paid no price for this shocking crime, and in my view, is being encouraged to believe

it can quite literally get away with murder" (pp. 1–2). Lundin argues that "the international reaction of unanimous condemnation was, however, neither strong enough nor accompanied by sufficiently strong efforts to curb this violation of international law" ("Chemical and Biological Warfare," p. 99).

32. Senate Committee on Foreign Relations, *Chemical Weapons Use in Kurdistan*, p. viii. Bulloch and Morris (*Gulf War*, p. 259) argue that the lack of UN action ignored the fears "expressed privately by some member states that failure to condemn Iraq would set a precedent for the use of chemical weapons. It certainly contributed to the belief in Baghdad that Iraq could proceed with its chemical attacks on the Kurds with little fear of reproach from the international community." They add that "the muted response by the UN and the international community to Iran's regular—and justified—complaints of the use by Iraq of gas seemed to have emboldened Saddam Hussein and his lieutenants to use chemical weapons against its own population, a ghastly precedent which may yet be repeated" (p. 260).

33. *New York Times*, July 2, 1988, p. A3.

34. "Paper Interviews 'Aziz on Kurds, Other Issues," Kuwait AL-QABAS, in Arabic, 31 October 1988, *FBIS NES*, November 2, 1988, p. 27.

35. See "Report on Use of Chemical Warfare Denied," "Source Denies Allegations," "Report Called 'Unfounded,'" "INA Cites Turkish Official," all Baghdad, INA, in Arabic, September 5, 1988, *FBIS* NES, September 6, 1988, p. 33; and "Hammadi Denies Use of Chemical Weapons," Manama, WAKH, in Arabic, September 9, 1988, *FBIS* NES, September 9, 1988, p. 15.

36. Human Rights Watch/Middle East, *Iraq's Crime of Genocide*, pp. 241–242.

37. "WAKH Reports Khayrallah 15 September Press Conference," Manama, WAKH, in Arabic, September 15, 1988, *FBIS* NES, September 16, 1988, pp. 23–24.

38. *Le Monde* (Paris), November 10, 1988, p. 12.

39. Kratochwil Ruggie, "International Organization: A State of the Art on the Art of the State," p. 768.

40. "Foreign Minister Denies Chemical Weapons Use," Baghdad, INA, in English, September 17, 1988, *FBIS* NES, September 19, 1988, p. 17.

41. *New York Times*, July 2, 1988, p. A3.

42. "Paris Paper Interviews 'Aziz on Chemical Weapons," Baghdad, INA, in Arabic, January 18, 1989, *FBIS* NES, January 19, 1989, p. 21.

43. Senate Committee on Foreign Relations, *Chemical Warfare*, p. 47.

44. Ibid.

45. Ibid., p. 34.

46. Robinson, "Origins of the Chemical Weapons Convention," pp. 47–48.

47. UN Documents S\C. 3\SC. 3\7\Rev. 1.

48. *United Nations Disarmament Yearbook*, vol. 14 (1989), chap. 11.

49. Pierre Morel, "The Paris Conference on the Prohibition of Chemical Weapons," *Disarmament* 12:2 (Summer 1989), 127–144.

50. Quoted from Esmat Ezz, "The Chemical Weapons Convention: Particular Concerns of Developing Countries," in *Proceedings of the Thirty-ninth Pugwash Conference on Science and World Affairs* (Cambridge, Mass., 1989), p. 216.

51. As one author has remarked, "The major nations' unwillingness to eliminate their nuclear weapons while resisting further chemical (and nuclear) proliferation is seen in some Third World nations as the height of hypocrisy. It sends a message that the lesser nations aren't mature enough for the most powerful of military capabilities"; see Victor A. Utgoff, "Neutralizing the Value of Chemical Weapons: A Strong Supplement to Chemical Weapons Arms Control," in

Krause, *Security Implications of a Global Weapons Ban*, p. 97. See also Geoffrey Kemp, "The Arms Race after the Iran-Iraq War," in Karsh, *Iran-Iraq War*, pp. 269–279. He argues that "many countries in the Near East and South Asia express a profound irritation at what they perceive to be selective Western outrage over the use of chemicals. They believe that the United States, having failed to prevent India, Pakistan and Israel from building nuclear weapons is now trying to deny them the very weapons that provide some sort of counter balance to nuclear devices" (p. 277).

52. Morel, "Paris Conference," p. 142.
53. Foucault, "Nietzsche, Genealogy, History," pp. 85–86.
54. A military intelligence officer quoted in *Los Angeles Times*, February 21, 1991, pp. A1, A18.
55. According to the *Washington Times* of February 7, 1991, Iraq moved a special chemical weapon brigade, armed in part with FROG-7 and Katusha artillery rockets, into Kuwait several miles from the Saudi border around February 1. U.S. intelligence agencies suspected that the missiles and rockets were armed with tabun, anthrax, or mustard in the form of dust. The battleship *Missouri* shelled the brigade. The *Minneapolis Star Tribune* of March 12, 1991, reported that a limited stock of chemical artillery shells was found in the theater, but not a significant capability. A Czechoslovak unit reported detecting low levels of sarin nerve-gas in northern Saudi Arabia, January 19–24, 1991, and found a small patch of liquid mustard gas near King Khalid Military City. The Czechs first suggested that allied bombing of Iraqi chemical-weapons sites could have been responsible and, later, that tests carried out by units of allied Saudi Arabia might have been the source. U.S. officials disagreed with the former suggestion, contending that the winds were blowing in the wrong direction, and indicated it would ask coalition members if any had chemical stockpiles in the region; see *Chemical Weapons Convention Bulletin*, no. 23 (March 1994), 9, 11, 14. A staff report of the Senate Banking Committee presented evidence of detection of CW agents during the Gulf War, highlighting a chemical storage tank found in Kuwait; see *Chemical Weapons Convention Bulletin*, no. 30 (December 1994), 26. The British Ministry of Defence stated that the tank contained a rocket propellant; see *Chemical Weapons Convention Bulletin*, no. 27 (March 1995), 29. Testimony given by a U.S. soldier indicated that his unit had detected traces of mustard-type blister agents and low levels of Lewisite blister vapors. However, other experts have argued that the instruments used in these instances are subject to false alarms from petroleum-based hydrocarbons that were in the theater. A U.S. soldier is reported to have detected mustard gas on the uniform of a soldier who became blistered after checking an abandoned Iraqi bunker after the war ended. The U.S. Department of Defense initially maintained that there was no official confirmation that such agents entered the field of battle. See House Committee on Armed Services, *Use of Chemical Weapons in Desert Storm: Hearing before the Oversight and Investigations Subcommittee*, 103d Cong., 1st sess., 1994, pp. 9–12, 40–41, 43–44, 47, 63.
56. Investigations have been conducted to determine the sources of the illnesses suffered by many Gulf War veterans. Some veterans have said they are afraid that they will never receive proper treatment if the Defense Department does not admit that chemical and biological agents were used during the war. Official investigations initially ruled out chemical weapons as the source of the so-called Gulf War syndrome, but many were unsatisfied with the investigations. Philip Hilts, "Study on G.I.'s Ailments from Gulf War Is Called a Failure," *New York*

Times, January 5, 1995, p. A4. In August 1996 a Pentagon report acknowledged that the Czech detections of chemical agents during the Gulf War were credible and other detections could not be discounted. The Pentagon still insisted that it had no conclusive evidence that American soldiers were ever exposed to Iraqi chemical weapons, though it said it was exploring the possibility that small amounts of chemical agents passed over American troops at staging areas after American bombers destroyed Iraqi factories and arms depots near the Saudi city of Hafr al-Batin. Philip Shenon, "New Report Cited on Chemical Arms Used in Gulf War," New York Times, August 22, 1996, pp. A1, 15.

57. For the British position, see Hansard (Lords) written answers, October 26, 1994, as cited in Chemical Weapons Convention Bulletin, no. 30 (December 1994), 28. The wording of replies of U.S. officials to the question of the existence of chemical agents in the theater left open the possibility of accidental releases of chemicals, such as damage to stored chemical munitions. For example, the director of U.S. Central Intelligence, John Deutch, stated the view that "there was no standard chemical or biological weapons use." See Chemical Weapons Convention Bulletin, no. 29 (September 1995), 22.

58. Rick Atkinson, "No Chemical Arms Found on Battlefields," Washington Post, March 7, 1991, pp. A1, A35.

59. Ibid.

60. Ibid.

61. Ibid.

62. Ibid. Kenneth Timmerman has claimed that Saddam Hussein "actually gave orders to his field commanders to use chemical weapons against Allied forces but that these orders were not obeyed." See "The Iraqi Papers," New Republic, January 29, 1996, p. 14.

63. Philip Shenon, "Gulf War Illness May Be Linked to Gas Exposure, Pentagon Says," New York Times, June 22, 1996, pp. A1, 20; Shenon, "New Report Cited on Chemical Arms."

64. Scuds could not carry chemicals yet, according to an Iraqi engineer who lived in Baghdad and had formerly worked on improving the al-Husayn and al-'Abbas versions. Along with electronics difficulties, he named the inaccuracy of the Scuds as one problem, and attaching a heavy gas container would add to the missile's inaccuracy (Frankfurter Allgemeine Zeitung, February 4, 1991). According to Brad Roberts, Iraq would have to drop seven tons of chemicals per day to knock out an airfield, and since Scuds could carry only one-fifth of a ton of agent, it is "clear that the entire missile supply would be quickly exhausted were it to be used in a strategy aimed at closing coalition bases with saturation chemical attacks" (Washington Times, January 30, 1991).

65. Interview with General Wafic al Sammarai on PBS's Frontline, "The Gulf War," broadcast January 9–10, 1996. These PBS interviews are available on the World Wide Web at http://www.pbs.org.pages.frontline.

66. The resolution of April 3, 1991, demanded "the yielding by Iraq of possession to the Special Commission for destruction, removal or rendering harmless" nuclear, biological, and chemical weapons, as well as ballistic missiles with a range over 150 kilometers, missile warheads and launchers, and the production facilities for such weapons (UN document S/1995/208). Among the munitions that Iraq declared it had weaponized for chemical weapons purposes were artillery shells for mustard; aerial bombs for mustard, tabun, sarin, and CS; rockets for sarin; and Al Hussein missile warheads for sarin (UN Security Council Document S/1995/284, 10 April 1995, p. 14). Iraq also conducted flight tests of chemi-

cal warheads and deployed biological weapons in aircraft bombs, artillery shells, rockets, and twenty-five Al Hussein missiles (UN Security Council Document S/1995/864, October 11, 1995, pp. 15, 26).

67. Quoted from "ABC's Diane Sawyer Interviews Saddam Hussein," Baghdad, INA, in Arabic, January 30, 1990, *FBIS* NES, July 2, 1990, p. 9. He later clarified this position in a meeting with U.S. senators, stating that "if Israel strikes and uses atomic bombs, then we will use the binary chemicals." See "Saddam Husayn Addresses Visiting U.S. Senators," Baghdad, Domestic Service, in Arabic, April 16, 1990, *FBIS* NES, April 17, 1990, pp. 5–9.

68. As Saddam Hussein stated, "The binary chemical weapon is a sufficient deterrent." See "Saddam Calls for Comprehensive Disarmament," Paris, Radio Monte Carlo, in Arabic, April 12, 1990, *FBIS* NES, April 13, 1990, pp. 7–8.

69. "INA Reports 'Aziz Remarks on Chemical Weapons," Baghdad, INA, in Arabic, August 18, 1990, *FBIS* NES, August 20, 1990, p. 17.

70. *Washington Post*, March 7, 1991, pp. A1, 35.

71. Abdel Fatah al-Khereji quoted in "Iraq Tightens Grip on Kuwait," *Independent* (London), August 10, 1990, p. 1.

72. "We Are Not in a War," *International Herald Tribune* (Paris), August 9, 1990, p. 1.

73. According to Tom King, Secretary of State for Defence; see "Gas War Warning as Britain sends RAF Squadrons," *Independent* (London), August 10, 1990, pp. 1, 8.

74. "Cheney Warns Iraq on Chemical Arms," *International Herald Tribune* (Paris), August 15, 1990, p. 4.

75. "Salih Reportedly Threatens Using Chemical Weapons," Paris, Radio Monte Carlo, in Arabic, 22 December 1990, *FBIS* NES, December 24, 1990, p. 25.

76. *Washington Post*, January 7, 1991, p. A1.

77. *Washington Times*, February 8, 1991.

78. *Los Angeles Times*, February 21, 1991, pp. A1, 18.

79. "Commander 'Prepared' for Chemical Weapons Threat," Riyadh, Television Service, in Arabic, August 28, 1990, *FBIS* NES, August 29, 1990, p. 20.

80. *Los Angeles Times*, February 21, 1991, pp. A1, A18.

81. *Christian Science Monitor*, August 14, 1990, pp. 1–2. Perhaps because of his undue candor, Dugan was relieved of his duties soon thereafter.

82. "Shamir Did Not Support Ne'eman's CW Remarks," Jerusalem, Domestic Service, August 2, 1990, *FBIS* NES, 90–149, p. 33.

83. "Cheney Warns Iraq on Chemical Arms," *International Herald Tribune* (Paris), August 15, 1990, p. 4.

84. As he continued, any confirmed use of chemical weapons would be a "matter for talks" among the allies. France would not respond with either chemical or nuclear arms, "although we could do so," according to French chief of staff Maurice Schmitt. See *Washington Times*, December 3, 1991; *Arms Control Reporter* 1991 704.E-2.27, citing Francois Cornet in Paris Antennae-2 television 4.2.91.

85. *Los Angeles Times*, February 21, 1991, pp. A1, 18.

86. Senior U.S. officials indicated the United States had decided against using nuclear or chemical arms to destroy Iraqi military installations or retaliate against Iraqi poison gas or germ warfare attacks: "The decision not to use 'weapons of mass destruction' in the Middle East crisis reflects high confidence in the overwhelming firepower of U.S. conventional forces, plus a desire not to compound the already unpredictable political consequences of a potential military conflict" (*Washington Post*, January 7, 1991, p. A1).

87. *Los Angeles Times*, February 21, 1991, pp. A1, 18.

88. See interviews conducted by PBS, *Frontline*, "The Gulf War."
89. *Washington Post*, January 7, 1991, p. A1.
90. Interview, *Frontline*, "The Gulf War." Rolf Ekéus, Executive Chairman of the UN Special Commission, has stated that he was told that Iraq did not use its biological weapons because "they were afraid of a nuclear riposte by the Americans" (*Chemical Weapons Convention Bulletin*, no. 30 [December 1995], p. 17).
91. UN Security Council Document S/1995/864, October 11, 1995, p. 11.
92. See Stephen R. Covington, "The Evolution of Soviet Thinking on the Utility of Chemical Warfare in a Major European Armed Conflict," in Krause, *Security Implications of a Global Chemical Weapons Ban*, pp. 9–10.
93. *Boston Globe*, February 17, 1991, p. 20.
94. "'Mother of Battles' Airs Saddam CNN Interview," Baghdad, Mother of Battles Radio Network, in Arabic, February 2, 1991, *FBIS NES*, February 6, 1991, p. 21.
95. Testimony of Brad Roberts in Senate Committee on Foreign Relations, *Chemical Warfare*, pp. 60–61.
96. "AL-RA'Y Comments on Paris Conference," Amman, AL-RA'Y, in Arabic, January 10, 1989, *FBIS NES*, 89–009, January 13, 1989, p. 47.
97. One of the lessons of the Gulf War, according to W. Seth Carus, is that "it is clear that chemical weapons are not the 'poor man's atomic bomb.' Whatever the true military effectiveness of chemical weapons, they are not able to induce the fundamental changes associated with nuclear weapons." See his article, "The Proliferation of Chemical Weapons Without a Convention," in *Chemical Disarmament and U.S. Security*, ed. Brad Roberts (Boulder, Colo.: Westview, 1992), pp. 47–56; see also Ronald F. Lehman, "Concluding the Chemical Weapons Convention," in the same volume, pp. 1–13. The conversion of Brad Roberts is interesting. Earlier he had contended that CW were in fact the poor man's bomb: "The risks of chemical proliferation have been overstated by some, who incorrectly have conceived of such weapons as "the poor man's atomic bomb" even when aimed at U.S. targets." See his "Framing the Ratification Debate," in *Chemical Disarmament*, pp. 119–149.
98. Charles C. Flowerree, "Implementing the Chemical Weapons Convention," in Roberts, *Chemical Disarmament*, pp. 107–117.
99. "Velayati Interviewed on Toxins, Foreign Credit," Paris, Liberation, in French, January 10, 1989, p. 18, *FBIS NES*, January 17, 1989, p. 70.
100. "Hashemi-Rafsanjani Speaks on Future of IRGC," Tehran, Domestic Service, in Persian, 6 October 1988, *FBIS NES*, October 7, 1988, p. 52.
101. The director of U.S. Central Intelligence Robert Gates revealed in December 1992 that Iran is suspected of having an active chemical weapons program, producing at least several hundred tons of agents. See *Chemical Weapons Convention Bulletin*, no. 19 (March 1993), p. 13; and "Chemical Weapons in the Middle East," *Arms Control Today* 22:8 (October 1992), p. 44. Iran is also believed to be attempting to acquire chemical missile capabilities, as reported in *New York Times*, April 8, 1993, p. A9.
102. "Majlis Speaker on Acquiring Chemical Weapons," Tehran, IRNA, in English, October 19, 1988, *FBIS NES*, October 19, 1988, pp. 55–56.
103. "Spokesman Affirms 'Right' to Chemical Weapons," Tehran, IRNA, March 14, 1991, *FBIS NES*, 91–051, March 15, 1991, p. 45.
104. For an explanation of the factors leading to agreement on the CWC, see Thomas Bernauer, *The Chemistry of Regime Formation: Explaining International Cooperation for a Comprehensive Ban on Chemical Weapons* (Aldershot, Eng.: Dartmouth Publishing, 1993).

105. Article XXII. The text of the convention is reprinted in *Arms Control Today* 22:8 (October 1992).
106. Statement of Michael Moodie in Senate Committee on Foreign Relations, *Chemical Weapons Convention: Hearings before the Committee on Foreign Relations*, 103d Cong., 2d sess., 1994, p. 103.
107. Foucault, *Discipline and Punish*, p. 180.
108. See, e.g., the statements in Senate Committee on Foreign Relations, *Chemical Weapons Convention*, p. 163.
109. Foucault, *Discipline and Punishment*, pp. 182–183.
110. UN Document S/Res/687 (1991).
111. The term is Foucault's; see *Discipline and Punish*, p. 187.
112. Senate Committee on Foreign Relations, *Chemical Weapons Convention*, pp. 174, 97.
113. Eisenhower did not consider the United States bound by this retaliation-only policy. By the end of the Vietnam War, however, public and international pressure had swung U.S. policy back to a commitment to the Geneva Protocol.
114. The reason for the exclusion is that toxicity only relates to animals and not to plants. For an indispensably insightful commentary on the understandings of the treaties provisions, see Walter Krutzsch and Ralf Trapp, *A Commentary on the Chemical Weapons Convention* (Boston: Martinus Nijhoff, 1994).
115. Krutzsch and Trapp, *Commentary*, pp. 23–24.
116. This definition is known as the General Purpose Criterion.
117. Krutzch and Trapp, *Commentary*, p. 25.
118. *Congressional Record* (daily edition) June 24, p. S7635; cited in *Chemical Weapons Convention Bulletin*, no. 25 (September 1994), 23.
119. *Chemical Weapons Convention Bulletin*, no. 23 (March 1994), 11–12, and no. 24 (June 1994), 20.
120. Ibid., no. 23 (March 1994), 10.
121. As of August 1996, significant other nonsignatory states include North Korea, Taiwan, Bosnia-Herzegovina, Macedonia, Yugoslavia, and Angola.
122. On the nuclear taboo, see Price and Tannenwald, "Norms and Deterrence"; and Nina Tannenwald, "Dogs That Don't Bark (Ph.D. diss., Cornell University, 1995).

Chapter 7. On Technology and Morality

1. Hale, "Gunpowder and the Renaissance," p. 127.
2. Ibid., p. 117.
3. Haber, *Poisonous Cloud*, pp. 295–296.
4. Ibid., p. 317.
5. Cited in *Portable Nietzsche*, p. 74.
6. Matthew Meselson, "The Myth of Chemical Superweapons," *Bulletin of the Atomic Scientists* 47:3 (April 1991), 12–15.
7. This is not to say that the nuclear taboo is unproblematic. Mutual self-interest does not explain why a taboo developed in conflicts between nuclear and nonnuclear powers such as Korea, or why low-yield nuclear weapons that have yields on par with the most destructive conventional explosives are subject to the taboo. See Price and Tannenwald, "Norms and Deterrence," and N. Tannenwald, "Dogs That Don't Bark."
8. For applications of such interest-driven approaches to international regimes,

see Robert Keohane, *After Hegemony* (Princeton University Press, 1984), and selected essays in *International Regimes*.

9. Applications of such an approach to weapons issues include John Ellis, *Social History of the Machine Gun* (Baltimore: Johns Hopkins University Press, 1986); Donald McKenzie, *Inventing Accuracy* (Cambridge: MIT Press, 1990); and Susan Wright and Stuart Ketcham, "The Problem of Interpreting the U.S. Biological Defense Research Program," in Wright, *Preventing a Biological Arms Race* (Cambridge: MIT Press, 1990), pp. 169–196.

10. From this large literature on the philosophy and sociology of technology, I will confine myself to noting *The Social Construction of Technological Systems*, ed. Wiebe Bijker, Thomas Hughes, and Trevor Pinch (Cambridge: MIT Press, 1987); *Sojourns in the New World*, ed. Tom Darby (Ottawa: Carleton University Press, 1986); *Technology and Responsibility*, ed. Paul Durbin (Dordrecht: D. Reidel, 1987); George Grant, *Technology and Empire* (Toronto: Anansi, 1969) and *Technology and Justice* (Toronto: Anansi, 1986); and Langdon Winner, *Autonomous Technology: Technics Out-of-Control as a Theme in Political Thought* (Cambridge: MIT Press, 1977).

11. An exception was the plan by a Jewish group to exact revenge on the Germans for the Holocaust by using the "poor man's bomb." During World War II, the group intended to poison the water supplies of German cities. The initial attempt failed, and the war ended before another attempt could be made. The group then poisoned bread baked for German prisoners of war, injuring an estimated two thousand. "The Avengers," ABC News broadcast on *Nightline*, August 16, 1996.

12. Senate Committee on Foreign Relations, *Chemical Weapons Convention*, pp. 51–52.

13. Senate Committee on Foreign Relations, *United States Policy toward Iraq*, p. 51.

14. As argued in SIPRI, *CBW and the Law of War*.

15. Alexis de Tocqueville, *The Old Regime and the French Revolution*, trans. Stuart Gilbert (Garden City, N.Y.: Doubleday, 1955), p. 177.

Selected Bibliography

Documents and Government Publications

Congressional Record. 67th Cong., 2d sess., 1922. Vol. 62, pt. 5.
——. 69th Cong., 1st sess., 1926. Vol. 68, pt. 1.
German Chemical Warfare [in World War II]. Part II: Civilian Aspects. Aberdeen Proving Ground, Md.: Historical Office of the Chief of the Chemical Corps. Draft translation, MS.P=004a, 1956. [Part I. *See* Ochsner, Lt. Gen. H.] Part II includes:
  Dwilling, Dr. "What Data Were Available to the German Intelligence Service concerning Chemical Warfare and Chemical Warfare Equipment on the Part of the U.S.A. and the Other Allied Countries?" Pp. 361–394.
  Ehmann, E. "Organizational and Industrial Functions of the Army Ordnance Office in the Army High Command in the Field of Chemical Warfare Agents." Pp. 508–530.
  ——. "What Was the Value Attached by the German Command to the Use of Guided Missiles in Warfare, and Specifically in Chemical Warfare?" Pp. 403–419.
  Fischer, Dr. Hans. "Administrative and Operational Control of Chemical Warfare in the German Armed Forces." Pp. 3–4, 8–65.
  ——. "German Doctrine and Viewpoint on Tactical and Strategical Advantages and Disadvantages of Chemical Warfare." Pp. 1–3.
  ——, and Dr. Schmidt. "What Offensive and Defensive Means Were Available to Germany for Conducting Chemical Warfare?" Pp. 5–7, 65–319.
  ——, and Dr. Wirth. "What Were the Plans and Intentions of the German High Command in the Question of Using Chemical Warfare? What Were the Reasons for Refraining from the Use of Chemical Warfare?" Pp. 7–8, 319–61.
  Schmidt, Dr. "On Gas Psychoses during the War." Pp. 394–402.
League of Nations. *Proceedings of the Conference for the Supervision of the International Trade in Arms and Ammunition and in Implements of War.* Geneva, 1925.

Ministry of Munitions. *History of the Ministry of Munitions.* Vol. 11: *The Supply of Munitions, Part II: "Chemical Warfare Supplies."* London: HMSO, 1921.

Ochsner, Lt. Gen. Herman. *History of German Chemical Warfare in World War II. Part I: The Military Aspect.* Aberdeen Proving Ground, Md.: Historical Office of the Chief of the Chemical Corps, MS. P=004, 1949.

U.S. Congress. House. Committee on Armed Services. *Use of Chemical Weapons in Desert Storm: Hearing, before the Oversight and Investigations Subcommittee.* 103d Cong., 1st sess., 1994.

U.S. Congress. House. Committee on Foreign Affairs. *Chemical Biological Warfare: U.S. Policies and International Effects: Hearings before the Subcommittee on National Security Policy and Scientific Developments.* 91st Cong., 1st sess., 1970.

U.S. Congress. Senate. *Chemical Warfare: Arms Control and Nonproliferation: Joint Hearing before the Committee on Foreign Relations and the Subcommittee on Energy, Nuclear Proliferation and Government Processes.* 98th Cong., 2d sess., June 28, 1984.

U.S. Congress. Senate. *Chemical Weapons Convention: Hearings before the Committee on Foreign Relations.* 103d Cong., 2d sess., 1994.

U.S. Congress. Senate. *Munitions Industry: Hearings before the Special Committee Investigating the Munitions Industry.* 73d Cong., pt. 11: December 6, 7, and 10, 1934; pt. 12: December 11 and 12, 1934.

U.S. Congress. Senate. *United States Policy toward Iraq: Human Rights, Weapons Proliferation, and International Law: Hearing before the Committee on Foreign Relations.* 101st Cong., 2d sess., June 15, 1990.

U.S. Congress. Senate. Committee on Foreign Relations. *Chemical Weapons Use in Kurdistan: Iraq's Final Offensive.* 100th Cong., 2d sess., 1987, S. prt., 100–148.

U.S. Congress. Senate. Subcommittee on Disarmament. *Disarmament and Security: A Collection of Documents, 1919–1955.* 84th Cong., 2d sess., 1956.

U.S. Department of State. *Conference on the Limitation of Armament.* Washington, D.C.: Government Printing Office, 1922.

U.S. Department of State. *Foreign Relations of the United States 1921.* Vol. 1. Washington, D.C.: Government Printing Office, 1936.

U.S. Department of State. *Foreign Relations of the United States: The Paris Peace Conference, 1919.* Vol. 5. Washington, D.C.: Government Printing Office, 1946.

U.S. War Department. *Annual Report, 1917.* Vol. 1. Washington, D.C.: Government Printing Office, 1918.

White, Andrew D. Collected papers, Olin Library, Cornell University, Ithaca, N.Y.

Secondary Sources

Adas, Michael. *Machines as the Measure of Men.* Ithaca: Cornell University Press, 1989.

Adelman, Kenneth. "Chemical Weapons: Restoring the Taboo." *Orbis* 30:3 (Fall 1986), 443–455.

Angerer, Jo. *Chemische Waffen in Deutschland: Misbrauch einer Wissenschaft.* Darmstadt: Hermann Luchterhand Verlag, 1985.

Auld, S. J. *Gas and Flame in Modern Warfare.* New York: George Doran, 1918.

Badoglio, P. *The War in Abyssinia.* New York: G. P. Putnam's Sons, 1937.

Barker, A. J. *The Civilizing Mission.* New York: Dial Press, 1968.

Bernauer, Thomas. *The Chemistry of Regime Formation: Explaining International Cooperation for a Comprehensive Ban on Chemical Weapons.* Aldershot, Eng.: Dartmouth Publishing, 1993.

——. *The Projected Chemical Weapons Convention: A Guide to the Negotiations in the Conference on Disarmament.* New York: United Nations Institute for Disarmament Research, 1990.

Bijker, Wiebe, Thomas Hughes, and Trevor Pinch, eds. *The Social Construction of Technological Systems.* Cambridge: MIT Press, 1987.

Bradley, Omar N. *A Soldier's Story.* New York: Henry Holt, 1951.

Brauch, Hans Günter, and Rolf-Dieter Müller, eds. *Chemische Kriegführung — Chemische Absrüstung: Dokumente und Kommentare.* Berlin: Berlin Verlag, 1985.

Brophy, Leo, and George Fisher. *The Chemical Warfare Service: Organizing for War.* Washington, D.C.: Office of the Chief of Military History, Department of the Army, 1959.

Brown, Frederic. *Chemical Warfare: A Study in Restraints.* Princeton: Princeton University Press, 1968.

Bull, Hedley. *The Anarchical Society.* New York: Columbia University Press, 1977.

——, and Adam Watson, eds. *The Expansion of International Society.* Oxford: Clarendon Press, 1984.

Bulloch, John, and Harvey Morris. *The Gulf War.* London: Methuen, 1989.

Campbell, David. *Politics without Principle.* Boulder, Colo.: Lynne Rienner Publishers, 1993.

——. *Writing Security.* Minneapolis: University of Minnesota Press, 1992.

Carnesale, Albert, and Richard Haass, eds. *Superpower Arms Control: Setting the Record Straight.* Cambridge, Mass.: Ballinger, 1987.

Churchill, Winston. *The Grand Alliance.* London: Cassell, 1950.

——. *Their Finest Hour* London: Cassell, 1949.

——. *The World Crisis.* Vol. 2. London: Scribner, 1923.

Clarke, I. F. *Voices Prophesying War: Future Wars 1763–3749.* Oxford: Oxford University Press, 1992.

Cordesman, Anthony, and Abraham Wagner. *The Lessons of Modern War.* Vol. 2: *The Iran-Iraq War.* Boulder, Colo.: Westview Press, 1990.

Cross, Charles. "Explanation and the Theory of Questions," *Erkenntnis* 34 (March 1991), 237–260.

Darby, Tom, ed. *Sojourns in the New World.* Ottawa: Carleton University Press, 1986.

Davis, Calvin DeArmond. *The United States and the First Hague Peace Conference.* Ithaca: Cornell University Press, 1962.

Del Boca, Angelo. *The Ethiopian War, 1935–1941.* Chicago: University of Chicago Press, 1969.

Der Derian, James. *On Diplomacy.* Oxford: Basil Blackwell, 1987.

Doty, Roxanne Lynn. "The Social Construction of Contemporary International Hierarchy." 2 vols. Ph.D. diss., University of Minnesota, 1991.

Douglas, Lawrence. "The Submarine and the Washington Conference of 1921." *Naval War College Review* 26:5 (March/April 1974), 86–100.

Doyle, Michael. "Kant, Liberal Legacies, and Foreign Affairs," Parts I and II. *Philosophy and Public Affairs* 12 (Summer and Fall, 1983), 205–235, 323–353.

Durbin, Paul, ed. *Technology and Responsibility.* Dordrecht: D. Reidel, 1987.

Ellis, John. *The Social History of the Machine Gun.* Baltimore: Johns Hopkins University Press, 1986.

Elshtain, Jean Bethke. "Critical Reflections on Realism, Just Wars, and Feminism in a Nuclear Age." In *Nuclear Weapons and the Future of Humanity,* edited by Avner Cohen and Steven Lee, pp. 255–72. Totowa, N.J.: Rowman and Allanheld, 1986.

Ezz, Esmat. "The Chemical Weapons Convention: Particular Concerns of Developing Countries." In *Proceedings of the Thirty-ninth Pugwash Conference on Science and World Affairs*, pp. 214–218. Cambridge, Mass., 1989.

Fair, Stanley. "Mussolini's Chemical War." *Army* 35:1 (January 1985), 44–53.

Fauchille, Paul. *Traité de Droit International Public.* Vol. 2. Paris: Rousseau, 1921.

Fleming, Peter. *Operation Sea Lion.* New York: Simon & Schuster, 1957.

Flowerree, Charles. "The Politics of Arms Control Treaties: A Case Study." *Journal of International Affairs* 37:2 (Winter 1984), 269–282.

Fotion, Nicholas, and G. Elfstrom. *Military Ethics: Guidelines for Peace and War.* London: Routledge & Kegan Paul, 1986.

Foucault, Michel. *Discipline and Punish.* New York: Vintage Books, 1979.

——. *The History of Sexuality.* Vol. 1: *An Introduction.* New York: Vintage Books, 1990.

——. "Nietzsche, Genealogy, History." In *The Foucault Reader*, edited by Paul Rabinow, pp. 76–100. New York: Pantheon Books, 1984.

——. *Politics, Philosophy, Culture.* New York: Routledge, 1990.

——. *Power/Knowledge: Selected Interviews and Other Writings, 1972–1977.* Edited by Colin Gordon. New York: Pantheon Books, 1980.

Foulkes, C. H. *Gas! The Story of the Special Brigade.* London: William Blackwood & Sons, 1934.

Fries, Amos, and Clarence West. *Chemical Warfare.* New York: McGraw Hill, 1921.

Fukuyama, Francis. *The End of History and the Last Man.* New York: Free Press, 1992.

Garner, James. *International Law and the World War.* London: Longmans, Green, 1920.

Gentili, Alberico. *De Iure Belli Libri Tres* [1612]. Vol. 2. Translated by John C. Rolfe. Oxford: Clarendon Press, 1933.

Geyer, Hermann. "Der Gaskrieg." In *Der Grosse Krieg: 1914–1918*, edited by Max Schwarte, pp. 485–528. Leipzig: Johann Ambrolius Barth, 1922.

Gibbons, Michael. "Interpretation, Genealogy, and Human Agency." In *Idioms of Inquiry: Critique and Renewal in Political Science*, edited by Terence Ball, pp. 137–67. Albany: State University of New York Press, 1987.

Goldgeier, James, and Michael McFaul. "A Tale of Two Worlds: Core and Periphery in the Post–Cold War Era." *International Organization* 46:2 (Spring 1992), 467–491.

Gong, Gerrit W. *The Standard of 'Civilization' in International Society.* Oxford: Clarendon Press, 1984.

Grant, George. *Technology and Empire.* Toronto: Anansi, 1969.

——. *Technology and Justice.* Toronto: Anansi, 1986.

Green, L. C. "Lawful and Unlawful Weapons and Activities." In *Essays on the Modern Law of War*, edited by L. C. Green, pp. 151–73. New York: Transnational Publishers, 1985.

Groehler, Olaf. *Der Lautlose Tod.* Berlin: Verlag der Nation, 1978.

Grotius, Hugo. *The Law of War and Peace.* Translated by Francis Kelsey. New York: Bobbs-Merrill, 1925.

Haber, L. F. *The Poisonous Cloud.* Oxford: Clarendon Press, 1986.

Haldane, J. B. S. *Callinicus: A Defence of Chemical Warfare.* London: Kegan Paul, Trench, Trubner, 1925.

Haldane, John. "Ethics and Biological Warfare." *Arms Control* 8:1 (May 1987), 24–35.

Hale, J. R. "Gunpowder and the Renaissance: An Essay in the History of Ideas." Charles H. Carter pp. 113–144. In *From the Renaissance to the Counter-Reformation*, edited by New York: Random House, 1965.

——. *War and Society in Renaissance Europe, 1450–1620.* New York: St. Martin's Press, 1985.

Hall, William Edward. *A Treatise on International Law.* Edited by A. Pearce Higgins. Oxford: Clarendon Press, 1924.

Hallissy, Margaret. *Venomous Woman*. New York: Greenwood Press, 1987.

Hamm, Manfred R. "Deterrence, Chemical Warfare, and Arms Control." *Orbis* 29:1 (Spring 1985), 119–163.

Hanslian, Rudolf, ed. *Der Chemische Krieg.* Vol. 1. Berlin: E. S. Mittler & Son, 1937.

Harbord, J. *The American Army in France, 1917–1919.* Boston: Little, Brown, 1936.

Harbour, Frances. *Chemical Arms Control: The U.S. and the Geneva Protocol of 1925.* Case Studies in Ethics and International Affairs, no. 4. New York: Carnegie Council on Ethics and International Affairs, 1990.

Harris, Elisa. "CBW Arms Control: A Regime Under Attack?" *Arms Control Today* 16:6 (September 1986), 8–13.

Harris, Paul. "British Preparations for Offensive Chemical Warfare 1935–1939." *Journal of the Royal United Services Institute for Defence Studies* 125:2 (June 1980), 56–62.

Harris, Robert, and Jeremy Paxman. *A Higher Form of Killling.* New York: Hill and Wang, 1982.

Haydon, F. Stansbury. "A Proposed Gas Shell, 1862." *Journal of the American Military History Foundation* 2:1 (Spring 1938), 52–54.

Heller, Charles. *Chemical Warfare in World War I: The American Experience, 1917–1919.* Fort Leavenworth, Kan.: Combat Studies Institute, 1984.

Hoy, David Couzens, ed. *Foucault: A Critical Reader.* Oxford: Basil Blackwell, 1989.

Hughes, Charles Evans. "Possible Gains." *Proceedings of the American Society of International Law.* Washington, D.C., 1927.

Hull, William I. *The Two Hague Conferences.* Boston: Ginn, 1908.

Inter-Parliamentary Union. *What Would Be the Character of a New War?* London: P. S. King & Son, 1931.

Irwin, Will. *The Next War.* New York: E. P. Dutton, 1921.

Jochnick, Chris, and Roger Normand. "The Legitimation of Violence: A Critical History of the Laws of War." *Harvard International Law Journal* 35:1 (Winter 1994), 49–95.

Johnson, James Turner. *Just War Tradition and the Restraint of War.* Princeton: Princeton University Press, 1981.

Kalshoven, Frits. *Belligerent Reprisals.* Leyden: A. W. Sijthoff, 1971.

Karsh, Efraim. *The Iran-Iraq War: A Military Analysis.* Adelphi Papers, no. 220 (London: Institute for Strategic Studies, Spring 1987).

——, ed. *The Iran-Iraq War.* New York: St. Martin's Press, 1989.

Kaufman, Robert. *Arms Control during the Pre-Nuclear Era.* New York: Columbia University Press, 1990.

Keeley, James. "Toward a Foucauldian Analysis of International Regimes." *International Organization* 44:1 (Winter 1990), 83–105.

Kelly, Joseph Burns. "Gas Warfare in International Law." *Military Law Review* (July 1960). Department of the Army pamphlet no. 27-100-9. Pp. 1–67.

Krasner, Stephen, ed. *International Regimes.* Ithaca: Cornell University Press, 1983.

Kratochwil, Friedrich. "Regimes, Interpretation and the 'Science' of Politics: A Reappraisal." *Millenium* 17:2 (Summer 1988), 263–284.

——, and John Gerard Ruggie. "International Organization: A State of the Art on the Art of the State." *International Organization* 40:4 (Autumn 1986), 753–775.

Krause, Joachim, ed. *Security Implications of a Global Weapons Ban.* Boulder, Colo.: Westview Press, 1991.

Krause, Joachim, and Charles K. Mallory. *Chemical Weapons in Soviet Military Doctrine.* Boulder, Colo.: Westview Press, 1992.

Krepon, Michael, and Dan Caldwell, eds. *The Politics of Arms Control Treaty Ratification.* New York: St. Martin's Press, 1991.

Krickus, Richard J. "On the Morality of Chemical/Biological War." In *War, Morality, and the Military Profession*, edited by Malhan Wakin, pp. 410–424. Boulder, Colo.: Westview, 1986.

Krutzsch, Walter, and Ralf Trapp. *A Commentary on the Chemical Weapons Convention*. Boston: Martinus Nijhoff, 1994.

Kunz, Rudibert, and Rolf-Dieter Müller. *Giftgas Gegen Abd el Krim: Deutschland, Spanien, und der Gaskrieg in Spanisch-Marokko, 1922–1927*. Freiberg: Rombach, 1990.

Lapid, Josef. "The Third Debate: On the Prospects of International Theory in a Post-Positivist Era." *International Studies Quarterly* 33:3 (September 1989), 235–254.

Lawrence, T. J. *The Principles of International Law*. Boston: D. C. Heath, 1923.

Lefebure, Victor. *The Riddle of the Rhine, Chemical Strategy in Peace and War*. New York: E. P. Dutton, 1923.

Legro, Jeffrey. *Cooperation under Fire: Anglo-German Restraint during World War II*. Ithaca: Cornell University Press, 1995.

Leipmann, Heinz. *Poison in the Air*. Translated by Eden and Cedar Paul. Philadelphia: L. B. Lippincott, 1937.

Leonard, James F. "Rolling Back Chemical Proliferation." *Arms Control Today* 22:8 (October 1992), 13–18.

Lewin, Louis. *Die Gifte in der Weltgeschichte*. Berlin: Julius Springer, 1920.

Lorimer, James. *The Institutes of the Law of Nations*. Edinburgh: Blackwood & Sons, 1883.

Low, Seth. "The International Conference of Peace." *North American Review* 169:5 (November 1899), 625–639.

Lundin, S. J. "Chemical and Biological Warfare: Developments in 1988." In *SIPRI Yearbook 1989: World Armaments and Disarmament*, pp. 99–130. Oxford: Oxford University Press, 1989.

——, J. P. Robinson, and Ralf Trapp. "Chemical and Biological Warfare: Developments in 1987." In *SIPRI Yearbook 1988: World Armaments and Disarmament*, pp. 101–125. Oxford: Oxford University Press, 1988.

Machiavelli, Niccolò. *The Prince*. Translated by Leo Paul S. de Alverez. Irving: University of Dallas Press, 1980.

Mahan, Alfred. "The Peace Conference and the Moral Aspect of War." *North American Review* 169:4 (October 1899), 433–447.

Mallison, W. T. "The Laws of War and the Juridical Control of Weapons of Mass Destruction in General and Limited Wars." *George Washington Law Review* 36:2 (December 1967), 308–346.

Mandelbaum, Michael. *The Nuclear Revolution*. Cambridge: Cambridge University Press, 1981.

May, Michael. "The Proliferation of Chemical Weapons and the Military Utility of Chemical Warfare: A Case Study of the Iran-Iraq War." Ph.D. diss., Syracuse University, 1993.

McElroy, Robert. *Morality and American Foreign Policy*. Princeton: Princeton University Press, 1992.

McKenzie, Donald. *Inventing Accuracy*. Cambridge: MIT Press, 1990.

McNeill, William. *The Pursuit of Power: Technology, Armed Force, and Society since A.D. 1000*. Chicago: University of Chicago Press, 1982.

Meselson, Matthew. "The Myth of Chemical Superweapons." *The Bulletin of the Atomic Scientists* 47:3 (April 1991), 12–15.

Mohan, C. Raja. "Chemical Weapons in the Gulf: A Dangerous Portent." *Strategic Analysis* 8:1 (April 1984), 71–80.

Moon, John Ellis van Courtland. "Chemical Warfare: A Forgotten Lesson." *Bulletin of the Atomic Scientists* 45:6 (August 1989), 40–43.

——. "Chemical Weapons and Deterrence: The World War II Experience." *International Security* 8:4 (Spring 1984), 3–35.

——. "Controlling Chemical and Biological Weapons through World War II." In *Encylopedia of Arms Control and Disarmament*, edited by Richard Dean Burns, pp. 657–74. New York: Charles Scribner's Sons, 1992.

——. "Project Sphinx: The Question of the Use of Gas in the Planned Invasion of Japan." *Journal of Strategic Studies* 12 (1989), 303–323.

Morel, Benoit, and Kyle Olson, eds. *Shadows and Substance: The Chemical Weapons Convention*. Boulder, Colo.: Westview Press, 1993.

Morel, Pierre. "The Paris Conference on the Prohibition of Chemical Weapons." *Disarmament* 12:2 (Summer 1989), 127–144.

Morgan, J. H., trans. *The War Book of the German General Staff*. New York: McBride, Nast, 1915.

Mueller, John. *Retreat from Doomsday: The Obsolescence of Major War*. New York: Basic Books, 1989.

Müller, Rolf-Dieter. "World Power Status through the Use of Poison Gas? German Preparations for Chemical Warfare, 1919–1945." In *The German Military in the Age of Total War*, edited by Wilhelm Deist, pp. 171–209. Warwickshire, Eng.: Berg Publishers, 1985.

Nehamas, Alexander. *Nietzsche: Life as Literature*. Cambridge: Harvard University Press, 1985.

Nietzsche, Friedrich. *Human, All-Too-Human*. Translated by Marion Faber. Lincoln: University of Nebraska Press, 1986.

——. *On the Genealogy of Morals*. Translated by Walter Kaufmann and R. J. Hollingdale. New York: Vintage Books, 1989.

——. *Thus Spoke Zarathustra*. In *The Portable Nietzsche*, edited and translated by Walter Kaufmann, pp. 103–439. New York: Penguin, 1982.

——. *Twilight of the Idols*. In *The Portable Nietzsche*, edited and translated by Walter Kaufmann, pp. 463–563. New York: Penguin, 1982.

——. *The Use and Abuse of History*. Translated by Adrian Collins. New York: Macmillan, 1957.

O'Brien, Terrence. *Civil Defence*. London: Her Majesty's Stationery Office, 1955.

O'Brien, William V. "Biological/Chemical Warfare and the International Law of War." *Georgetown Law Journal* 51:1 (Fall 1962), 1–63.

O'Connell, Robert. *Of Arms and Men: A History of War, Weapons, and Aggression*. Oxford: Oxford University Press, 1989.

Oldendorf, W. H. "On the Acceptability of a Device as a Weapon." *Bulletin of the Atomic Scientists* 18:1 (January 1962), 35–37.

Partington, J. R. *A History of Greek Fire and Gunpowder*. Cambridge: W. Heffer & Sons, 1960.

Pershing, John. *My Experiences in World War I*. New York: Frederick A. Stokes, 1931.

Pozdnjakow, V. "The Chemical Arm." In *The Red Army*, edited by Basil Liddell Hart, pp. 384–94. New York: Harcourt, Brace, 1956.

Prentiss, A. M. *Chemicals in War*. New York: McGraw-Hill, 1937.

Price, Richard. "A Genealogy of the Chemical Weapons Taboo." *International Organization* 49:1 (Winter 1995), 73–103.

——. "Interpretation and Disciplinary Orthodoxy in International Relations." *Review of International Studies* 20 (April 1994), 201–204.

——, and Nina Tannenwald. "Norms and Deterrence: The Nuclear and Chemical Weapons Taboos." In *The Culture of National Security: Norms and Identities in World*

Politics, edited by Peter Katzenstein, pp. 114–152. New York: Columbia University Press, 1996.

Quester, George. *Deterrence Before Hiroshima.* New Brunswick, N.J.: Transaction Books, 1986.

Raudzens, George. "War-Winning Weapons: The Measurement of Technological Determinism in Military History." *Journal of Military History* 54:4 (October 1990), 403–433.

Read, James Morgan. *Atrocity Propaganda: 1914–1919.* New Haven: Yale University Press, 1941.

Richter, Donald. *Chemical Soldiers: British Gas Warfare in World War I.* Lawrence: University Press of Kansas, 1992.

Roberts, A. A. *Poison in Warfare.* London: William Heinemann, 1915.

Roberts, Adam and Richard Guelff. *Documents on the Laws of War.* Oxford: Clarendon Press, 1982.

Roberts, Brad, ed. *Chemical Disarmament and U.S. Security.* Boulder, Colo.: Westview Press, 1992.

Robinson, Julian Perry. "Chemical and Biological Warfare: Developments in 1984." In *SIPRI Yearbook 1985: World Armaments and Disarmament,* pp. 159–219. New York: Taylor and Francis, 1985.

——. "Chemical and Biological Warfare: Developments in 1985." In *SIPRI Yearbook 1986: World Armaments and Disarmament,* pp. 159–179. Oxford: Oxford University Press, 1986.

Rolin, Alberic. *Le Droit moderne de la guerre.* Vol. 1. Bruxelles: Albert DeWit, 1920.

Rose, Steven, ed. *CBW: Chemical and Biological Warfare.* Boston: Beacon Press, 1968.

Rosecrance, Richard. *The Rise of the Trading State.* New York: Basic Books, 1986.

Royse, M. W. *Aerial Bombardment and the International Regulation of Warfare.* New York: H. Vinal, 1928.

Saunders, D. "The Bari Incident." *United States Naval Institute Proceedings* 93 (September 1967), 35–39.

Scarry, Elaine. *The Body in Pain.* Oxford University Press, 1985.

Schwarzenberger, Georg. *The Legality of Nuclear Weapons.* London: Stevens & Sons, 1958.

Scott, James Brown, ed. *The Hague Peace Conferences of 1899 and 1907.* Vol. 1: *Conferences.* Baltimore: Johns Hopkins Press, 1909.

——, ed. *The Hague Peace Conferences of 1899 and 1907.* Vol. 2: *Documents.* Baltimore: Johns Hopkins Press, 1909.

——, ed. *Instructions to the American Delegates to the Hague Peace Conferences and Their Official Reports.* New York: Oxford University Press, 1916.

——, ed. *The Proceedings of the Hague Peace Conferences.* New York: Oxford University Press, 1920.

——, ed. *The Reports to the Hague Conferences of 1899 and 1907.* Oxford: Clarendon Press, 1917.

Sprout, Harold, and Margaret Sprout. *Toward a New Order of Sea Power: American Naval Policy and the World Scene, 1918–1922.* Princeton: Princeton University Press, 1940.

Steer, George. *Caesar in Abyssinia.* Boston: Little, Brown, 1937.

Stockholm International Peace Research Institute (SIPRI). *The Problem of Chemical and Biological Warfare.* Vol. 1: *The Rise of CB Weapons.* Stockholm: Almqvist & Wiksell, 1971.

——. *The Problem of Chemical and Biological Warfare*. Vol. 3: *CBW and the Law of War*. Stockholm: Almqvist & Wiksell, 1973.

——. *The Problem of Chemical and Biological Warfare*. Vol. 4: *CB Disarmament Negotiations, 1920–1970*. Stockholm: Almqvist & Wiksell, 1971.

——. *The Problem of Chemical and Biological Warfare*. Vol. 5: *The Prevention of CBW*. Stockholm: Almqvist & Wiksell, 1971.

Stone, Julius. *Legal Controls of International Conflict*. New York: Rinehart, 1959.

Tannenwald, Nina. "Dogs That Don't Bark." Ph.D. diss., Cornell University, 1995.

Taylor, Charles. "Interpretation and the Sciences of Man." In *Interpretive Social Science: A Second Look*, edited by Paul Rabinow and William Sullivan, pp. 33–81. Berkeley: University of California Press, 1987.

Thomas, Andy. *Effects of Chemical Warfare: A Selective Review and Bibliography of British State Papers*. Philadelphia: Taylor and Francis, 1985.

Thomas, Ann Van Wynen, and A. J. Thomas. *Development of International Legal Limitations on the Use of Chemical and Biological Weapons*. Vol. 2. Prepared for the U.S. Arms Control and Disarmament Agency, 1968.

——. *Legal Limits on the Use of Chemical and Biological Weapons*. Dallas: Southern Methodist University Press, 1970.

Thuillier, Henry. *Gas in the Next War*. London: Geoffrey Bles, 1939.

Tompkins, John. *The Weapons of World War III: The Long Road Back from the Bomb*. Garden City, N.Y.: Doubleday, 1966.

United Nations. *United Nations Disarmament Yearbook*. Vol. 14, 1989.

van Creveld, Martin. *Technology and War*. New York: Free Press, 1989.

——. *The Transformation of War*. New York: Free Press, 1991.

Vattel, Emer de. *Le Droit des gens*. Leiden: Aux depens de la compagnie, 1758.

Vinet, E. "La Guerre des gaz et les travaux des services chimiques francais." *Chemie et Industrie* 2:1 (January 1, 1919), 1377–1415.

Waitt, Alden. *Gas Warfare*. New York: Duell, Sloan & Pearce, 1942.

Waley, Daniel. *British Public Opinion and the Abyssinian War*. London: Maurice Temple Smith, 1975.

Walzer, Michael. *Just and Unjust Wars*. New York: Basic Books, 1977.

Wendt, Alexander. "Anarchy Is What States Make of It: The Social Construction of Power Politics." *International Organization* 46:2 (Spring 1992), 391–425.

West, Clarence J. "The History of Poison Gases." *Science* 49:1270 (1919), 412–417.

White, Andrew D. *The First Hague Conference*. Boston: World Peace Foundation, 1912.

Winner, Langdon. *Autonomous Technology: Technics Out-of-Control as a Theme in Political Thought*. Cambridge: MIT Press, 1977.

Wright, Susan. "The Military and the New Biology." *Bulletin of the Atomic Scientists* 41:5 (May 1985), 10–16.

——, and Stuart Ketcham. "The Problem of Interpreting the U.S. Biological Defense Research Program." In *Preventing a Biological Arms Race*, edited by Susan Wright, pp. 169–196. Cambridge: MIT Press, 1990.

Index

Abyssinia 101, 102, 105–107, 112. *See also* East Africa; Ethiopia; Italo-Ethiopian War
Adas, Michael, 37, 182n
Addis Ababa, 103
Afghanistan, 5, 107, 139
Africa, Africans, 21, 199n. *See also* East Africa
Algeria, 4, 144
Anbari, Abdul Amir, 151
Anglo-French Declaration, 111
Angola, 212n
Antonescue, Marshal, 127
Arthur, Stanley, 146
Asia, 21
Asphyxiating gas. *See* Gas, asphyxiating
Asphyxiating shells: at Hague, 15, 18, 32–33, 35–40, 43–44, 168; and World War I, 48, 50, 53, 68
Asquith, H. H., 53
Atomic bomb, 79, 125. *See also* nuclear weapons
Atkinson, Rick, 209n
Auld, S. J., 61, 189n
Austrialia, 103
Austria-Hungary, 32
Aziz, Tariq, 134, 207n; and Gulf War, 148, 150; position on CW use, 140, 142–143. *See also* Gulf War; Hussein, Saddam; Iraq

Bacterial warfare, 79
Bacteriological warfare, 92, 111, 134, 152–153
Badoglio, P., 198n
Baghdad, 205n, 207n, 209n, 210n
Baker, A. J., 197n
Baker, James, 148
Balfour, 75, 194n
Basra, 139
al-Batin, Haf, 209n
Bauer, Max, 184n
Belgrade, 36
Beitz, Charles, 183n
Belgian, 61
Bernauer, Thomas, 211n
Bijker, Wiebe, 213n
Bingham, Hiram, 93
Biological warfare, 50, 82; allegations World War I, 190n; and poison, 25, 28, 29
Biological weapons, 14, 31; compared with chemical weapons, 67, 91, 205n; and Geneva Protocol, 90; and Iraq, 150, 155, 177n, 178n, 208n, 209n, 210n, 211n; Japanese use of, 107, 196n, 201n; as "poor man's bomb," 143, 144, 153, 160, 162; taboo against, 181n
Biological Weapons Convention, 134
Borah, Senator, 94, 195n
Boulogne, 53
Bows, 2, 25, 70, 81, 115